U.S. Policy and Low-Intensity Conflict

Reviewed for Perspectives

U.S. Policy and Low-Intensity Conflict

Potentials for Military Struggles in the 1980s

Edited by
Sam C. Sarkesian
and
William L. Scully

Transaction Books
New Brunswick (U.S.A.) and London (U.K.)

Library of Congress Catalog Number: 80-24071
ISBN: 0-87855-851-9
Printed in the United States of America

Library of Congress Cataloging in Publication Data
Main entry under title
U.S. policy and low intensity conflict.
  Bibliography: p.
  Includes index.
  1. United States—Military policy.   2. Limited war.   3. Intervention
(International law)
I. Sarkesian, Sam Charles.   II. Scully, William L., 1940-
UA23.U547   355′.033073   80-24071
ISBN 0-87855-851-9

Table of Contents

Preface   vii

Introduction   *American Policy and Low-Intensity Conflict: An
               Overview*   1
               Sam C. Sarkesian

Chapter 1   *The Employment of Force: Political-Military
               Considerations*   17
               George K. Osborn and William J. Taylor, Jr.

Chapter 2   *The Employment of Force: Political Constraints and
               Limitations*   49
               David W. Tarr

Chapter 3   *U.S. Capabilities for Military Intervention*   69
               Howard D. Graves

Chapter 4   *Lessons of Modern History: The British Experience*   95
               Dennis Duncanson

Chapter 5   *Lessons of Modern History: The French Experience*   127
               Jacques L. Pons

Chapter 6   *Low-Intensity Conflict: The Soviet Response*   149
               Roger Hamburg

Chapter 7   *Low-Intensity Conflict: The U.S. Response*   175
               Frank N. Trager and William L. Scully

Bibliography   199
About the Authors   207
Index   211

Preface

Since the withdrawal from Vietnam, the United States has not developed a realistic political-military policy for the employment of force in nonnuclear contingencies. The failure to do so has important ramifications for international perceptions of our political will and military resolve, as well as our ability to respond to threats to U.S. interests. Even though recent events have reawakened interest in force employment, American military capability and political will to employ forces short of nuclear or major conventional conflict remain questionable and suspect.

Debate continues as to the reasons underlying this apparent failure of American policy: arguments range from the Vietnam syndrome and leadership weakness to the futility of force employment. Regardless of the American position or the lack thereof, world events will not wait. Events in Iran and Afghanistan in 1979 and 1980 show the instability in the Third World and the character of Soviet political-military policy. Such events reinforce the view that the Third World environment will continue to pose threats to United States interests. It seems unnecessary in such circumstances to advocate a coherent American policy response. Yet the fact remains that American political-military strategy is inadequate to respond to Third World security threats. This weakness is particularly evident in America's posture and policy with respect to low-intensity conflict—conflicts that are characteristic of the Third World.

To probe these matters and assess American policy options, a group of scholars and practitioners met at Loyola University of Chicago in November 1979. At this workshop a number of papers were presented and discussed, analyzing important factors in American policy and the conduct of low-intensity conflict. The results of the workshop are presented in this volume with some revisions and additions. This volume, however, is not intended as an exhaustive assessment of all the major aspects of nonnuclear conflict. What we hope to do is stimulate a serious debate on American policy in nonnuclear conflicts by examining major characteristics of nonnuclear conflict, the conflict phenomenon in general, U.S. security interests, and various American policy options.

We were encouraged to organize the workshop and pursue an examination of the subject by various individuals in the military, high government circles, and academia. Though it would be impossible to list all the names of those who assisted us, we do wish to publicly acknowledge our gratitude for their assistance and support. The following groups, however, must be singled out for their generous assistance and support of the workshop and this volume: The U.S. Army War College (Carlisle Barracks, PA), the National Strategy Information Center (New York, NY), the National Security Education Program of New York University, the Institute for Political Philosophy and Policy Analysis of Loyola University's Department of Political Science, and Loyola University (Chicago, IL).

The Editors

INTRODUCTION

American Policy and Low-Intensity Conflict: An Overview

Sam C. Sarkesian

The Loyola Workshop on Low-Intensity Conflict (November 1979)

Four major issues provoked substantial debate and some disagreement among the participants of the workshop. First, there was little agreement on the meaning of the term "low-intensity conflict." It was evident that the term could mean different things to different people, depending on the organizational perspective and anticipated level of involvement in the conflict. For example, to the individual soldier, there may be little sense in labelling any type of combat "low-intensity," when survival on the battlefield is rarely low-intensity. From the point of view of the policy maker, low intensity could be meaningful in terms of level of combat expected, the limits placed on force employment, and the restrictions on the scope and number of parties involved in the combat area. There is also the possibility that protagonists may view the conflict differently, creating serious asymmetry. One side may consider the conflict as a limited one, while the other may see it as a struggle for survival and consider it a total war.

Second, there was little agreement as to the specifics of policy to be adopted in responding to low-intensity conflict. (There was consensus,

1

however, that the United States must be prepared to respond.) But the force composition, the circumstances under which a force would be employed, and the areas into which such forces should be introduced if necessary remained major issues throughout most of the workshop. It was generally thought that no force could be specifically tailored beforehand for a particular contingency in a particular country or situation; for example, a military force could not be structured specifically to respond to a low-intensity conflict in Venezuela. Rather, it was felt that a force posture should be developed that had the flexibility to respond to low-intensity conflict in several areas in a variety of forms. Participants agreed that political leaders had to develop and articulate clear purposes for the use of military force—purposes, it might be added, that have or can develop the necessary domestic support.

Third, there was disagreement regarding the quantity and quality of the hardware and logistical backup available for response to nonnuclear contingencies. This disagreement was also reflected in the discussions over the type of training, force structures, and command and control procedures needed. Additionally, there was lack of agreement regarding American ability to intervene rapidly and ability to escalate once troops were committed. Such disagreements were probably due to more fundamental disagreements regarding the specifics of policy and the meaning of low-intensity conflict; nevertheless, they were particularly significant in considering mobility and support after intervention.

These observations must be considered within the context of the overall consensus and intellectual value of the workshop. Two countervailing points need to be made in this respect. There was a clear recognition that military capability, national will, and political-military policy need to be integrated. Underlying this was the belief that American military intervention could not be undertaken without a proportionate level of popular support.

A positive, although less clear, result of the workshop was the intellectual experience and interaction between participants. There is much to be said for simply "thinking" about policy in a setting removed from the pressures of day-to-day operational requirements, particularly when such thinking is a result of debate, discussion, and assessment among participants from varying backgrounds and interests. No book can truly reflect the breadth and depth of this kind of intellectual exchange.

Definition and Concept

Aware of the difficulty in defining and conceptualizing the term, we nevertheless have formulated a working definition of low-intensity conflict to use as the cornerstone of our analysis—noting that such a definition and conceptualization will undoubtedly be revised during the course of the analysis. "Low-intensity conflict," as used here, refers to the range of activities and operations on the lower end of the conflict spectrum involving the use of military or a variety of semimilitary forces (both combat and noncombat) on the part of the intervening power to influence and compel the adversary to accept a particular political-military condition. Employment of force is a concept closely related, but broader in scope and in policy option. The employment of force is not exclusively concerned with combat, but includes a variety of methods and strategies in which military force or its perceived use can influence the environment and actions of other states without necessarily resorting to battle. It encompasses the threat of force (without employment or combat), the employment of force (without combat), and the use of force in combat. Employment of force and low-intensity conflict, as concepts, blend into one another. It is difficult to develop credibility for a policy for force employment without being prepared to commit forces to combat. A foreign state (or states) must be convinced that the state employing force is also prepared to use it in combat. Nevertheless, for the purpose of methodological clarity, distinctions are made between the two concepts. Additionally, it is necessary to identify characteristics of the environment in which low-intensity conflict is likely to occur, as well as the character of the states in the Third World that compose the environment in which forces may be employed.

The Third World Environment

A number of scholars have recognized the fallacy of placing all of the Third World states in one category, inasmuch as there exists a variety of distinctions that can be made between the developing states (for example, that between oil producers and oil consumers). However, there are common characteristics that are particularly important in developing American political-military policy. The most obvious is that most developing areas are likely to remain unstable and have a high degree of revolutionary potential. There are many reasons for this, but four predominate: the diffusion of political power, lack of legitimate governing structures, the politicization in a modern context of historical ethnic and geographic animosities, and the introduction of technology. As one observer concludes:

> The third world of one hundred less developed countries (LDCs) has come to dominate the rhetoric of the U.N. and other international agencies, but its real power standing is remarkably weak.... The under-developed world is riven with internecine conflicts, domestic upheavals and a mounting burden of surplus, unskilled people. Governed by military juntas, one-party dictatorships or repressive oligarchies, they resent the "free trade imperialism" and the neocolonial exploitation that they associate with either the former empires or the domineering dollars of the West.... Most of the LDCs can not realistically hope

to raise their opportunities for work or to expand the bare necessities for survival (for their burgeoning populations). It will not be surprising if they resort to regional wars, as in the horn of Africa, simply to let off steam and to ease their population pressures. They might yet prove that the dire predictions of the Reverend Malthus were flawed by optimism.[1]

Equally important, conventional armies of developing states may not, in the long run, wield the coercive power nor have the military capability to defend the state. The availability of modern weaponry and the ethnic diversity within the various developing states provide clusters of political-military groups that can easily be arrayed against the existing government and intervening forces. "People's War," in its broadest sense, is the most likely conflict phenomenon in such an environment.

The instability created by these developments provides opportunities for solving problems through use of force by indigenous groups or by the intervention of foreign states to protect their own interests. The most critical result is that existing governments and/or ruling elites are usually placed in a fragile power position. Events in Iran and Afghanistan are cases in point.

Involvement in such an area presents a policy quagmire for the West and the United States. But though it may seem prudent for the United States to avoid serious involvement in such areas, energy needs and geopolitical considerations may require it.

Low-Intensity Conflict

The conflicts that are most likely to occur in the Third World areas are of the low-intensity variety. They are limited geographically, in the number of participants, and in the nature and scope of military operations. If "visible" intervention from external sources should occur in low-intensity conflicts, nationalistic passions are likely to be aroused, with a high propensity for the development of a "People's War." A "fluid" battle area, not bound by conventional considerations and enmeshed in the political-social fabric of the political system, is likely to create difficulties for the intervening power that may be insurmountable in terms of "conquest" or "victory." Moreover, combat can include both rural and urban areas, and occur against forces who possess sophisticated weapons. In these circumstances, the political-psychological dimensions of military operations predominate over tactical considerations. Additionally, conventional means of ascertaining military progress may be irrelevant, as may also be the case with conventional military training and doctrine. In broad terms, low-intensity conflicts are usually limited wars and/or wars of insurgency on a scale smaller than Vietnam, but are something more than isolated acts of terrorism. As such, they demand a political-military response rather than an exclusively police operation.

Employment of Force

This refers to the various uses of military force, short of combat, to achieve a particular goal (coercive diplomacy). It is used as a "signal" to the foreign country or countries of the seriousness of the issue at hand from the point of view of the state employing force and the fact that national security is at stake. Employment of force can include a variety of measures ranging from a show of naval force through increasing military assistance to the commitment of advisors.[2] Employment of force must, however, be buttressed by a policy of resolve and may require the commitment of military units to combat—low-intensity conflict. Failure to follow through beyond force employment (as that term is used here) when circumstances require it may be a signal to the foreign state or states of the lack of resolve, military inadequacy, or both, on the part of the employing state. The erosion of credibility and policy is sure to follow.

The Conflict Spectrum

The relationship between various types of conflicts is shown on the accompanying diagram. The diagram also displays the perceived strategic dimension and capability of the United States. The United States has a reasonably adequate capability to conduct short-duration surgical operations and limited conventional wars in the fashion of Korea. Additionally, the United States has a reasonable capability and credibility to maintain a strategic nuclear posture with respect to NATO and vis-à-vis the Soviet Union. Increasingly, the United States is developing, along with its NATO allies, a nonnuclear conventional capability in Europe. However, for limited wars of Guerrilla types II and III and Vietnam types, the United States lacks not only credibility but military capability. Thus the United States appears to have an adequate capability and credibility for conflicts on the extreme ends of the spectrum. For the vast middle range (consisting primarily of low-intensity conflicts and limited wars) however, the United States appears to have limited capability and minimal credibility. And it is in this range that most future conflicts are likely to occur.

Assuming the validity of the conflict spectrum and the political-military capability of the United States, three issues predominate. What should be the political-military policy of the United States to develop a credible force-employment capacity and a response to low-intensity conflict? What political constraints and limitations must be considered? What are the military requirements and capabilities necessary to carry out political-military policy? Let us briefly examine each of these issues, deferring the question of policy until the last.

Diagram 1

Conflict Spectrum

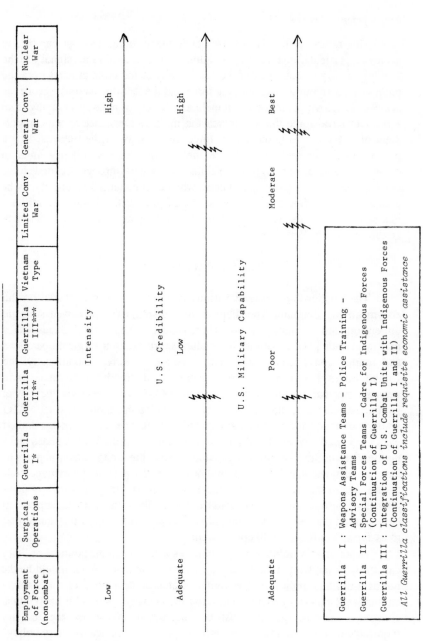

Political Constraints and Limitations

Political forces and pressures, both domestic and international, play a crucial role in the capacity of the United States to employ force and to engage in low-intensity conflict. Most are aware of the constraints imposed by the domestic environment. These were clearly manifested during the American involvement in Vietnam. Congressional-Executive relationships, the state of domestic politics, the attitudes of the populace regarding threat perceptions and force employment, and the "mind set" of policy makers are important political ingredients in determining the boundaries of political-military policy. For example, it may be one matter to commit a team of Special Forces to a particular area and to provide military and economic assistance. It is another matter to commit a battalion-size combat unit in the same area. As the United States learned (one hopes), without the requisite popular support and the consensus of important political actors force employment has little hope of achieving intended policy goals. In this respect, there are a number of observations about America's Vietnam experience that need to be considered.

Relevance of the Vietnam Experience

There is a considerable body of opinion in both military and civilian quarters that places little value on the United States' experience in Vietnam to the conduct of future low-intensity conflicts. Though it is true that policy makers should not be bound by the past, it is also true that to forget the lessons of Vietnam is to invite similar results. If one reviews the history of the United States' military operations against the Seminole Indians (1836–43), in the Philippines (1898–1901), and in Vietnam (1964–72), one is struck by a number of similarities regarding political-military problems, military operations, and insurgency forces. Unfortunately, there has been little historical analysis for purposes of developing doctrinal guidelines. Indeed, the military has a singularly short institutional memory. It has had to relearn lessons that should have been historically ingrained in the institutional posture. To avoid mistakes of the past, therefore, there is a need to examine the doctrinal relevance *and* irrelevance of Vietnam, both political and military, and assess its applicability to policy and program guidelines for future low-intensity wars. Using such assessments, we can designate conceptual frameworks and examine doctrinal feasibility to provide guidelines and historical-experience factors for military and civilian decision makers.

This is not the appropriate place for a reexamination of the United States involvement in Vietnam. The literature abounds with such studies.[3] Several observations, however, are relevant and appropriate for our purposes. First, the Vietnam war developed into an asymmetrical relationship between the United States and the Viet Cong/North Vietnamese. While we conducted a limited war, for the revolutionaries it was a total war. Second, conventional military wisdom, training, and professional education were apparently inadequate to meet the challenges of the political-military dimensions characteristic of revolutionary wars. Third, American domestic political attitudes were crucial in affecting the American military role in Vietnam. Equally important, the crescendo of criticism from domestic political groups had a decided effect on the policy options available to the political leadership. All of these factors reinforced the asymmetry of the relationships in Vietnam. Fourth, American military intervention in support of a governing elite or political system that does not have some minimum level of internal support is likely to erode any existing public support. This does not necessarily mean that such intervention is doomed to failure. Rather, it means that American intervention must be a balanced political-military one, primarily concerned with the reinforcement and legitimation of the existing system. Fifth, the American experience in Vietnam remains an important influence in the world perspective of military and civilian leaders and as such, has a decided impact on political-military strategy. The result is a very cautious approach that borders on a "never-again" attitude. Sixth, the Vietnam involvement stimulated a military preoccupation with the "conventional" environment of European wars. This is manifested in hardware and tactics as well as in professional military education and training. A further consequence is that perceptions of military capability and of the imperatives of political-military policy appear to have become closely wedded to a "conventional" mind set, where issues appear clearer and military capability and policy seem to have a more understandable goal.

Regardless of recent events, therefore, the American military intervention still weighs heavily in the minds of important political actors. As Osgood notes,

> ...the popular disaffection with the Vietnamese war does not indicate a reversion to pre-Korean attitudes towards limited war. Rather it indicates serious questioning of the premises about the utility of limited war as an instrument of American policy, the premises that originally moved the proponents of limited war strategy and that underlay the original confidence of the Kennedy Administration in America's power to cope with local Communist incursions of all kinds.[4]

Most important, as demonstrated in Vietnam, the employment of force for any length of time requires popular support. Without it, military intervention of any type will quickly lose its legitimacy.

As Ravenal points out,

> The ... condition that will complicate the enforcement of international order is the lack of consensus in domestic support not when our system is free from

external pressure, but precisely when it most needs steady support. Few societies—especially one such as the United States—will hold together in foreign exercises that are ill-defined or, conversely, dedicated to the maintenance of a balance of power. . . . The lack of public support might not prevent intervention, but it might critically inhibit its prosecution.[5]

Superpower Relationships

The security relationships between the United States and the USSR are obvious elements in determining the nature of America's use of force and policy to respond to low-intensity conflicts. It is common knowledge that the cornerstone of United States-Soviet security relationships is deterrence—mutually assured destruction capability. If the past is any guide, neither superpower intends to use nuclear weapons in conflicts not directly and immediately affecting its own survival. By and large, the use of nuclear weapons is conceivable only in the European context and possibly the confrontation along the Sino-Soviet border. Comparable nuclear threats and military balance are absent in non-European areas. From a strategic point of view, the applicability of deterrence in the context of the Third World necessitates a military capability not exclusively rooted in nuclear weaponry.

The Soviet Union seems to have grasped this fact and shaped its military capability to expand its nonnuclear flexibility, apparently without surrendering any of its nuclear effectiveness. It is, for example, able to influence politics and events in Africa and the Middle East by a variety of strategies and methods. It has developed a political-military capability to exploit limited wars in various regions and support or deter insurgency wars as its policy dictates. It is difficult to predict the long-range benefits, if any, to the Soviet Union. In the short run, however, the Soviet Union has projected political resolve and strengthened its political-military credibility in areas outside of the European context.

Since the denouement in Vietnam, the United States, unlike the Soviet Union, has displayed a decreasing capability and credibility to influence political-military matters outside of the European area. Focusing primarily on Europe, the United States has strengthened its NATO commitment and is developing an increasingly effective nonnuclear capability for large-scale battles likely to occur in the Central Plains of Europe. Few would argue the need for such a posture. Without a strong political-military base in Europe, political-military policy in other areas would be seriously jeopardized. Nonetheless, it appears that this preoccupation on the battles in Europe has caused the neglect of other areas—areas with a potential for serious security problems for the United States. Even with a reawakened interest in low-intensity conflict because of the Iranian crisis of 1979 and 1980 and Soviet incursions into Afghanistan in 1979 and 1980, the United States has not as yet demonstrated the political resolve nor military posture to respond to threats outside of the European context. Though the development of an American "Rapid Deployment Force" has been announced, there remain outstanding issues of force composition and structure, the effectiveness of logistical backup, and combat effectiveness of such forces. Moreover, the United States has yet to demonstrate its ability to integrate political, military, and economic instruments into a coherent policy, effective in the Third World. This cannot be accomplished overnight or by one-time actions. The credibility of such a policy is a result of a pattern of consistent actions reflecting purposeful policy goals that are understood by other states.

In sum, the ability to deter is not exclusively based on nuclear capability. Successful deterrence policy requires a credible nonnuclear capability, among other things. It does not necessarily follow that nonnuclear forces must engage in conflict. An existing credible nonnuclear capability, combined with purposeful political strength, is likely to have important political overtones in any crisis or confrontation.

Policy Constraints

It is conceivable that once the United States intervenes, it will opt not to raise the intensity of the conflict beyond "low intensity." If so, the United States must be prepared to withdraw if the conflict goes beyond low-intensity proportions. If the decision to remain is taken, then the character of the conflict may develop into a Vietnam- or Korea-type conflict, with a possibility of escalation and superpower confrontation. Serious attention must therefore be given to the political impact of force employment on the domestic political system.

The international ramifications of force employment are no less serious. The reaction of allies and potential aggressors must be included as part of the political calculus. Similarly, the political repercussions within the target area must be weighed in terms of intended outcome. It is difficult to isolate the target area. Intervention usually affects contiguous areas and regional balances of power, as well as nationalistic and racial sensitivities. No intervention can be undertaken without creating unforeseen political and social consequences that may be to the disadvantage of the intervening power. In such circumstances, multilateral employment of force may be the desired method, yet unilateral force employment may be the only possibility.

There are serious questions that must be answered before undertaking force employment. In less than clearly perceived crises and major wars, these questions limit the scope of force employment and narrow the range of policy options for the American policy elite. These questions include, but are not limited to, the following: Under what conditions will Congress, the public and other political actors support U.S. military intervention? Once intervention takes place, can the United States withdraw at an appropriate time without creating a sense of defeat or abandonment? What are the likely consequences of intervention? What are the consequences of withdrawal without accomplishing policy goals? Should intervention be attempted without clear domestic political support?

Military Requirements and Capabilities

Military requirements and capabilities are dictated by the national interest as translated into political-military policy. In its ability to employ force credibly and engage in low-intensity conflict, the American military appears inadequate. We have already identified a number of political reasons for this situation. There are also a number of military considerations, including the prevalence of a "conventional" military wisdom, perceived costs in resources, and the nature of military planning and organization.

Underlying American military philosophy is the assumption that military formations trained for conventional battle are adequate to engage in low-intensity conflict. Moreover, this "generalist" attitude prevails throughout the military system. Simply stated, "common" service training for appropriate military units is considered adequate to respond to almost all contingencies. The fact of the matter is that the highly sociopolitically sensitive character of low-intensity conflict and force employment require a dimension that is hardly touched in standard military training or professional education. Additionally, military planners probably find it difficult to reallocate funds and shift priorities. The costs of developing and maintaining adequate military posture for force employment outside of the European context may be too high, requiring reduction of the high-technology and capital-intensive posture required for modern nuclear and major conventional wars.

As a result, military planning for force employment usually means reliance on *ad hoc* command structures devised from existing conventional formations and military forces composed of conventionally trained and equipped units. Similarly, planning for force employment as a result of imminent commitment usually means a conventional thought process re-flected in conventional response—reliance on well-established procedures. To respond successfully, planning, training, organization, and equipment must be part of an ongoing military program. Command structures and combat formations must be accustomed to operate as an integrated unit. This requires an assessment of existing military formations and the degree to which current forces can respond to low-intensity conflict and force employment. Subsequently, adjustments can be made to rectify major weaknesses.

For example, Ranger battalions and Special Forces units in the Army may need to be restructured to develop a combined light infantry force capable of low-intensity conflict. Such restructuring may require a Special Forces-type organization with a capability generally associated with Ranger battalions. Additionally, doctrines need to be developed, along with professional education, aimed at developing a deep understanding of the political-social character of Third World areas and how these translate into the complex environment of low-intensity conflicts.

The American military, to be sure, must prepare for a range of potential crises. The starting point for such preparation is a clear policy and military programs that are placed in a "real-life" context. A number of scenarios should be developed based on the criteria and considerations discussed earlier. Such scenarios need not, nor can they, include every conceivable contingency. Enough scenarios should be developed, however, to cover a range of the major types of intervention, for example, less-than-Korean-type limited war, various types of insurgency (Guerrilla I, II and III), and Vietnam-type operations.

Moreover, forces-in-being cannot be structured to respond to every possible low-intensity contingency. What is needed is an examination and assessment of prototype forces (including political and military command structure) that can be quickly shaped to meet the most likely crises. This necessitates flexibility in the organization, innovative command systems, highly mobile and reactive forces, and a responsive decision-making structure.

Contingency planning must also be based on something more than "vault" plans. This refers to the tendency of military planners to develop plans for every conceivable contingency, with little reference to the issues of national will, political considerations, and prevailing military posture. These plans are then filed in "vaults" to be used when an appropriate contingency arises. Such plans may be useful for clear crises, for example NATO-Warsaw Pact conflict, but they quickly lose their validity when applied to force employment and low-intensity conflict—unless such plans are constantly revised in a dynamic way. What this means is that there must be ongoing military training and education programs to insure that appropriate military forces develop and maintain knowledge of the Third World, and understand the ambiguities and complexities characteristic of military intervention in a Third World context.

For example, it is conceivable that a realistic scenario considers the occupation of the Panama Canal by a hostile power or group in the 1980s. To be sure, most expect a conventional United States military response, but without serious consideration of insurgency warfare, a response to the occupation of the Panama Canal based solely on conventional operations would in the long run create conditions destructive of the very purpose of the policy. Major considerations in such a scenario should include, among other things, the type and number of U.S. military formations required for the recovery of the canal, the expected nature of the military operations, the political-social conditions in Panama, identification of friendly and hostile groups within the target area, the anticipated reaction of Latin American states, domestic and international political ramifications, the long-range political goal, the expected costs in manpower and material, and the effect on America's military posture elsewhere. Similar questions should be raised in each scenario, regardless of the target area. The important point, however, is that military requirements and capabilities as they are reflected in "forces-in-being" must be realistically integrated into plans.

Military requirements are impossible to determine if they are not based on a consistent pattern of political-military policy that reflects clear national security interests. Attempting to develop military requirements in relation to military capabilities, isolated from clearly defined policy goals, simply relegates military requirements to some perceived imminent crisis or financial criteria. In the first instance, military requirements become the prisoners of wide fluctuations reflecting threat perceptions of the moment. In the latter case, military requirements may have little relationship to military capabilities and political-military policy.

Brent Scowcroft's observations with respect to Soviet-American relationships are particularly appropriate in this context.

> We must therefore learn to curb our fast shifting reactions to the Soviet Union, both of fear and complacency. It is this oscillation between these two poles, this lack of consistency and conviction that can do the most harm. It prompts us to waste valued resources and to strain our alliance understandings. These oscillations increase the chance of miscalculation and they lead to crash programs whenever anxiety rises. To cut back military efforts in periods of calm and to swell them in times of crisis is a most inefficient way to operate a defense establishment.[6]

Interestingly enough, the reaction of the Carter Administration in early 1980 to the Soviet intervention in Afghanistan is a case in point. Increased defense spending as contrasted to the reduction of defense in the preceding three years may well be "fast shifting reactions to the Soviet Union, both of fear and complacency."

Assessments of military requirements in the context of force employment and issues of low-intensity conflict, must, therefore, begin with such questions as: What mix of nuclear and nonnuclear forces is necessary to achieve political-military goals? What training and professional education should be introduced to prepare military units for nonnuclear contingencies? What logistical support is necessary to support military operations? What tactical doctrines are relevant? What should be the force structures and command and control arrangements? Under what conditions should the United States disengage following intervention, and what does this mean in terms of military capability? What are the costs, political as well as in terms of resources, for developing a credible nonnuclear capability?

Policy Guidelines

The translation of policy from the decision stage to implementation is a difficult task wrought with imponderables and miscalculations. But any policy must, at a minimum, integrate goals with programs and resources. American policy designed to respond to low-intensity conflict and force employment must be based on the recognition of the special character of nonnuclear contingencies and their relation to the credibility of American deterrence and interests. The identification of American interests must be clear, and articulated in understandable terms. Political-military strategy must be designed to protect those interests, with military posture and national will capable of supporting the strategy. Without a correlation of these elements, policy is doomed to failure. If these cannot be correlated, then the sights of policy must be lowered to reflect capabilities and political resolve realistically. Yet if policy goals remain crucial, then military capability must be strengthened and national will sensitized to the level necessary to reach the goals.

As one commentator has written,

> American power—economic, military and spiritual—must be shaped anew to protect free world interests. What is the meaning of war, what is our global strategy? We must recalibrate the mix of weapons and bases. We need to jar our allies to reconsider the purposes and forms of our alliances. We desperately need a new intelligence capacity. We need to recharge our technology and leap ahead of Soviet weaponry. We need an energy strategy for survival, not for re-election.

> We must certainly decide where and how we can wage the most effective "bloodless" battle to discourage terrorism and aggression. But we must, too, decide where and how we best can fight if blood must be shed.[7]

In the final analysis, the cornerstone of effective policy is the balancing of military posture, national will, and national interests. Successful policy is rarely the sole result of scientific application of this balance derived from mathematical assessments. It generally is the result of the meshing of the science of policy making with the art of leadership. This requires wisdom based on political acumen, intellectual sensitivity, and a sense of history. What makes it more difficult is that the "meshing" of science and art is necessary at many levels of the policy process and from a number of those involved in the instrumentalities for implementing policy. Therefore, military professionals as well as civilian policy makers and elected officials need the wisdom to know when and how to engage in "bloodless battles" and "where and how we best can fight if blood must be shed."

Notes

1. Walter Goldstein, "Which is the West That is Likely to Survive?," in Walter Goldstein, ed., *The Western Will to Survive* (Report of a Wingspread Conference, The Johnson Foundation, June, 1977), p. 20.
2. For an extremely useful account of one aspect of force employment, see Harry M. Blechman and Stephen S. Kaplan, *Force Without War: U.S. Armed Forces as a Political Instrument* (Washington, D.C.: Brookings Institution, 1978).
3. One of the most balanced accounts is Guenter Lewy, *America in Vietnam* (New York: Oxford University Press, 1978).
4. Robert E. Osgood, "The Reappraisal of Limited War," in Eugene Rosi, ed., *American Defense and Détente; Readings in National Security Policy* (New York: Dodd, Mead and Co., 1973), p. 466.
5. Earl C. Ravenal, "The Case for Strategic Disengagement," *Foreign Affairs* 51 (April 1973): 513.
6. Brent Scowcroft, "Western Security in the Coming Years," in Goldstein, p. 14.
7. Hugh Sidey, "Carter Must Accept Today's Perilous Truths," *Chicago Sun-Times*, 6 January 1980, p. 12.

CHAPTER 1

The Employment of Force: Political-Military Considerations*

George K. Osborn and William J. Taylor, Jr.

International Security Environment

The international security environment in the early and mid-1980s is likely to be a mix of suspicion-riven and tenuous standoff between the superpowers and extreme instability in the non-Western, nonindustrial world. It appears reasonable to assume that "central wars" (those involving the Soviet Union and the United States) are low-probability events. This means mutual deterrence will be effective, and neither superpower will be tempted to resort to compellence *in extremis*, *à la* Cuba, 1962.[1] Admittedly, there is a period of uncertainty, beginning as early as 1982 and extending somewhat beyond 1985, during which Soviet leaders might try compellence, but if U.S. development and deployment schedules already in train are pursued the temptation should be minimal. In addition, it is not highly probable that the advanced industrial states will forego all international economic integration and resort to the beggar-thy-neighbor policies of the 1930s—although one must be more than somewhat concerned about the ability of both national and international institutions to function effectively under continued, probably greater stress.

The mild optimism concerning central-war deterrence reflected above, however, does not extend to the non-Western, nonindustrial part of the globe, that is, the states making up the so-called Third and Fourth Worlds, where the modernization process releases simultaneously political, economic, cultural and social forces that are potentially volatile. Here one might anticipate relatively high instability to be reflected in endemic violence, both inter- and intranational. However, anticipation and prediction are two different matters.[2] Paradoxically, such violence—evidence of the inability of political institutions to function or adapt effectively—probably will occur across the spectrum of wealth, from the rich and developing states to the poor and stagnating or retrogressing. Many states with a plethora of resources (of the right or marketable sort) may be unable to cope with the demands of forced-draft development. Many of those that are resource-poor and at the mercy of the weather probably will be unable to cope with the demands of nondevelopment. Those in the middle range will have some of the problems of those toward both ends of the spectrum.

In these circumstances, some might think it desirable if the exogenous powers, that is, the superpowers and their industrialized friends and neighbors in the Council of Mutual Economic Assistance (COMECON) and the Organization for Mutual Cooperation and Development (OECD), would adhere rigorously to the principle of nonintervention in the internal affairs of sovereign states and to the less sweeping but appealing slogan of "regional solutions to regional problems" for international violence. One might make a convincing case that even if indifference were not feasible, certainly diffidence, self-restraint, and patience might be. Alternatively, it might be hoped that violence in the Third and Fourth Worlds that impinges on the relations of those states with those in the First and Second could be treated within some existing institutional framework—say the United Nations Conference on Trade and Development (UNCTAD), for one—and other violence could be left to play itself out in the local theater, perhaps not unnoticed or ignored, but without audience participation. Such forebearance is not likely to result, for reasons sketched below.

First, whatever the long-range desires, hopes, and plans of this and succeeding leadership groups in the Soviet Union, it is reasonably clear the near-term goals of the Soviet state include global recognition of the Soviet position as the leading superpower and the prestige, including the deference of other states, that goes with such a position. If the USSR were able to demonstrate superpower status across the spectrum of power and capabilities it might be acceptable to others, though others might view such power with considerable ambivalence. But clearly the USSR is not able to do so. Whatever the lingering appeal of Marxian socialism in the world, the ideological appeal of Marxism-Leninism in the operational mode explicated by the historical development of the USSR has little appeal outside its boundaries. Sometimes, indeed, it has little appeal even within its boundaries. Further, the USSR uses trade or economic aid to gain influence elsewhere only with difficulty (though with some limited success). The Soviet economy can produce neither the goods nor the capital to compete broadly in that arena with the other advanced industrial states. As a model for economic development for those who desperately need such development, the USSR is not very attractive—in spite of showcase examples such as steel mills (in India), stadiums (in Indonesia), and hotels (in Burma). What the USSR does have, however, is military power and an increasing capability to use it in a wide variety of forms—direct transfers of hardware, technology transfer, provision of advisors (Soviet, but also Cuban, German, and others), and intervention by USSR military forces and/or proxies. In short, relatively high levels of instability in Third and Fourth World states will tempt the USSR to intervene to enhance its superpower status by demonstrating its responsibility for the development of a stable world order (of its liking). Any such intervention frequently, though not necessarily always, will take on military form because : (1) the USSR lacks capabilities in other forms of power; (2) the Soviet leadership appears to recognize the continuing utility of military force (for example, in Afghanistan in December 1979); and (3) the Soviets do not appear to be deterred from using military force by such intangibles as "world opinion."[3]

Second, OECD members do have interests—vital and otherwise—in various parts of the nonwhite, non-Western, southern world. These range from historic associations through the spectrum of economic interests from investments (including loans) and access markets and raw materials to vital security interests in specific geographic areas or sites. The latter may be derivative from other interests, primarily economic, but they nevertheless are real and may be "vital," that is, interests worth fighting to protect or secure. Where sociopolitical disorder threatens any such interests, OECD states, individually and collectively, certainly will be tempted to intervene. For OECD, despite the legacies of anticolonialism, the choice of instruments of intervention is much wider than it is for the USSR. The appeal of such ideas (not ideologies) as freedom and human dignity, the concepts embodied in the American Declaration of Independence or the French Declaration of the Rights of Man, remains strong. A broad spectrum of economic capabilities is available, although the state of the economies of the Western industrialized countries in the early 1980s may cast some doubt on the extent of these capabilities. The tactics of usage may be difficult to fathom and master. In any case, the temptation to resort to military intervention will remain, and it would seem foolhardy to ignore this fact, even though some might prefer to do so.

Third, protagonists in Third and Fourth World conflicts are likely to seek help where they can find it. They will search for patrons to assist them in external or internal struggles for power, and they may not be very particular about the overt and covert motivations of the patrons. In most cases, to be sure, the local parties will attempt to avoid the more onerous aspects of client-patron relationships, but frequently this probably will not lead them to eschew available external assistance. Hence the simple temptation to intervene for reasons sketched earlier in this paper will be reinforced by positive appeals for assistance couched in terms calculated to invite internvention.

Low-Intensity Conflict

This brief introduction to the internal-security environment of the 1980s may serve as a prologue to the definition of low-intensity conflict. It is easier to proceed with definition itself in negative terms, that is, to say what low-intensity conflict is not rather than what it is. Obviously it is not central war involving both the home territories and military forces of the superpowers, nuclear or nonnuclear. It is not large-scale conventional war between NATO and Warsaw Pact forces. It is not limited conventional war on the scale of Korea or (at least on the side of the United States and other "Free World Forces") Vietnam, 1965-75. It is conflict in which exogenous actors have limited objectives, even though those of endogenous participants may be less limited. It is conflict in which the military component may superficially obscure more fundamental socioeconomic-political issues and goals. It is conflict most likely to arise in the Third and Fourth Worlds in the 1980s. It could involve high risks of escalation into regional or even global (central-superpower) wars, but such risks probably will not be high or obvious at the outset.

Low-intensity conflict is not to be equated with insurgency and counterinsurgency, at least as those also ambiguous terms have been defined operationally in the literature and programs of the 1960s and 1970s.[4] It is conceivable that the exogenous interventions in low-intensity conflict might include some or even all of the programmatic aspects of counterinsurgency as they are commonly understood, but it is as likely that the forms of intervention, at least by the United States, would include threats (both deterrent and compellent), raids, shows of force (that is, demonstrations), *coups de main*, and so forth, extending to use of surrogates (for example, the role of Belgians, French, and Moroccans in Shaba Province of Zaire in 1977 and 1978). Especially in the case of the United States, intervention in low-intensity conflict probably would be characterized by: (1) use of forces in being without immediate substantial augmentation or mobilization to reconstitute a strategic reserve; (2) limited objectives (for example, secure freedom of navigation through vital straits (Hormuz, Malacca?) rather than stop the spread of communism at the Kra Isthmus (roughly between Chumphon—east—and Ranong—west—Thailand) or prevent Tudeh seizure of power in Teheran; (3) careful tailoring of intervention forces to limited objectives; and (4) strict political control over intervention forces at every stage.

With respect to time limitations, limited objectives may include them or not, at least *ab initio*, but military planners probably are going to have to plan disengagement under both favorable and unfavorable conditions from the very first moments of the planning process. The time dimension is important. Recent research indicates that the "success rate" in applying military force erodes sharply over time,[5] and, as the experiences of Korea and Vietnam suggest, piecemeal commitment ("Salami tactics") does not achieve optimum results. In the locality of low-intensity conflict, high-intensity resolution may be in order.[6] In the time dimension, one might suggest seizure and indefinite retention of Simonstown without direct regard for an insurgency interventionist scenario in southern Africa.[7] Simonstown (South Africa) is the only modern naval base on the Cape Route, useful in providing antisubmarine protection to shipping lines or as a base for launching submarine warfare.

The "intensity" of conflict could be measured in a variety of ways. Depending upon the scenario, the possible variables might be:

• Lethality of weapons systems employed, that is, systems deployed or weapons fired;
• Amount of death and destruction;
• Numbers of people involved, for example, advisers, combatants, noncombatants;
• Quantity of material resources introduced, for example, weapons, military supplies, economic assistance;
• Rates at which resources are introduced and "expended";
• Opportunity costs of resources involved;
• Rate of actual and perceived progress toward political-military objectives.
• Length of time "conflict" continues;
• Public (domestic and international) perceptions of all of the above, based upon official and news-media reports.

It is important to note that "intensity" will be in the eye of the beholder and will always be relative to:

• Degree of psychological commitment by the contenders and interested third parties;
• Resource bases available to contenders;
• Information available to contending governments, leaders, and their bodies politic;
• Nature of the domestic polities of the contenders;
• Cost/risk calculations by the contenders and interested third parties.
• Positional relation to the conflict, for example, political decision makers or military commanders directly involved, civilian noncombatants in *locus rei sitae* or as interested observers in distant polities. Different actors using different indicators may differ in their perceptions of intensity.

The point here is that the ways in which these variables combine will be critical in establishing the symmetries and asymmetries central to conflict termination. If the object of the employment of force is a negotiated settlement, then it is important that the contender's objectives be limited and somewhat flexible in the range between maximum safe objectives and minimum tolerable outcomes. The mix of relevant variables might be very different if the object of force is outright capitulation. It will be important for U.S. decision makers and field operatives to understand the differences.[8] And that understanding should occur prior to the commitment of military force.

The issue of coupling (and its opposite, decoupling) presents something of a dilemma. It is probable that the United States would prefer generally to decouple low-intensity conflict situations from other more intense levels of conflict on a hypothetical superpower-escalation ladder. This might be especially important in those cases where the United States itself or its allies, surrogates, and close friends are involved, either directly or as intervening parties. In such cases national-security decision makers probably would insist that each case be regarded as *sui generis*, at least insofar as relations with the other superpowers are concerned (the assumption implicit here, that there will be only one other superpower, appears reasonable for the 1980-85 period). At the same time, however, it could be preferable (desirable?) to insist on coupling in cases where the USSR itself or its allies, surrogates, and close friends are involved, either directly or as intervening parties, and insist that each case be treated as rending the seamless web of peace.

One obvious way to avoid the dilemma, of course, would be to insist that it does not exist. In this interpretation, the definition of conflict is what the United States declares it to be; the problem disappears because its very being is denied. There are two principal objections to such a simple (simplistic?) solution. First, there must be considerable doubt of its viability in the conduct of foreign policy by a democratic state.[9] Second, any state could pursue this solution only if it had overwhelming superiority across the full spectrum of capabilities in the international arena, a situation unlikely to obtain even if willed and pursued actively and creatively.

Of course, one might argue that neither superpower is likely to initiate intervention plans with a clear intent to risk central war. Rather, in relative terms, each would tend to view such intervention as presenting an opportunity to advance or protect interests on the cheap. Starting from the latter proposition, one may construct hypothetical escalation ladders in which firebreaks appear to be clearly demarcated, risks may be calculated with reasonable precision, and probabilities of escalatory linkage discounted at several levels. Unfortunately, history presents a good many examples of how the pressure of events in a dynamic situation may lead to bizarre outcomes made logical in the cold light of conflict. Thus, those who believe themselves in control of events find themselves in turn controlled by those very events. This is not likely, of itself, to deter action though it might inhibit hubris.

In the case of the United States, the trauma of the Vietnam experience leads some to conclude that any form of intervention, especially any military intervention (including arms and arms technology transfer), takes the first step on the slippery slope leading inevitably to disaster. Aside from the absurdity of the metaphor itself, firmly embedded in automaticity or inevitability, such a conclusion can be dangerous if it prevents or precludes recognition of interests and potential means of advancing or protecting them. It is not necessary for the United States, or indeed any other state, to assume the role of international gendarme in the absence of a legitimate global order. What is necessary, rather, is that the lack of such an order be recognized as a form of order itself—legitimacy accorded the principle of state sovereignty— in which conflicts of interests between states, as well as within them, will from time to time result in resort to the use of force. Not all of the instances in which the use of force occurs or is imminent—and certainly not all of the conflicts of interests—impinge on our ability to continue on our experiment with democracy. International politics is not, as reductionists sometimes would have it, a simple, zero-sum game, but it is a game which few states can afford to ignore, as well as one from which winners cannot withdraw and hope to preserve their winnings. The issue of a choice between American involvement or noninvolvement on a large scale in world affairs holds little relevance. As a general rule, America's interests and the reality of the nation's massive economic and military power dictate a course of involvement in world problems. What require attention are the circumstances and form of American involvement.

Further, the world of 1980-85 will not be one in which the United States has global interests and capabilities while its friends and allies only have regional ones. The realization that total military capabilities, important as they may be, are not the only forms of disposable power in international politics should assist the United States and others in appreciating the flexibility of choice they have among instrumentalities to effect policy. This realization also should contribute to better definition of interests. However, clarity is not necessarily simplicity. Indeed, what might be called alliance or coalition politics must be more complex under conditions where power is more diffuse and disparities in capabilities are less pronounced. From a parochial perspective, as the United States persuades others to share the responsibilities of power because it is in their interests to do so, the United States will have to accept limitations on autonomy. This may engender serious domestic political conflict within the United States because of the discomfiture perceived by both the internationalists and the neoisolationists prominent in development of foreign and national security policy.

Widespread low-intensity conflict in the Third and Fourth Worlds, sensitivity to the requirements of successful coalition politics, appreciation of the difficulties involved both with linking and unlinking, recognition that intervention or nonintervention must be a product of careful evaluation of interests, willingness to use surrogates where feasible, and so on, should not obscure another important factor. The United States should be very cautious about contributing to the growth of regional powers to become permanent surrogates to serve the interests of American foreign policy. It is essential to recognize, in advance, that the stability of such regional powers itself may be temporary. Worse, U.S. attempts to strengthen them and expand their influence may produce even greater internal instability in the state in question. In such efforts, explicit in the case of the Shah of Iran and less clear but implicit in such cases as Indonesia, Zaire and the Republic of Korea, may well represent a natural tendency to confuse means and ends, to convert temporary alliances into permanent interests, to mistake transitory stability for legitimate order, and to make the stronger power the prisoner or hostage of the weaker (as with Germany and Austria-Hungary in 1914 or the United States and the Republic of Vietnam in 1954-75). Though the parallel is not perfect, it might be well to recall the ambivalence of United States responses to the evolution of unity in Europe despite our commitment to the North Atlantic Alliance—both phenomena being based on clear appreciation of interests—before pursuing further the implementation of the so-called Nixon and Ford Doctrines.

To be sure, force (or, to be explicit, military force) is by no means the only instrumentality even of coercive power, or more generally of power available to influence the course of world events, including the complex and probably conflict-prone world of the coming decade. However, even if one regards war (in Clausewitz's dictum, "the use of force to compel an adversary to do our will") as the *ultima ratio regum*, that it is ultimate should not exclude it from consideration.[10] Thus, though one should not forget that willingness to use force may involve bloodshed and death, including that of seemingly innocent bystanders, the arguments for abnegation of the employment of force in the real, as opposed to some hypothetical, world are far from compelling. One need not accept the arguments of Bernhardi or become a Nietzschean to consider using military force in a world in which the absence of legitimate order itself legitimizes force; one need only accept the real world of power politics.[11]

Making the Critical Links: Interests and the Use of Force

The issue of linkage, touched upon earlier, deserves further adumbration because of the necessity to understand the role of interests. Indeed, it may be argued that linkage in an objective sense can only be understood when it is tied to specific interests. If this cannot be done, the concept of linkage loses its value. For example, Dulles's proclamation of the massive-retaliation doctrine helped justify a U.S. defense budget in which so-called conventional forces would receive reduced emphasis while the importance of strategic (central-war retaliatory) forces was magnified. The intellectual underpinning, for what it was worth, was that the United States could not afford sufficient forces, especially manpower, to meet the Soviets with force at every point they might choose to stir up trouble. Given Dulles's penchant for viewing international politics as a zero-sum game and Eisenhower's determination to contain growth in defense spending, the defense-budget decisions may have made sense. However, linking every event that might take place on the international scene to central attacks on the Soviet Union simply lacked credibility. Similarly, as Henry Kissinger pointed out in 1979, linking the defense of NATO Europe to a U.S. willingness to engage in Mutual Assured Destruction is to perpetuate shibboleth.[12]

The above suggests, then, that for linkage to be credible it must be related specifically to interests as well as to the capability to protect or advance the interests and the will to do so.[13] If any of these elements is absent, or is so vague or general as to raise serious doubts in the minds of attentive observers, linkage is defective; commitment will be questioned. At the same time, failure to protect or advance specific interests, to develop the capabilities to do so, and the absence of a clear will must be taken to indicate absence of linkage or the erosion or disappearance of an erstwhile linkage. These interrelationships clearly are complex enough in themselves, but they must be treated in the context of the dynamics of an international arena in which interests do change (though not as rapidly as some might have it), in which the capabilities required to protect or advance interests change (probably more rapidly than the interests), and in which the will, especially in a democracy, is subject to the vagaries of the political process.

A major difficulty arises here because of the possibility that interests will become confused with the means of protecting or advancing them. Interests do tend to be of very long standing and frequently are articulated only in general terms. Indeed, it is rare, at least relatively, that one can state interests even with a degree of specificity approaching that of Great Britain's near-permanent interest in guaranteeing the channel coast of Europe against domination by a single power. It should be noted, in this case, that the single power threatening domination of the channel coast became hostile without regard for past conduct or promises of future conduct. The general nature of formulations of interests opens the way for some to overlook the distinction between means and ends. For example, there can be little doubt that a relatively long-term United States interest in preventing single-power hegemony in East and Southeast Asia perpetuated U.S. involvement in Vietnam and maintenance of diplomatic relations with Taiwan long after these means lost their utility. In the one case, the inferences one might properly draw from the reality of the Sino-Soviet split and the evolving tripartite relationship between Hanoi, Moscow and Peking were discounted; in the other, the profound nature of the shift in China's perception of the principal threat to its security was not appreciated by many.

It is true also that subsidiary interests may be highly specific. For example, most thoughtful Americans would concede that access to oil in the Persian Gulf demands free navigation of the Straits of Hormuz by oil tankers. Careful investigation, however, reveals that this specific interest is derived from, and therefore subsidiary to, other more general United States interests: economic survival of NATO allies, Japan and other OECD members, freedom of navigation of all international straits, and so forth. It may be less clear the United States has a specific interest in guaranteeing nonhostile control of Simonstown, but the same general interest of NATO allies and that of the broad interest in freedom of navigation on the high seas combine in this case to merit concern if not action. Subsidiary interests likely will be more transitory than interests generally, and it is important to recognize change as it takes place.

Commitments generally are taken as the objective demonstrations of interests. This provides further opportunity for confusion. Given the apparent general nature of some interests and frequent lack of specificity in defining subsidiary interests, it is convenient to look at commitments (that is, actual or programmed deployments of capabilities) as evidence for a manifestation of interests. Although the old political saw, "show me your programs and I'll tell you your policy," may have analytical applications, there may be disutilities in approaching commitments and interests from the same perspective. There is nothing inherently wrong in such a process, but there is a margin of error to be recognized. First, the sum total of commitments may not be the whole of interests—the whole may be greater than the sum of its parts. Second, states frequently do not have the resources available to commit to protecting or extending interests. Third, in specific cases, commitments and interests may be out of phase, i.e., the general interest may be unchanged while commitments may not shift as rapidly as the dynamics of a particular political context operate.

In a sense, then, ambiguity begets ambiguity. States and statesmen search for certainty, for certainty lies at the heart of credibility: will a state do what is says it will do or what external observers think it should do to protect or advance its interests? Will the United States embark on MAD if faced with a *casus belli* under the North Atlantic Treaty (especially if it appears the central sanctuary otherwise might be preserved)? What will the United States do if passage through the Straits of Hormuz is interdicted? Will the United States support its NATO ally, Norway, if the latter takes a strong stance in the face of Soviet nibbling at Spitzbergen? One is reminded of Chamberlain's statement, less than a year before the outbreak of World War II in Europe:

> How horrible, fantastic, incredible it is that we should be digging trenches and trying on gas masks here because of a quarrel in a far-away country between people of whom we know nothing.[14]

Thus, interests, commitments, and credibility become blurred, the one confused with the others. States attempt to realize their interests and recognize those of others; commitments take on an autonomy of their own as hard, objective evidence of specific interests, and credibility must be demonstrated, both in terms of specific interests and commitments and as proof that other interests are "real" and that commitments will be carried out when the occasion arises. All of these must be understood and appreciated not only by the individual state and its people but also by actual or putative allies, friends, and enemies. And, this must take place in a future world in which conflict will be endemic.

In the United States, as in any democratic state, and especially in the modern age of multimedia, national security decision makers carry the heavy responsibility of justifying the use of military force. An important part of that justification is to demonstrate the linkage between American involvement in military conflict and the pursuit of some clear U.S. interest. The longer the conflict and the greater the expenditure of U.S. resources, the greater the justification required to pacify the almost inevitable opposition. This is nothing new; every military conflict in which Americans have been involved has had its domestic critics. The information and education revolution in the United States have merely magnified the tasks of providing a clear rationale for resort to force. This is not necessarily a cause for lament, for American public opinion on foreign policy matters may be more sophisticated than some might think.[15] It is entirely possible for public opinion to sharpen the focus of policy makers on the nature of U.S. interests in a particular situation.

It is not possible to address here all U.S. interests which might be of such a nature as to justify commitment of American resources to one or more variants of low-intensity conflict. However, one can generalize about certain broad interest categories. We must deal with the range of "threats" which conceivably might be posed for the United States in the first half of the 1980s. Threats should not be treated in the abstract, but as challenges to U.S. interests. The most fundamental of these interests is "national survival," variously referred to in such amorphous terminology as "self-preservation," "military security," or "political security," and most clearly pursued in the currency of U.S. and allied military forces and related plans, programs, and budgets to support them. Fundamental too are national interests in "economic well-being" and "national prestige." But beyond these general notions of national interest, one must come to grips with the more specific interests beyond America's shores that, if threatened directly, would invite American responses somewhere along a spectrum of low-intensity conflict.

National interests are notoriously difficult to define. In the 1980s they may be more so. As Henry Kissinger stated recently about the relationships between NATO and the Soviet Union:

> If present trends continue, the 80's will be a period of massive crisis for all of us. . . . In a world of upheaval and rapid changes, enough opportunities will arise in which the relative capacity and the relative willingness of the two sides to understand their interests and to defend their interests will be the key element.[16]

Because the Soviet Union is America's most dangerous opponent in military-strategic terms for the early 1980s, how the Soviet leadership defines and defends Soviet interests will condition, but should not dictate, U.S. interests as well as American capabilities and propensities to resort to military force. Additionally, American policy makers must continually reassess U.S. regional interests in Europe, Asia, the Middle East, Sub-Saharan Africa and Latin America.

The Soviet Union

The most immediate challenge across the spectrum of U.S. interests in the early 1980s will continue to be presented by the Soviet Union in the form of continued expansion and modernization of its armed forces. With or without a SALT II agreement, the Soviets will continue to attempt to overcome feelings of insecurity, at a minimum, by outproducing the United States in a quest for absolute nuclear and conventional security or at least a position of equality on a global scale. If this is perceived by others as Soviet superiority it will be serious enough; if it is perceived by the Soviet leadership as superiority it could be disastrous. Either condition could produce Soviet political advantages in regions where vital U.S. interests reside.

In 1978, the Soviets were less interventionist in outlying geographic regions than in the preceding three years, concentrating instead on strengthening the Soviet strategic periphery from Norway in the west to Afghanistan in the south, and to Japan to the east. Soviet activity in the Northern Theatre could be viewed as threatening U.S. vital interests in Western Europe, although few in the United States perceive this.[17] One analyst of Soviet affairs provides an explanation:

> In its drive for control over Western Europe, its prime target, the Soviet Union is engaged in giant flanking movements designed, by means of southern and northern pincers, to envelop this continent and sever it from the United States, its main protector. . . . The northern pincer is pushed forward in a less dramatic fashion and therefore attracts less attention. There its objective seems to be primarily military. It aims at establishing Soviet control over the waterways used by Soviet Naval forces both for entry into the North Atlantic and for the deployment of submarines targeted on the territorial United States. . . . When completed, this movement will place Scandinavia behind Soviet forward lines.[18]

The challenge to United States interests is twofold. The first is military-strategic; the same Soviet military capabilities devoted to control of access to the North Atlantic can be used to deny United States reinforcement of Western Europe by sea in time of war. The strategic position of Norway is critical in the region. The second is psychopolitical; the Soviets seek political advantages from military power, and those advantages could take the form of "Finlandization" of European nations on NATO's northern flank.[19] Similar Soviet practices with respect to Turkey lend credence to this view.

Translation of American values in the international system calls for a world characterized by: (1) peace and stability in international politics; (2) multiple power centers and prevention of hegemony by adversary powers; (3) evolutionary change in global politics; (4) free trade and guaranteed access to markets and resources; and (5) the promotion of the democratic spirit and respect for human rights throughout the world. The Soviets will attempt to upset these features of the system where political costs appear minimal and the dividends high. Interventions will take many forms—military advisors and arms transfers that destabilize regional balances, promotion of armed conflicts by "proxy," support of terrorism in selected areas, exports of nuclear energy technology, and support for economic actions directed against the United States and its allies. The rising strength of Soviet military capabilities absolutely and relative to the strength of other Soviet capabilities is ominous.[20]

East Asia

The principal U.S. interest in Asia will remain the traditional one of preventing the domination of the Asian region by any single nation or alliance. Stated conversely, the United States seeks "a stable system of independent nations in Asia . . . that will increase the chances of maintaining a stable equilibrium among the United States, Japan, China, and the Soviet Union."[21] At the highest level of strategic generalization the principal U.S. interest seems assured. The probable cost of Soviet or People's Republic of China "domination" of the Asian land mass is central Sino-Soviet war.

Although lacking in capability to project military power in the near term, the pivotal East Asian actor for the 1980s will be the PRC, the government of which rules nearly a quarter of the human race. From the American perspective, political-military balance in Asia and elsewhere may depend largely on *judicious* use of the "China card," as a means of leverage against the Soviet Union. The PRC clearly will play a leading role in Asia and, as economic and technical development takes place in the latter 1980s and 1990s, might be expected to seek control of the entire deck in which the China card resides.

Normalization of relations with the PRC and the conditions of Asian balance this suggests for the early 1980s facilitates other important interests of the United States. U.S. trade with Asia grew to $60 billion in 1977, exceeding trade with Western Europe. America and Japan (with the second largest economy in the world) are the two largest investors in Asia. China's new drive for economic and technical development portends vast new markets for American business, though promise may obscure reality. Keeping doors open for American business enterprises will be even more important in the 1980s than in 1900. Asian nations depend largely upon future Japanese and American investments and economic assistance for sustained growth. Japan has relied upon the United States for protection of those investments and raw material resources as well as its own security. A militarily "secure" Japan that perceives no advantages from rearming has been a vital interest of the United States shared by other nations of Asia. These reciprocal U.S.-Japanese interests may change in the early 1980s as Japan rearms to establish its own capability to protect its absolutely vital interest in access to oil at a reasonable price, and as the United States encourages Japan to assume responsibility for a greater share in its security interests. .

Important if not presently vital among U.S. interests is finding solutions to mitigate the future efforts of North-South conflict. A "developing" nation (by Western standards) of 950 million people, and yet already a major power in Asia with influence in many parts of the developing world, China may prove pivotal in the development of global institutions to cope with the resource, population, environmental, and economic problems of the interdependent world of the 1980s.

Maintaining the peace in Northeast Asia, where the interests of Japan, the PRC, the United States, and the USSR meet, has been difficult enough. However, in Southeast Asia, where the interests of the same powers overlap, the situation is complicated further by recent attempts to increase Soviet presence, by older, unresolved conflicts among the smaller states, and by the attempts of the Socialist Republic of Vietnam to assert hegemony over the Indochina peninsula, if not further afield.

South Asia

U.S. policies toward South Asia have fluctuated over time. Interests have appeared to be a product of shifting attention. When Asian members of the Southeast Asia Treaty Organization were needed (1954), when Chinese expansion into the area was feared (1962), when the existence of Pakistan may have been threatened (1972), or when outright seizure of Afghanistan appeared imminent (1980), the United States was attentive. At other times, attention was diverted elsewhere, and it was difficult to discern what, if any, American interests were involved. U.S. economic involvement, despite sizeable sums of assistance, has remained relatively small.

The possibility exists, however, that the USSR (like its predecessor) will attempt to use South Asia to buttress its drive for global dominance in international politics. This could be done from the sea, using South Asian bases to support operations in the Indian Ocean and its littoral, or from the land, constructing client regimes to provide access from land and outflanking U.S. interests to both east and west. Soviet acquisition of port facilities and air bases in South Asia no doubt would call for reassessment of interests.

The specter of the breakup of India into a number of ethnolinguistic, warring states, or the outburst of a rural-versus-urban war in India could present a situation of low-intensity conflict similar to that facing sub-Saharan Africa. The interests of the United States in such cases no doubt would be influenced by the degree to which other exogenous powers intervened or showed restraint, but there can be little doubt the United States would be forced to examine its interests carefully and make critical decisions about what to do.

The Middle East

For strategic purposes, the Middle East may be considered the large arc of territory from Egypt to Iran, a region where "more important and yet different interests converge ... than in any other area of the developing world."[22] The Assistant Secretary of State for Near Eastern and South Asian Affairs stated U.S. interests in the region succinctly in 1979:[23] (1) Avoidance of confrontation with the Soviet Union; (2) security and well-being of Israel; (3) supply of Middle Eastern oil at reasonable prices; (4) close and friendly ties with key moderate Arab nations; (5) humanitarian concerns. For analytical purposes, U.S. interests in the Middle East can be categorized in three broad, sometimes overlapping categories: economic interests, strategic interests related to the global Soviet-American competition for influence and security, and interests related to Israel.[24]

Since the mid-1970s, U.S. economic interests in the Middle East have been based primarily on oil. Approximately 60% of the world's proven oil reserves are located in the Middle East, the great majority of it concentrated around the Persian Gulf littorals. The Middle Eastern countries accounted for about half of world oil production. The United States consumes 30% of the world's oil production and imports approximately 40% of its daily oil needs. Of that import total, about 40% is Middle Eastern oil. Although the U.S. economy would not collapse were it deprived of those imports, it would suffer severe dislocations which could lead to equally severe domestic political and social disorders.

Key allies such as Japan and the NATO countries are far more dependent on Middle Eastern oil that the United States. Japan must import over 90% of its total energy needs (over 5 million barrels per day) from the Middle East, while the NATO countries import anywhere from 60% to 80% of theirs. A serious interruption in the supply of oil could mean economic collapse for those countries. Since the economic health and political stability of Western Europe and Japan are vital to U.S. national security, it is very much in the interest of the United States to ensure that they, like the United States itself, have access to adequate supplies of Middle East oil at reasonable prices.

The rapid rise in the price of oil since the early 1970s has led to the transfer of unprecedented sums of money to the governments of the Middle Eastern oil-producing countries. For example, Saudi Arabian oil revenue rose from $655 million in 1965 to over $62 billion in 1979. Iranian oil revenue rose from $522 million per year to over $20 billion per year during the same period. The United States has a vital interest in making sure that such enormous sums are used constructively, and in ways which will eventually bring them back into the economies of the industrialized nations. Were such funds not "recycled," the resulting drain of capital would quickly create severe economic problems for the United States and its closest allies.

Many of the Middle Eastern countries have substantial surplus funds in excess of economic developmental needs. Large amounts have been deposited in U.S. banks which, in turn, can invest them in the U.S. economy. Recently, there have been some attempts by the producing countries to invest directly in the U.S. economy. Such efforts generally have met with little success. The United States has a strong interest in convincing the major oil-producing countries to invest their surplus revenues constructively. The existence of large, uncommitted amounts of hard currency that can be used to speculate on the world money market or, alternatively, to subsidize political unrest definitely is not in the interest of the United States.

Since World War II, and especially during the last decade, the Middle East has been an area of strategic competition between the United States and the Soviet Union. Traditionally, the primary U.S. strategic goal in the Middle

East has been simply to keep the Russians out of the region. U.S. policy makers felt that any significant Soviet political or military presence there would pose a threat to the security of NATO's southern flank, and they wanted to ensure that the Soviets did not gain control of the region's oil resources. U.S. policy in the Middle East tended to be reactive in nature; whenever Soviet influence appeared to be increasing, the United States attempted to devise means to counter it. The policies adopted varied substantially, depending on the nature of the perceived Soviet threat.

The desire to minimize, if not actually eliminate, Soviet influence in the Middle East remains. In fact, in the 1970s, it has been intensified by the Soviet naval buildup in the Indian Ocean, the Soviet role in the Horn of Africa, and, more recently, by possible Soviet flanking movements in South Asia. Since approximately 1970, however, that desire has been tempered increasingly by a reluctance to become involved in direct military confrontation with the Soviet Union anywhere. A series of events, starting with the commitment of Soviet pilots and missile troops in Egypt in 1970 and culminating with President Nixon's global alert in October, 1973, apparently has convinced both U.S. and Soviet policy makers that the danger of a confrontation is very real. Given the climate of "detente" and the Carter Administration's focus on SALT, the desire to avoid a superpower confrontation over the Middle East probably is a vital U.S. strategic interest in the region. Thus, the methods used by both sides in competing for influence there will be limited. However, U.S.-Soviet competition in the region will not be eliminated, especially if the Soviet Union becomes a net importer of oil by the 1990s, as some analysts suggest.[25]

One of the most consistent features of U.S. policy in the Middle East has been a strong commitment to Israel's security and well-being, despite occasional differences such as the American reaction to the invasion of Egypt in 1956. U.S. policy makers have sought to justify the "special relationship" with Israel in several ways. For example, Israel has been characterized as a reliable U.S. ally, bridgehead and source of emergency military bases in an otherwise Anti-American region. Alternatively, Israel has been viewed as a sort of regional policeman that could be used to keep radical, pro-Soviet states such as Nasser's Egypt in line. U.S. support for Israel often has been justified as essential to maintaining the credibility of U.S. commitments abroad. Too, the U.S. commitment to Israeli security is partly a function of U.S. domestic policies.

Despite its overwhelming victory in 1967, Israel was incapable of using its military superiority to obtain a secure peace. Furthermore, as Israel became increasingly isolated after the 1967 war, its demands on the United States increased. By 1973, the United States had supplied Israel with over $2 billion worth of military equipment. During the 1973 Arab-Israeli war, Israel received an additional $2 billion worth of U.S. arms, some of which were taken directly from U.S. operational reserves in Germany. By 1974, the United States again was using its influence to obtain a mutually acceptable settlement to the Arab-Israeli conflict. By 1979, the prospects for peace between Israel and Egypt, if not between Israel and its other Arab neighbors, appeared good.

Such massive arms transfers, particularly those involving licensing and production agreements enabling Israel to produce sophisticated U.S. military equipment on its own, have begun to create a strategic rationale for close U.S.-Israeli relations which previously did not exist. Since 1973, a primary Israeli security goal has been to acquire sufficient military resources to conduct a successful three-week "war of annhiliation" against the combined forces of Egypt, Syria, Jordan, Iraq, and Saudi Arabia without having to rely on external (that is, United States) support. By 1977, U.S. military aid probably had enabled Israel essentially to achieve that goal. The military predominance thus gained in the region could reduce pressures toward diplomatic flexibility that might otherwise affect Israeli policy makers. It is possible, too, that Israel now has the option of redressing perceived changes in the regional balance of power by lauching a "preventive war" without having to worry about short-term U.S. pressures or restraints. Such a war would have disastrous effects on U.S. economic and strategic interests throughout the Middle East. Consequently, it is now very much in the interests of the United States to ensure that the conditions that could lead to such a war do not arise.

Sub-Saharan Africa

Black Africa promises to loom large in the troubled 1980s. The views on U.S. interests there vary significantly. One school of thought defines U.S. interests in terms of countering directly any Soviet attempts to increase their influence in the region. A second school envisions massive doses of economic assistance to help Africans solve African problems. A third view is that Africa is not fundamental to U.S. interests and that, in any case, American capabilities in sub-Saharan Africa are limited.[26]

U.S. strategic interests in sub-Saharan Africa are relatively low in relation to interests in other areas. It is not a crossroads of world power or trade, nor a natural battlefield for the great powers. It is underdeveloped for the most part. No African nation constitutes a military threat to the United States or to America's non-African allies. Only a few African nations can be said to possess even significant regional power. Nevertheless, the United States has critical concerns in Africa on several levels.[27]

Strategic position is of major importance. The huge African continent sits astride one of the world's key shipping lanes, the route for Middle Eastern oil to Europe and America. This makes its littoral states of geopolitical interest to Western oil-importing powers and, consequently, to their potential Soviet adversary. The African coastline is similarly important for communications with the Indian Ocean, where superpower rivalry continues to grow.

Sub-Saharan Africa is a cockpit for power rivalries. Nearly a third of the world's sovereign nations are on the continent, and Africa has contributed to a transformation of the character and scope of international affairs since the mid-1960s. African nations play a large role in seeking change in the international order through increasingly active participation in conferences of nonaligned nations, in the U.N. and its specialized agencies, in the North-South dialogues on aid, trade and investment, and in numerous other forums. The United States has an interest in African support in such functional areas as the international environment, the future of the oceans, nuclear non-proliferation, energy, and population growth.

Africa's role in the world economy is small by U.S., European or East Asian standards. Africa accounts for only 5% of world trade, for instance. U.S. trade and investment in Africa constitute a very small proportion of America's national product. However, two factors raise the economic importance of Africa well above the basic relative data. First, America's European allies have a significant stake in the African economies. Relative to GNP, West European interest in trade and investment in Africa is five to ten times that of the United States. Second, all the Western industrialized nations have become more dependent on African fuels and nonfuel minerals. Nigeria, for example, has become a leading supplier of American oil imports. But the more crucial concern south of the Sahara is Western access to Africa's underdeveloped mineral deposits. In the noncommunist world, African sources yield over half the production of seven crucial minerals—chromium, cobalt, industrial diamonds, germanium, manganese, platinum and vanadium—and are a major source of several other commodities. European dependence on these minerals considerably exceeds that of the United States with its sizable strategic stockpiles and mineral wealth. However, the location of most of the mineral deposits in the troubled areas of southern Africa posits difficult policy constraints on all Western powers.

Ironically, the very weaknesses that preclude African states from posing a security threat to the United States contribute to situations conducive to regional strife and outside intervention. The general instability of African regimes rests upon a host of problems such as poverty, tribalism, secessionist and irredentist movements, and inadequate political institutionalization. Competing with the notion that these are African problems best left to Africans is the fear that Soviet exploitation of such instability has sharply risen to the detriment of U.S. interests in Africa and, more broadly, of U.S. credibility worldwide. U.S. post-Vietnam retrenchment and the marked expansion of Soviet global military capabilities have heightened Africa's role in the East-West balance. Of particular concern to the United States has been Soviet and Cuban willingness to intervene militarily in local conflicts such as Angola (1975) and Ethiopia-Somalia (1977–78). Sub-Saharan Africa is an unstable area of conflict.

The growing U.S. interest in Africa is not only material and strategic; it bears strong threads of cultural, social, and moral values as well. Fundamental American norms of independence, patriotism, and peaceful order find sympathy with American anticolonialism, nationalism, and pan-African solidarity. Other values—democracy, human rights, free enterprise—encounter fewer parallels in the numerous single-party and military regimes of Africa. Thus, with respect to the values African governments represent, U.S. interests vary. The issue of majority rule in southern Africa, however, brings all these values into focus. Both the size of the American black population and the postwar emergence of the civil-rights struggle give the United States a vital moral interest in southern Africa. Strategic and economic interests certainly accentuate the urgency U.S. policy makers attach to finding solutions to the struggle in Namibia (South-West Africa) and Zimbabwe, and the early 1980s may see the struggle erupt over South Africa itself. But perhaps of greater significance, there also is a moral imperative that affects the content of U.S. policy in those crises and America's antiapartheid stance toward South Africa.

Latin America

For many years, Latin America has been accorded a low priority in U.S. foreign policy. This may be the result of a simple lack of consensus concerning the nature of American interests in the region. A former chairman of the Joint Chiefs of Staff testified in congressional hearings that

> Latin America's geographical proximity to the United States, its economic potential, and its existing commercial relationships with the United States make it an area of prime strategic significance.[28]

However, a respected scholar on Latin American affairs wrote in 1973:

> the effect of this policy or that policy on *our* ends and *our* interests in Latin America is extremely hard to predict, and may even verge on the indeterminate. But no matter, since our interests in Latin America are not very important anyway.[29]

Between the poles represented by these views, the United States has significant economic, strategic, and political interests in the region. Latin America possesses important raw materials, such as oil, copper, tin and bauxite. Although many of the raw materials of strategic significance have been stockpiled by the United States or are available from other sources, Latin America's importance as a source cannot easily be dismissed. For example, the region continues as a low-cost producer of raw materials and is an important supplier of strategic items to some of America's allies who do not possess the same degree of self-sufficiency as the United States. Latin America also is less likely than some other resource-rich developing areas to fall under the control of the Soviet Union. On balance, Latin American resources constitute a marginal interest for the United States.

Although declining, American private capital investment in Latin America is significant, valued at approximately $22.2 billion in 1975. These investments traditionally have been in raw-materials extraction, but increasingly are concentrated in manufacturing, commerce, and banking. American private enterprise also sells growing amounts of technology to Latin America. The United States has an important, but not vital, interest in protecting existing American investments in Latin America. Despite the political problems of previous nationalizations of American foreign investment, the prospect that future investments will be forthcoming is an important factor in keeping Latin American governments more friendly to Washington than they otherwise might be.

Strategically, defense of the Panama Canal's capability to deploy warships and strategic goods has assumed far less importance to America's security. This is confirmed by the renegotiated Panama Canal treaty in which Washington agreed gradually to transfer the canal to Panama between 1979 and 2000. Nevertheless, as the Panama Canal debates remind us, potentially there are important political-military considerations for the 1980s surrounding the way in which the transfer occurs.

Maintenance of sourthern flank security in its own hemisphere remains a vital United States interest. Resources employed in constructing warning systems facing an opponent based in the Western Hemisphere would not be available for the defense of Western Europe, Japan or the Middle East or for other lesser contingencies elsewhere. Consequently, as the September-October 1979 furor over a Soviet brigade in Cuba reminds us, the American government (at least Congress) remains adamant that the Soviet Union live up to the 1962 understanding that it not place "offensive" weapons on Cuba. The same rationale of defense opportunity costs also helps to explain a U.S. interest in preventing historic rivalries between South American countries from degenerating into armed conflict. War in Latin America would not only divert American energies away from the delicate European and Asian balances, but might also create situations in which a Latin American country might seek assistance from the Soviet Union. Brazil probably will emerge as the pivotal nation in Latin America. The economic boom of the 1970s, the growth of the Brazilian navy and arms industry, and the growth of Brazil's dependency on external resources, especially oil, lead to concerns about projections of Brazilian economic and military power beyond its borders.[30]

Finally, the United States has "psychopolitical" interests in Latin America. Despite predictions of increasing tensions between Latin American nations and the United States,[31] Latin Americans remain culturally closer to the North Atlantic region than to the socialist bloc or to African, Asian and Middle Eastern states. Despite their different cultural mix of Hispanic and Indian traditions, and their antagonisms toward the "colossus to the North" notwithstanding, Latin Americans have a closer bond with the populace of the United States than do the peoples of most other continents. The fact that the President and Congress raised human rights issues more vocally in Latin America than elsewhere in the mid-1970s suggests an American expectation that Latin Americans, because of their European roots, should live up to the highest ideals of "Western" civilization. At the same time, unfortunately, it suggests that many Americans have not given up the "white man's burden" when it comes to hemisphere neighbors.

Western Europe

One might wonder why it is relevant to discuss U.S. interest in Western Europe in the context of low-intensity conflict. There are at least two good reasons. First, there is no a priori reason why one should discard immediately the concept of U.S. participation in coalition low-intensity conflict. The degree of congruence between U.S. interests and the interests of U.S. allies obviously will condition related possibilities. Second, the degree of congruence of U.S. and allied interests will have a bearing on the nature of international support accorded American involvement in low-intensity conflict—as the American involvement in Vietnam should remind us.

Other debates over the nature and extent of U.S. interests notwithstanding, there has been little disagreement over the proposition that the physical security and economic prosperity of Western Europe constitute a vital interest of the United States. Western Europe being the well-spring of the American cultural heritage, the focus of the overwhelming share of American direct investment abroad (Canada is the nation with the highest U.S. direct investment), and the cornerstone of American foreign policy for three decades, policy makers and public alike understand the nature of American interests in Western Europe. There is a deep commitment to protecting those interests, although there are and will continue to be, *inter alia,* disagreements and tensions concerning the means the United States will employ to fulfill its commitments in time of peace and war. American interests in Western Europe have been reciprocal:

> For the United States, Western Europe has represented not only a vital extension of the American economic system but also a bulwark against geopolitical encroachments on that system by the Soviet Union. For Western Europe, the United States has been not only the sole credible source of military security, but—notwithstanding Europe's increasing prosperity—the ultimate provider of her economic security as well.[32]

Nonetheless, the ledger of the Atlantic Partnership in recent years has perhaps shown more political debits than credits. By 1979, it had become clear that the European Monetary System was born out of Western European rejection of the American economy and the dollar as the mainstay of the Western economic system. European leaders are especially disenchanted with what they perceive to be a lack of American presidential leadership in failing to maintain a stable dollar, and in failing to lead Congress in forging an adequate U.S. energy policy upon which many pin their hopes of economic recovery from simultaneous inflation and recession.[33]

There were genuine achievements in NATO in 1977 and 1978. The NATO Long Term Defense Program was approved by heads of state and government in Washington. Following the American lead, NATO ministers agreed in Brussels to a 3% rise in defense costs in real terms. NATO members took some confidence, albeit transitory, from the encouragement of the American President and his reaffirmation of the U.S. commitment to defend Western Europe with strategic nuclear forces if necessary. In 1979, this renewed confidence appears to have been diminished by the impact of statements from the former Secretary of State, Henry Kissinger:

> It is absurd to base the strategy of the West on the credibility of the threat of mutual suicide. ... And therefore I would say, which I might not say in office, the European allies should not keep asking us to multiply strategic assurances we cannot possibly mean or if we do mean, we should not want to execute because if we execute, we risk the destruction of civilization.[34]

These were disheartening public revelations, however valid, at a time when the Soviets were reportedly strengthening Europe's central front and when the American ability to reinforce in Europe was called into question by estimates of inadequate strategic airlift and estimates of increasing Soviet capability in the Northern Theatre to interdict American sealift via the North Sea.[35] But they reminded us that although by mid-1979 there were still few questions in America about U.S. vital interests in Western Europe, there were serious concerns on both sides of the Atlantic as to how the United States could, should, or would pursue those interests.

Whether or not Kissinger is right makes a real difference. Vital U.S. interests in Western Europe are not new. A denial or serious public questioning by a prominent American of U.S. resolve to fire nuclear weapons to save Western Europe and U.S. vital interests there was new. And the critical issue surfaced at a time when European confidence in American military capabilities (relative to Soviet deployment of SS-20 missiles) already was in decline. Kissinger's statement highlighted the argument between those who see NATO plus U.S. strategic retaliatory capabilities as a deterrent by their very existence, and those who prefer to emphasize the importance of "war waging" capabilities. Nearly a generation ago, De Gaulle came down in between, essaying the "force de frappe" as a mechanism for guaranteeing the United States use of its strategic retaliatory forces by moving the *casus belli* decision from America (Washington) to Europe (Paris). Now, Kissinger and others may have made the point to induce Western European nations to strengthen their own conventional defenses. There are other conceivable outcomes—European nuclear capabilities, Soviet invasion, Soviet political, economic, and psychological penetration of Western Europe (Finlandization), or European adaptation of the Swedish or Swiss strategic models.

Although there has been a decline in American willingness to intervene abroad since the end of the Vietnam war,[36] some Western European states have been less reluctant. In recent years, the French have intervened in Chad, Mauritania, Zaire's Shaba province (using U.S. heavy-lift aircraft), and the Central African Republic, and the Belgians have intervened in Shaba. The performance of German Federal Republic antiterrorist forces at Mogadishu is yet another example. At least in the public realm, there have not been any Western multilateral contingency preparations for interventions in the developing world.[37] However, where there is a congruence of well-understood vital or important Western (to include Japan) interests in areas where challenges to those interests are likely, such contingencies appear within the realm of feasibility.

Western interests in access to sufficient quantities of oil at reasonable prices would appear to justify multilateral contingencies for intervention. Despite evidence that the Western European nations have unilaterally sought agreements to secure access to oil, it is certainly conceivable that field or shipping closures by terrorists in some areas, or unilateral or cartel actions by oil-producing states could confront the industrialized nations of the West with common domestic crises that call for concerted intervention.

Contingency planning for multilateral interventions would, no doubt, not only identify inadequacies in national capabilities but also underline the importance of standardization and interoperability of weapons systems, which has heretofore been treated solely in the context of NATO defense.[38]

The Employment of Force

The general nature of the international environment discussed earlier was one in which armed conflict at the intra- and international levels will be widespread, and in which there exists Soviet determination to assert a global political role. The projection that the Soviets will, through use of military capabilities, pose difficult problems for the American interests, as we have defined them, does not require the United States to intervene militarily to settle every conflict, nor does it require the United States to counter every Soviet move tit for tat. The adjustments that will have to be made to live in the environment without sacrificing interests do not require the United States to assume the task of international gendarme.

At the same time, however, the vital and important interests of the United States and its friends and allies are likely to be threatened, and the ability to meet these threats will depend on having the means and the will to employ them. The collapse of the elite consensus on U.S. foreign-policy goals in the mid-1960s and the failure to forge a new consensus likely will inhibit or constrain severely both the development of means and the employment of those which are available. Thus, the employment of force by the United States probably will be highly selective, and when force is employed the tendency will be to seek positive results in a very short time. In and of itself, this is not a bad thing. However, there is some danger it could lead to reluctance to employ force until it is too late to achieve desired results quickly with minimum force. Those who make U.S. policy and those who carry it out will not find it easy to resolve this dilemma.

Assuming that the complex domestic political issues can be resolved and that no less complex alliance politics can be negotiated, it is not too difficult to forecast the ways in which force might be employed. The most obvious is presence—a normal, peacetime deployment of military forces, not only to demonstrate the existence of interests and awareness of them, but also to avoid the appearance of abandoning interests in the face of pervasive Soviet presence. For a variety of reasons, this peacetime presence can best be accomplished by naval task forces, including carriers and their associated aircraft, surface and subsurface ships of other types, and marine amphibious units.[39] In this connection, the erstwhile widespread presence of U.S. military missions ashore probably should be avoided (with certain exceptions) because they require excessive overhead and lead to "golden ghettos." Air deployments do have some place in the peacetime presence, but they are limited by overflight and basing rights. There probably is no requirement for permanent basing of ground combat forces abroad beyond existing alliance commitments, although this should not preclude such temporary deployments as combined maneuvers and exercises. Indeed, combined operations involving all services could be a useful program when and where the political climate is favorable.

Peacetime operations, that is, presence, could be augmented by demonstrations and raids. Demonstrations can be mounted easily, but with strategic-opportunity costs, by the redeployment of the peace establishment. For example, naval task forces could be reassembled from components visiting different ports or exercising individually, and both air and ground forces could be moved to friendly bases (where they exist) in the immediate area. Raids are different in that they require highly trained specialists who should have worked together in a variety of situations over an extended period. Counterterrorist operations or rescue of kidnapped individuals may be required fairly infrequently, but they need careful advance planning to achieve success. This is an area in which allied cooperation could pay handsome dividends. Between peacetime presence and demonstrations/raids and full-scale deployment of combat divisions, with their heavy equipment and associated tactical air support, lies much of the scale of low-intensity conflict. Here the United States should be prepared to augment local forces. Much of the augmentation can be accomplished through arms transfers and training of indigenous forces. The use of mobile training teams to supplement training in the United States or contractor training is a way of avoiding resident U.S. military missions.

Depending on the scenario, augmentation of local forces by U.S. combat units could pose severe problems in the domestic politics of the United States, including invocation of the provisions of the War Powers Act.[40] This is not, by itself, sufficient reason to eschew such actions where and when interests demand, but there are compelling reasons why it may require specially trained and equipped air and surface forces. Without exploring the details of force structure to be addressed elsewhere, it is obvious that lightly equipped mobile units, with self-contained communications and minimum logistic and administrative overhead, will be required; they will have to be trained to operate independently in cooperation with local forces, and to accept limitations on the application of force. Structuring and training such U.S. units will require development of specialized equipment and doctrine, and it will impose on all ranks a requirement for difficult psychological adjustments.[41] "General-purpose forces" in contemporary defense terms are *not* structured, equipped or trained for general purposes. Rather, they are configured and trained for warfare on the plains of central Europe. Units drawn from current general-purpose forces are ill-suited for low-intensity operations in such areas as North Yemen, the Omani heights, or the fiords of Northern Norway.

More importantly, if the United States is to develop and use military forces in the modes just discussed, policy makers and field commanders will have to adapt; good tactics grounded in bad strategy will not succeed. First, there must be a clear understanding of the political objective(s) to be served by employment of force. Second, it must be appreciated that every instance of the employment of force may not be successful as judged against political objectives. Third, failure to attain original political objectives should not result automatically in "more of the same": objectives may need adjustment, and this could lead to a decision to use losses (actual or potential) by withdrawal. Finally, in the case of the executive, political authority may have to be decentralized to very low levels.

Earlier in this chapter, it was posited that intervention in low-intensity conflict would require "strict political control over intervention forces at every stage." This is an important consideration. Although the Commander in Chief and the Secretary of Defense must, will want to, and will have the authority and technological capability to exercise strict political control over forces involved in local operations, they require something more than C^3 (command, communications, and control) in the common usage. They should require, in the locale of conflict, appropriately educated and experienced "regional experts"; individuals sensitive to the cultural, social, and political nuances of the area of operations, with specified delegations of political authority not commonly construed as part of the military "chain of command." Given trends in funding for civilian education for military officers, and given routine military assignment patterns and procedures, it is improbable that requisite expertise would be brought to bear by military officers. One is not talking about "political commissars," but about individuals with appropriate expertise. Although relevant examples are legion, one suggests the following:

(1) Language capability in local dialects;
(2) Ability to identify and know the degree of importance of religious shrines;
(3) Understanding of cultural taboos;
(4) Knowledge concerning local political institutions.

In this sense, the decentralized "political authority" mentioned above will involve making the tactics "fit" the environment, though other tactical questions may have to be resolved at the national level.

Conclusions

It is to be expected that the general interest of the USSR in demonstrating its status as a superpower and the specific interests of America and its allies and friends will come into conflict in the period 1980–85. In those areas where the U.S. interest is unknown or ambiguous in Soviet eyes, the possibilities of conflict may be high. At any rate, testing likely will take place. Faced with such uncertain certainty, the United States and its allies must be prepared to act across the spectrum of conflict with highly flexible military forces that can be tailored and used to meet the requirements of the specific situation. Soviet intentions in specific cases may be obscure, while in general it remains in doubt whether the USSR fundamentally remains dedicated to overthrow of the international order. In such circumstances, prudence demands political decisions to be made in the light of capabilities, in the hope that intentions may be clarified and behavior modified. Nowhere is this likely to be more difficult, politically and militarily, than in the arena of low-intensity conflict.

Notes

*This chapter has been cleared by the Office of the Chief of Information (OCINFO) for open publication. The views and conclusions expressed herein are solely those of the authors and do not purport to represent the policy of any government agency of the United States.

1. "Compellence" in the sense developed by Thomas C. Schelling in *Arms and Influence* (New Haven: Yale University Press, 1966), pp. 69–91.
2. A substantial amount of scientific research has been conducted, with moderate progress in recent years, on predicting the likelihood of international armed conflict. For an analysis of the current status of this research, see James H. Dixon, "Protracted Social Conflict: A Focus in Dynamic Processes," Ph.D. dissertation, University of North Carolina at Chapel Hill, 1980, chs. 2, 3.
3. Soviet activities in Angola, Ethiopia and Afghanistan are three cases in point. The reports of a multinational force in South Yemen (*Washington Star*, 7 September 1979), if confirmed, could represent a decision to field a Foreign Legion.
4. Cf. select bibliography at the end of the book.
5. See Barry M. Blechman et al., *Force Without War: U.S. Armed Forces as a Political Instrument* (Washington, D.C.: The Brookings Institution, 1978), p. 517.
6. The classic examples are the employment of the Guards in the French and Russian Revolutions. However, potential increases in weapons lethality in the 1980s could permit very low troop densities with very high technologies to take advantage of newer methods of attaining high intensity.
7. See Sir John Hackett et al., *The Third World War* (New York: Macmillan Co., 1978) for an explication of one variant scenario involving Simonstown.
8. Certainly this will be important in formulating conflict-termination strategies. See, for example, Morton H. Halperin, "War Termination as a Problem in Civil-Military Relations," *The Annals* 392 (November 1970): 86–95.
9. It is worth reviewing periodically what these persistent problems are. See, for example, Alexis de Tocqueville, *Democracy in America*, ed. J.P. Mayer, trans. George Lawrence (Garden City, N.Y.: Anchor Books, 1966), pp. 226–30, and Kenneth N. Waltz, *Foreign Policy and Democratic Politics* (Boston: Little, Brown & Co., 1967).

10. Cf. Carl von Clausewitz, *On War*, trans. Peter Paret and Michael Howard (Princeton: Princeton University Press, 1976), pp. 75, 259–60.
11. For another view, see "Force in Modern Societies: Its Place in International Politics," *Adelphi Papers* no. 102 (London: The International Institute for Strategic Studies, 1973).
12. Henry A. Kissinger, "NATO: The Next Thirty Years," remarks in Brussels, Belgium, 1 September 1979, transcribed by the Center for Strategic and International Studies, Georgetown University, pp. 10-11.
13. The authors recognize the notion that one might accrue some degree of deterrent or compellent value over an opponent out of sheer unpredictability. We reject the notion on the grounds that one's allies might not be reassured thereby.
14. Quoted in Carroll Quigley, *Tragedy and Hope* (New York: Macmillan Co., 1966), p. 637.
15. See Daniel Yankelovich, "Farewell to 'President Knows Best,'" in *America and the World 1978* (New York: Pergamon Press for *Foreign Affairs*, 1979), pp. 688-93.
16. Kissinger, "NATO: The Next Thirty Years," pp. 2,4.
17. See Marian Leighton, *The Soviet Union and the Northern Flank of NATO* (New York: The National Strategy Information Center, 1980).
18. Richard Pipes, "Soviet Political Dynamics," *Soviet Dynamics—Political, Economic, Military* (Pittsburgh: World Affairs Council of Pittsburgh, 1978), p. 27. Clearly, this is a "conservative" view; however, increasing numbers of analysts focusing on the Northern Theatre share the view.
19. The authors recognize that the case of Finland's relationship to the USSR is unique. The term "Finlandization" means only that the sheer weight of Soviet "presence" induces a nation's leadership to adopt policies conditioned by probabilities of Soviet response. See Nils Andrén, "The Nordic Balance: An Overview", *Washington Quarterly*, vol. 2., no. 3 (Summer, 1979).
20. Ideas in this passage are taken from a draft manuscript on "U.S. Interests and the Soviet Union" by Tyrus W. Cobb and Joseph Collins for Amos A. Jordan, William J. Taylor, Jr., and Associates, *American National Security: Policy and Process* (Baltimore: The Johns Hopkins University Press, forthcoming in 1981), ch. 16.
21. Cyrus W. Vance, *Department of State Selected Documents* no. 9, 15 January 1979, p. 1.
22. Harold H. Saunders, "The Challenge of Peacemaking," *Department of State Current Policy*, no. 108 (November, 1979), p. 1.
23. Ibid., pp. 2–3.
24. Much of the following is taken verbatim with permission from Major Roger T. Olson's draft manuscript, "The Middle East Cockpit," for Jordan, Taylor, and Associates, ch. 18.
25. See Tyrus W. Cobb, "The Soviet Energy Dilemma," *Orbis*, vol. 23, no. 2 (Summer 1979).
26. See "Black Africa: More Weight in U.S. Policy Scales?," *Great Decisions '79* (New York: Foreign Policy Association, 1979), p. 62.
27. Portions of this section are taken verbatim or in edited form from the draft manuscript "The United States and Africa," by Richard Witherspoon and Thomas P. Gorman for Jordan, Taylor, and Associates, forthcoming in *American National Security*, chapter 19.

28. Quoted in David J. Myers, "Brazil and the Latin American Balance," draft manuscript for Jordan, Taylor, and Associates, forthcoming in *American National Security*, chapter 20. Portions of this section are taken in edited form from the Myers manuscript.

29. Jerome Slater (quoted in Myers), "The United States and Latin America: Premises and Policies for the 1970s," unpublished paper, State University of New York at Buffalo, 1973.

30. See Gregory F. Treverton, "Latin America in World Politics: The Next Decade,"*Adelphi Papers* no. 137 (London: International Institute of Strategic Studies, 1977), pp. 58–67. See also Geoffrey Kemp, "The New Strategic Map," *Proceedings, Senior Conference 1976* (West Point, New York: U.S. Military Academy, 1976) pp. 38–39, and "Weapons Makers Seek Foreign Sales," *Latin America Regional Reports, Brazil*, (RB-79-01) 9 November 1979.

31. See Abraham F. Lowenthal, "The United States and Latin America: Ending the Hegemonic Presumption," *Foreign Affairs* vol. 55, no. 1 (October, 1976), pp. 209-10.

32. David Wyatt, "The European Initiative," in *America and the World 1978* (New York: Pergamon Press for *Foreign Affairs*, 1979), p. 572.

33. See James O. Goldsborough, "The New Entente Cordiale," *The New York Times Magazine*, 26 August 1979.

34. Kissinger, "NATO: The Next Thirty Years," pp. 10-11. The same point has been made by other noted strategic analysts; see, for example, Earl C. Ravenal, "NATO's Unremarked Demise," *Policy Papers in International Affairs* (Berkeley and Los Angeles: University of California Press, 1979), p. 14.

35. See Kenneth J. Coffey, *The Strategic Implications of the All-Volunteer Force* (Chapel Hill: University of North Carolina Press, 1979); see also Robert G. Weinland, "War and Peace in the North: Some Political Implications of the Changing Military Saturation in Northern Europe," a paper presented to the "Conference on the Nordic Balance in Perspective: The Changing Military and Political Situation," Center for Strategic and International Studies, Georgetown University, Washington, D.C., 15–16 June, 1978.

36. See Morris Janowitz and Ellen P. Stern, "The Limits of Intervention: A Propositional Inventory," in *Military Review*, vol. 58, no. 3 (March, 1978), pp. 18–19.

37. See *Strategic Survey 1978* (London: International Institute for Strategic Studies, 1979), pp. 14–17.

38. Israeli Defense Minister Shimon Peres was emphatic about the lack of United States or other Western forces capable of counterterrorist operations on "Meet The Press," 9 December 1979.

39. The spread worldwide of precision guided missiles poses special, but not insurmountable, problems in this respect. See Janowitz and Stern, "The Limits of Intervention," p. 16; see also the data on the spread of missile systems to Third World Countries in *The SIPRI Yearbook 1978* (Stockholm, Sweden: The Stockholm International Peace Research Institute, 1978), pp. 243–45, 249.

40. The *Mayagüez* incident of May 1975 provides at least some evidence that an important interest (protecting United States nationals and preserving United States prestige) pursued at low *strategic* cost/risk and executed quickly can be met with domestic approval. Of course, other costs (for example, 41 American dead to

rescue 40 crewmen), were significant. Conversely, the *Pueblo* incident of January 1968 might indicate that similar important interests might be temporarily abandoned because of relatively high strategic cost/risk and tactical infeasibility, even in the absence of a War Powers Act.

41. See Douglas S. Blaufarb, *The Counterinsurgency Era: U.S. Doctrine and Performance: 1950 to Present* (New York: The Free Press, 1977), pp. 298–301; Halperin, "War Termination", and Jeffrey Race, "Vietnam Intervention: Systematic Distortion in Policy-Making," *Armed Forces and Society*, vol. 2., no. 3 (Spring, 1976), pp. 377-96.

CHAPTER 2

The Employment of Force: Political Constraints and Limitations

David W. Tarr

The capacity of the armed forces of the United States to respond effectively at the lower end of the spectrum of violence is being searchingly questioned, especially in the aftermath of the seizure of the American embassy in Teheran and the Soviet invasion of Afghanistan at the end of 1979.[1] To engage effectively in "low-intensity conflict" requires, at first glance, special organization, training, and equipment to cope with various small-war contingencies. Having such capabilities undoubtedly constitutes an important aspect of overall national military capability. However, one must note, at the risk of a cliché, that capability is not everything. This paper represents a second glance at low-intensity conflict, aimed not at capability analysis but at the political and moral restraints on the development of such capabilities and on their employment in time of crisis.

The question addressed here is "What constraints and limitations, other than capabilities per se, operate on American decision makers when they face the prospect of committing American armed forces to low-intensity conflicts?" We begin with the assumption that U.S. participation in such events will constitute military intervention. That is to say, while many states may find themselves involved in low-intensity conflict as a result of attacks upon their borders or from internal upheaval, the United States is unlikely to experience violence of this sort directly. American borders are relatively secure, and domestic politics is relatively peaceful. Thus, to become involved in such events is to choose to intervene in them. We must fight "over there."

The United States continues to express world-order objectives, and is actively involved in a number of bilateral and multilateral security guarantees as well as less specific arrangements involving security policies of third parties. Although the United States has participated vigorously in such arrangements for more than three decades, it does so from a rather unique geopolitical perspective—reaching out across the Atlantic and Pacific to participate in the international affairs of Europe, Asia, and Africa. As our isolationist past has taught us, the United States has a choice. When violence looms, the United States may choose to intervene, or it may choose not to do so. Though this choice is technically faced by others as well (that is, whenever the issue does not involve violence on their territory), the great physical distance of the United States from many an event creates the opportunity or incentive to avoid American involvement, except under circumstances defined as compelling.

After the experience of World War II, the United States rejected its isolationist past and asserted a new, activist, internationalist posture. As leader of the Western world, the United States came to oppose Soviet expansion in particular, and the growth of communist influence in the world in general, in a process known as the "cold war." This effort drew the United States into extensive involvement with many nations of the world, and on a number of occasions, employment of its armed forces in a variety of tasks, ranging from alliance support activities (for example, peacetime deployment of forces to NATO) to military intervention in ongoing hostilities (for example, Korea, Vietnam).

Throughout this period, from 1945 to the present, tensions have existed within the American polity with respect to the wisdom and legitimacy of American military involvement abroad. Although a broad consensus of support for these policies existed over much of the span, there were sharp debates at several points of departure (for example, the "Great Debate" resulting from President Truman's decision to deploy U.S. troops to NATO, announced in 1950). The most acrimonious controversy followed American involvement in Vietnam. It is fair to say that the consensus that pertained to the cold war period had come undone by the 1970s, reflected in greater opposition to defense spending, disillusionment over foreign aid, and explicit reluctance for further involvements of the type that Vietnam represented.

On the other hand, some observers see a new departure in the 1980s, catalyzed by events in Iran and Afghanistan. We are still too close to these events to assess the long-term effects. Perhaps the "Vietnam syndrome" has diminished, but surely the deeper traditions and concerns remain. These are the topics of this chapter. When the United States is faced with a choice—to intervene or not—what are the parameters of constraints and limitations on such decisions, especially with respect to the potentially most ambiguous and confusing realm of violence, the realm referred to here as "low-intensity conflict"?

International Normative Restraints

In international affairs "military intervention" is, in the parlance of our day, often used pejoratively. It suggests wrongful involvement by forces not legitimately concerned; it often connotes unjustified interference. Given the fact that the insertion of American armed forces into a "low-intensity conflict" is, under most conceivable circumstances, *ipso facto* intervention, this poses some troubling dilemmas whatever the reasons for such action. Compared to circumstances of "self-defense," for example, military intervention requires special moral and legal justification to be acceptable to domestic constituencies and the international community. Otherwise, the interventionist forces will be vulnerable to broad international criticism and pressure.

A number of scholars have expressed the belief that normative restraints have been growing, at least in the West and possibly beyond, through the "Europeanization" of international norms; this process, now embodied in the Charter of the United Nations, is said to have reached significant heights.[2] Before this century, of course, in terms of both law and opinion, the use of force by one state against another was generally regarded as an expected and often a legitimate enterprise. Force was an instrument of state policy and its use, even for what might now be called "aggressive" purposes, had the sanction of the "laws of war" so long as the conduct of such wars fell within accepted norms.

A growing revulsion against the use of force can be traced back at least to the carnage of World War I, as Klaus Knorr observed in his essay on the subject.[3] The war-guilt clause in the Treaty of Versailles, the creation of the League of Nations, the Kellogg-Briand Pact, and (after the trauma of World War II), the war-crimes trials and the establishment of the United Nations may all be regarded as evidence of significant erosion in the legitimacy of the resort to force. This process has doubtless been furthered by the publicity attendant to more recent wars, especially during American involvement in the Southeast Asian conflict of the 1960s and early 1970s. Instantaneous global communication of pictures through television is a modern phenomenon carrying great impact, probably largely negative, especially with respect to the use of force by a great power against lesser powers. Moreover, the communication of the horrors of war by picture has probably been as important a factor in this century as any in butressing antimilitarism and antiwar sentiment.

Another factor deemed of great significance by a number of scholars is the possibility that industrial states have become more "inward looking" as they progressed toward more popular and responsive forms of government, as their people became more wealthy, more literate and more educated. The "low politics" of social welfare issues, according to this view, became more salient, and the "high politics" of international security less acceptable, to domestic constituencies growing more resistant to the hardships and sacrifices that military conflict entails. Military institutions and the military profession became less revered, more often opposed, by competing domestic demands. Thus, the military bureaucracy is rivaled by the growth of welfare-state bureaucracies. In short, the development in modern times of politicized populations and more responsive governments with greater scope of domestic social and economic responsibilities is thought to have furthered the shift in popular attitudes against militarism and war.

Writing in 1966, Klaus Knorr cited such factors as these in concluding that the dominant attitudes of the industrial world of the West have narrowed the legitimacy of the resort to force, characterizing this period as "an age of transition, with practices, values, and symbols of the pre-modern past, which die hard, still intermingled with those of the modern state."[4] He also concluded that such a shift in values is not confined to the West, but also applies to the nations of eastern Europe and the Soviet Union, although the restraints there are considerably fewer. Further, he argued that these normative restraints are least effective in the less-developed states, where most populations "are still governed by pre-modern modes of life, and live outside the universe of discourse that is concerned with matters of international order and disorder."[5] But even in those regions of the world, Knorr observed, the urban elites are

> "plugged in" on the international system of political communications and share in the complex and troubled attitudes toward war of the present age. Mankind is moving toward a common history and, in some limited respects at least, toward the rudimentary development of a universal conscience.[6]

This conception of a "global village" of urban elites and modern societies is widely perceived as resulting in increasingly powerful restraints against the resort to force, at least amongst the industrial states.

Knorr, of course, recognized not only that the normative shift, though profound, was incomplete, but also that the distribution of these restraints was uneven. Thus, he expected, along with most other observers, that conflict in the developing world would continue to be less restrained by normative considerations. Professor Knorr revised his thesis in 1977,[7] noting, among other things, that though normative restraints continue to be unevenly effected around the world, the "international distribution of military power is now far *less* uneven than it was, say, from the end of the fifteenth century to World War II."[8] In particular, the transfer of arms to the less-developed countries, the moral and political restraints against the use of force by the industrial states against the less developed, and the "powerful moral stigma attached to the use of nuclear weapons, especially against a nonnuclear opponent" all tend "to increase the utility of their [for example, the less developed states] military forces ... thereby making the distribution of military ... power less unequal than it would otherwise be."[9]

Overall, Knorr's assessment of the restraints on the use of force is far more pessimistic in 1977 than it was in 1966. But even in his earlier essay Knorr pointed out an important and decidedly pessimistic distinction: the erosion in the legitimacy of war applies to only *one* kind of war—*aggression!*[10] Thus, defense against aggression remains fully legitimate. Moreoever, wars for the "liberation of oppressed peoples" are exempt from normative restraints—"the first exception [aggression] being especially popular in the West, and the second in the Communist and in the ex-colonial countries."[11]

Now the cynic will quickly point out the futility of attempting to define either "aggression" or "wars of liberation" in terms that meet universal acceptance and will, no doubt, argue that it depends on whose ox is being gored. Yet the labeling of events, especially in these days of instant global communication, becomes a significant part of the process of international and national restraint. Domestic political constituencies and the so-called international community engage in normative "labeling" of military conflicts. The impact of such labeling can be enormous. If domestic political constituencies are inclined to reach the verdict that an American ally is the victim of "aggression," for example, support for an American military response is likely to be very high indeed, even if communist and/or Third-World spokesmen claim the American response is "aggressive." On the other hand, if elites in the United States and among Western allies, incline toward labeling a Third-World low-intensity conflict as a struggle for self-determination or independence[12] ("liberation"), the opposite is the case. Normative constraints will be very strong and a military response is likely to be subjected to widespread international disapprobation.

In the event of flagrant aggression, where a nation is subjected to an overt invasion by the armed forces of another state, self-righteous claims by the invading state may not carry much credibility among the political elites of the world—and rapid communication, under some circumstances, may make it impossible for political subterfuge to have much effect. But the very fact of the illegitimacy of the "aggressive" use of force today undoubtedly motivates the "aggressor" to resort to any of a variety of indirections, such as proxy actors or acts of prolonged provocation that produce the desired result of having the defenders undertake the actual (or at least visible) "first use" of armed forces—so that both (all) sides can charge "aggression."

In this context, let me now return to my opening observation: "intervention" is widely used pejoratively, yet most of the expected low-intensity conflict contingencies in which American military force might be applied are likely to be labeled as "military interventions." "Intervention" does not have as serious negative moral connotations as does "aggression," but unless it is convincingly justified at the outset to American opinion makers, public regard for such action is likely to erode in that direction, especially in view of the expected onslaught of criticism from unsympathetic international sources. Because the motivation by all parties to the conflict to claim legitimacy on the basis of charges of aggression or claims of liberation is high, and because the publicity attendant to American participation in the conflict is likely to be very intense,[13] the requirement for persuasive justification by spokesmen. of the American government will be under many imaginable circumstances most difficult to accomplish.

Even if conditions are right and the use of force by the United States is not likely to result in charges of aggression outside the communist bloc, the United States might be saddled with a further normative burden: as a "Goliath" in this world, our military actions may engender sympathy for the opponent "David," in what might be called the "underdog" phenomenon.[14] Quite apart from the question of the capacity of large states to use force effectively against small ones, there is the problem of "dual morality." The powerful states are expected to act with greater restraint than are the less powerful. This expectation may indeed range across the whole spectrum of conflict—for though (for example) the tactics of Khomeini in present-day Iran may be widely condemned, they do receive some international support, whereas such tactics are unthinkable on the part of the government of the United States. The Palestine Liberation Organization can openly admit to terrorist tactics. Cuba can export its troops to Africa, even on behalf of Soviet interests. Yet these actions still receive some moral support from elites not only in the Third World and the East, but in the West as well. In part, such support may have an ideological basis ("liberation"), but there is also the possibility that the less powerful can sometimes be forgiven their excesses; or, at least, there is less attention and perhaps a lower expectation of "responsible" behavior.

For whatever totality of reasons, the extreme attentiveness of the world to American military actions in general, and the higher expectations, in the West at least, of morally acceptable behavior on the part of the United States, possibly reinforced by potential development of sympathy for underdogs, are in themselves sufficient conditions for the sudden generation of rather substantial normative restraints upon American intervention in low-intensity conflict situations. American political leaders seem generally aware of the necessity for articulating morally compelling reasons when intervention is contemplated or undertaken, for they obviously want to obtain both international and domestic support, and to minimize opposition.

National Values and Intervention

All of these normative restraints play heavily upon the foreign-policy leadership of the United States. Americans tend to demand or expect that United States foreign policies be based on sound moral principles. Much has been written on this subject. "Realists,"[15] for example, have been especially critical of the alleged propensity toward excessive moralism and legalism in American foreign policy. Since the days of de Tocqueville, many foreign observers have noted, often critically, the moralistic overtones of American political attitudes. A more recent French commentator, Raymond Aron, has detected an ambivalent impulse in America: "the urge to power and moralism," which has been manifest in American foreign policy since the founding of the Republic.[16] And a great many observers have noted, often with distress, the tendency of American policy to swing from idealistic crusade to disillusionment and isolation.

John Spanier, author of one of the more popular undergraduate texts on American foreign policy[17] speaks of an American "style" of foreign policy, an approach characterized by an assumed harmony of interests among states, a depreciation of power, yet an impulse toward a "righteous" use of power to promote such principles as freedom, democracy, self-determination, and the end of "power politics"; in short, a tendency to place principle ahead of power, and to insist that the application of power be justified by higher moral principle:

> Above all, America has always considered itself a morally and politically superior society due to its democratic culture. This has meant that its attitude toward the use of power internationally has been dominated by the belief that the struggle for power did not exist or could be eliminated by crusading against those countries indulging in power politics. Moralism . . . proscribed . . . the use of power . . . [except] in confrontations with unambiguous aggression.[18]

Similarly, Stanley Hoffmann presents an analysis of America's style in the spirit of those already mentioned. In particular, he detects a tendency toward "moral imperatives" in American foreign policy, of which two are of special relevance to this discussion: "the principle of self-determination" and "the principle according to which no changes in the *status quo* should be perpetrated by force" (or the principle of peaceful change).[19] In both cases, Hoffmann finds a basic problem in application of the principle, and certainly the two imperatives could clash when "self-determination" is sought by means of force.

Whether moral principles have actually guided American foreign policy or have served (as some critics have argued) as window dressing for baser motives is beside the point in this discussion. We are not even concerned here with what role, if any, such principles should play in U.S. foreign policy. It seems sufficiently evident, empirically, that such values have concerned American political leaders, whether they have regarded themselves as pursing the realpolitik of Nixon (Kissinger) or the human-rights principles of Carter. Truman may have "masked" an unpopular policy, "containment," in a popular one ("I believe we must assist free peoples to work out their own destinies in their own way")—the Truman Doctrine—just as Lyndon Johnson was later to do in defense of his decision to intervene in the war in Vietnam. But virtually all presidents and secretaries of state (among other high spokesmen) have associated American foreign policies with avowed moral principles that serve to rationalize and justify U.S. foreign-policy behavior. Cynics may say that such language has been used to engender public support for actions otherwise not entirely supportable. Critics may argue that such principles have, in fact, been those of our leadership and have led us astray. Others may say we have "betrayed" our principles and should return to them. But whatever the case, the values claimed to be at issue obviously play a significant role in expanding or contracting restraints upon the latitude of actions of the leadership—whether one sees this as manipulation of the public or as a response to shared values. This has been especially true in those cases where presidents have decided to authorize the use of force in international affairs.

What indeed have been the rationales in recent history for the actual use of force by the United States to intervene in conflicts abroad? What values must be served (or at least addressed) as justifications? What must be avoided—that is, what values proscribe the resort to force? The identification of such values will not, of course, *explain* American interventions or noninterventions, only the values at issue.

Fortunately, there are a number of studies in the literature that address this topic. In many respects the best theoretical work for our purpose here is that of Herbert J. Tillema,[20] for his is a theory of *restraints* upon the use of force by the United States. It is therefore worth summarizing.

The first category of constraints examined by Tillema is that of those associated with the process of threat perception, and here he finds that since 1945 the U.S. leadership has consistently adopted an operational code which defines serious threats in terms of communism and the need to contain it. Thus a perceived danger of a communist government's being imposed in a country that does not have one is hypothesized as a necessary condition for overt military intervention by the United States: the communist threat.

A second category of constraints emanates from the international system. Here Tillema identifies two major tacit agreements that restrain both the United States and the Soviet Union: they will avoid fighting each other directly, and they will refrain from using nuclear weapons against nonnuclear countries. Thus, he predicts that the United States will not intervene with force where such actions might violate those agreements.

The third set of restraints concerns the nature of the foreign-policy decision-making process. The complexity of the problems has resulted in group decision making, complex organizations, and the use of experts. The president can, of course, oppose action, or he can permit another actor, such as the Secretary of State or Congress, to "veto" it. In most cases an incremental response to crisis is likely, and something short of overt military intervention, that is, something less drastic, will be attempted first. If it works, intervention will not occur; if it does not, it is still possible that some other actor will assume the burden (the United Nations, an ally, and so on), or it may be concluded, after the first step by the United States, that local actors are strong enough to survive without overt intervention. Thus the decision-making process tends to restrain the resort to force incrementally, and to make it the last resort.

The final set of restraints identified by Tillema are *moral* restraints—the national values that militate for and against the resort to force (that is, the "rightness" and "wrongness" of force). He finds a basic ambivalence, founded in the Judeo-Christian tradition, between regarding force as sometimes morally wrong and at other times justifiable—"immoral because of the death and destruction that will result," and yet sometimes morally justified in terms either of self-defense or in the defense of others. He reduces the justifications for the resort to force used by American leaders to three: (1) there must be a "deadly conflict going on that should end"; (2) the host country's government must request United States intervention; and (3) some "outside nation" must have already intervened. According to Tillema's theory, all three of these justifications are necessary, else overt military intervention will not occur.

Inasmuch as we have already discussed the growth of international normative restraints, it might be useful to develop this analysis further in the context of American values. According to Klaus Knorr, the only justifications remaining for the use of force today are defense against aggression and liberation of oppressed peoples. Tillema's theory suggests we might now say that these norms are applied by American policy makers to legitimize military interventions as follows: Communist governments oppress people; furthermore, the intervention of communist forces against other countries constitutes aggression; thus, American counterintervention (that is, defense against aggression and prevention of oppression) is morally legitimate, and—assuming official invitation by the government in question—legal as well.

We noted Stanley Hoffmann's thesis in similar vein, that the United States tended toward two "moral imperatives," "self-determination" and "peaceful change." Again, these principles are compatible with Knorr's distinction between aggression and liberation, and with Tillema's hypothesized required conditions for U.S. intervention—among them the attempt to accomplish change by force of arms and prior military intervention by a third party attempting to replace a noncommunist government with a communist one.

In short, it seems that there is some consensus, among the observers cited at least, of the central constraining values that must be invoked to legitimize American military interventions: protecting the right of others to self-determination; opposition to aggression; violation of the principle of peaceful change; legal action (invitation by the authority in power versus subversion, insurgency, and so on); and the existence of a communist threat.

It is hardly surprising, then, that many observers find a connection between these basic values and the cold war moral imperative—opposition to communism. During the height of the cold war, Americans tended generally to perceive the communist threat as endangering these central principles. Communism seemed only to be achievable through violence, not by peaceful political processes. Communist governments appeared to extend their power by aggression—both direct, as in Korea, and indirect, through the subversive activities of their agents. Communism seemed to make a mockery of the principle of self-determination, and by extension, of democracy itself. In short, from the American moral perspective, the communist countries were aggressive, violent, illegal, and undemocratic.

But perceptions shift, allowing the possible development of greater ambivalence: with the development of efforts at "peaceful coexistence" and "detente," with the shift in China's alignment from anti-American to anti-Soviet, with the failure of the American enterprise in Southeast Asia, with the rise of "Eurocommunism," the American image of the "communist threat" was bound to change.

The greatest catalyst for change, no doubt, was the disillusioning experience of the Vietnam War. All the salient principles discussed here were invoked in the attempt to legitimize American participation in that conflict. Citizens at home argued, while men abroad fought and died for those principles. And in the end the whole shaky venture collapsed. There is a strong consensus today that American participation in the Vietnam War was not only a mistake, but immoral. A public opinion poll sponsored by the Chicago Council on Foreign Relations, conducted in 1978, found in its public sample that when respondents were asked whether the "Vietnam War was more than a mistake; was fundamentally wrong and immoral," 72% agreed, 47% of them strongly, and only 7% disagreed.[21] Although by itself that result is hardly conclusive evidence of a changed perception, in the context of other results from that poll, the editor found it reasonable to conclude that "both the public and the leaders displayed an ambivalent attitude toward the role of communism and communist governments in the world today." Although they were concerned about growing Soviet power, "both groups were less concerned about the role of a communist government in China or the possibility of communist governments coming to power through elections in Western Europe."[22]

One might draw two tentative conclusions from this. First, the Vietnam War experience has seriously tarnished the "communist threat" rationale as a legitimizing symbol for future American military interventions in the Third World. Second, the public may be beginning the process of discerning a difference between the ideological issues associated with the "communist threat" and the military dangers of a specific "Soviet threat." If the ideological dimension is subsiding, or at least becoming more complex, the requirements for legitimizing future American military interventions will change. One might imagine future circumstances in which an alleged "communist threat" would no longer be a sufficient rationale for American intervention. Will the underlying principles (self-determination, defense against aggression, opposition to violent change) remain as moral restraints? Presumably they would, and as such they may function as fairly strong curbs against unilateral American responses to low-intensity conflicts, whatever the perceived role of communist forces. The 1980s are likely to bring a great many conditions for conflict, and though the East-West ideological division will continue to exist, the structure and distribution of power in the world of today and tomorrow suggests the further growth of independent centers of decision making, aligned in multidimensional ways. Fewer issues leading to conflict are likely to relate directly to East-West, "good guys"-"bad guys" dimensions comparable to the cold war period. Thus the "communist threat" is likely, by itself, to be a less persuasive rationale in the 1980s than in previous decades.

If, indeed, this analysis is correct—that "cold war" rationales no longer adequately mobilize support for interventionist options—there are likely to be increasing possibilities for political division within the American society over the issue of the morality of resorting to force. A narrowing defintion of "self-defense" (for example, defense of the United States rather than of our international interests) may gain strength as American world-order objectives are challenged. Recent misgivings of younger Americans over the issue of draft registration are instructive, as a generation unaccustomed to conscription reacts to its prospect in 1980. The 1980s are not the 1930s, but the reduced efficacy of the communist threat to catalyze public support of defense measures reveals a significant political void: there does not presently exist a widely shared public rationale *for* American military involvement in low-intensity conflicts, beyond a rather vague preference for peaceful change and an ill-defined anxiety about vulnerable resources, especially petroleum.

By way of contrast, prior to the Vietnam experience there existed a strong domestic consensus supporting American international leadership, initiative, and military strength. United States foreign policy was based on a military posture of strategic nuclear supremacy, which was presumed to deter a wide range of aggression from Soviet and/or communist sources. Beneath the level of strategic weapons a corollary doctrine operated: American armed forces were expected to play an active and sustaining role in building and maintaining an international security system of alliances, military bases, economic and military assistance programs, and the like, to extend military deterrence as far down the spectrum of conflict as possible, to build up local defense capabilities, and to promote stability, democratic values, and peace. Deterrence and containment were linked in a global security system that explicitly included the promise to use American armed forces in response to aggression.

All of this derived from assumptions and expectations concerning the nature of the communist threat. But these assumptions and expectations have changed, not only as a result of the experience in Southeast Asia, but also because perceptions of the U.S.-Soviet power equation have altered. At the strategic level, the doctrine of nuclear superiority has given way to that of strategic parity—based on an acceptance of Soviet rough equivalence in nuclear power, and even of a preference for such equality as a contribution to international stability (mutual deterrence). The implications of strategic parity for deterrence and defense at various levels of potential confrontation and conflict are only now coming to be appreciated. At any rate, the doctrine of superiority represented a posture of power that probably enhanced public confidence in the efficacy of American international involvements.

Today, below the level of strategic arms competition, the rationale for supporting an international security system of alliances, overseas bases, widely deployed naval power, and programs of economic and military assistance is seriously wanting. Only in western Europe, where deterrence and defense objectives seem justified by the evident military capability of the Soviet Union and the Warsaw Pact nations, does the rationale of the 1960s retain validity and support. Beyond that region—exactly in those parts of the world where less intense conflicts are most likely—the cold war rationale appears insufficient. That is, the corollary some have labeled "Pax Americana"—according to which the United States might lead the effort to contain communism and to promote stability and political and economic development in a secure environment, lest the nonindustrial world be subverted or conquered by communist forces—has significantly less domestic and international support.

This lack of confidence in the efficacy and, to some extent, legitimacy of American power abroad is an important constraint on military policy, and one of particular sensitivity for the problem of prospective participation by U.S. armed forces in future low-intensity conflicts. These comments should not be read as a call for a military doctrine of intervention, however, but simply as an observation concerning the changing parameters of choice.

Other Constraints

Normative constraints based on underlying political and moral perspectives probably change slowly. There are other constraints that should at least be touched upon in a discussion such as this. For example, how are decisions to intervene processed through the political system? Does it make any difference how the issue arises and what the nature of the problem is? What role does public opinion play? What about electoral politics?

Let us look first at the patterns by which such issues are processed. Many foreign policy problems are not identified as problems until government spokesmen announce them. A classic case of inadvertent, or perhaps improper, handling of issue definition was the announcement by Senator Frank Church of the presence of a Soviet military brigade in Cuba. When a problem is so identified, there is an immediate impression given that something will be done about it. As a general rule, it would be imprudent in international affairs to admit that a problem exists, if one can avoid it, until one is prepared to do something. Thus, for example, the State Department persisted in denying that there were North Vietnamese troops in Cambodia in 1966—even though there was ample evidence to the contrary—because the United States was not prepared to do anything about it and did not want to encourage pressure to do something about it.[23] Perhaps the most celebrated instance of controlling information until policy makers were ready for action was the Cuban missile crisis of 1962, when the Kennedy Administration kept its knowledge of Soviet missile emplacements secret until the United States was ready to announce its response.

Information about and definition of many problems are, of course, well beyond the control of U.S. policy makers. Crises often take the leadership by surprise, even if there is forewarning—consider the attack on South Korea in 1950. Often there is no warning. In many cases the attendant publicity itself defines the issue as one that requires an American response—consider the sudden construction of the Berlin Wall in 1961 or the seizure of the U.S.

Embassy in Iran in 1979. Thus, how the story surfaces has some impact on expectations of response.

Moreover, the nature of the issue partly determines which organizations will be assigned responsibility for developing a response. The growing involvement of the United States in Vietnam is perhaps *the* classic case of incremental increases in U.S. entanglement short of the use of force (that is, from 1954–64), whether one subscribes to the "quagmire" explanation for American involvement or not. Certainly, everything *short* of force was tried first in Vietnam. Many of these programs did not receive very much public attention or even critical congressional scrutiny.

In general, we see a pattern of deferring decisions to use force if it can be avoided, if so the problem is "assigned" to one or several functional organizations—most likely dealing with military assistance and foreign aid, as well as regional and country specialities. On the other hand, the greater the sense of urgency, the more likely will the president and top advisers become involved in formulating, reviewing, and deciding upon responses. Thus, crises may be thrust upon top decision makers, while other issues are handled "routinely" within the bureaucracy—unless the president or other high official decides to make an issue out of something. One might have thought, for example, that the announced existence of a Soviet "combat" brigade in Cuba was a situation of this variety. In short, the way in which issues are identified tends to determine how they are handled and at what level of government.

It is interesting that Tillema's theory of intervention constraints does not include public opinion as a significant factor. The reason may be that most studies show that public opinion tends to react to international events rather than to function as keenly felt pressure on policy makers. Again, it all depends upon the situation. Obviously, if there is time for the expression and measure of opinion, it will somehow make its weight felt. However, the foreign-policy-making system tends to resist outside pressures.[24] As a result, public opinion per se is unlikely to function as a kind of "prior restraint" upon policy makers faced with an immediate crisis and serious consideration of military action. On the other hand, as may have been the case with the Mayagüez operation (1975), pressure to act forcefully may be greater in one instance if previous setbacks have created a backlog of resentment, shame, or anger, or if the president is regarded as lacking in leadership or resolve.

In any case, public opinion tends to be regarded by policy makers as mercurial and ephemeral. Moreoever, whatever the polls may show at any moment about levels of support in terms of such indicators as defense spending, foreign aid, international military involvement, and the like, the underlying tendency is for opinions to fluctuate wildly in response to immediate real international stimuli, regardless of contrary prior views solicited in the abstract. Thus, a finding that less than 50% of a national sample favor the "use of United States troops" if the "Soviets take West Berlin"[25] is not likely to impress a president faced with that as a real-world crisis. He probably would care very little about opinion in a crisis of that dimension. Moreover, opinions would doubtless have reacted sharply (probably in favor of a military response) anyway.

One of the most important phenomena in this regard is the inclination of the American public to "rally round the flag" in crisis. As John E. Mueller has shown,[26] a decision to resort to force is likely to result in very high initial levels of support, even though that support probably will decline as a function of the length and costs of the conflict. Although decisions to use force abroad have been taken by every American president since Franklin D. Roosevelt, each leader and his advisers surely understood the inevitable controversy that would be raised by such actions. Although each case is different, it is unlikely, overall, that concern for adverse public response will, by itself, deter presidents from decisions to underake military action abroad. The circumstances that have led to such decisions have been regarded as too important in terms of U.S. security interests to weigh against anticipated impact on public opinions. In most respects, the influence of public reaction has been heavier in the conduct of these military actions than in the decisions themselves.

That is not an insignificant point, however. Presidents Truman and Johnson paid heavily for "their" wars. The advisability of "short" wars has been institutionalized in the War Powers Act of 1973, which requires termination of American interventions abroad in 60 to 90 days unless congressional authorization to continue combat operations is obtained. The common political wisdom derived from the "lessons" of Korea and Vietnam is clearly to avoid similar events in the future, but by all means to avoid *lengthy* military engagements. The trouble with hindsight is, of course, that it may not result in foresight.

Thus, opinions generated by military interventions abroad might ultimately be translated into election results. The Tonkin Gulf decision undoubtedly enhanced Lyndon Johnson's position in the 1964 election, but the ensuing war, culminating in the Tet Offensive, did him in by 1968. Such lessons are not lost upon the next generation of politicians. They know that support for such decisions is time- and result-sensitive. People rally around the president because "he is the only one we've got." But he is also the most central figure to blame when things go wrong. The next military intervention by the United States is unlikely to resemble either the Korean model or that of Vietnam. The "never again" club has too many members.

Thus, beneath the fickleness of today's opinions may lurk the deeper "moods" that (so some have hypothesized) fluctuate more slowly, perhaps due to a kind of "imprinting," as Bruce Russett has put it, of a whole generation to the pivotal events of their time.[27] Perhaps Russett is right that we have seen a transition involving a "change of minds and change of bodies," in which the attitudes based on the experiences of World War II have been challenged and supplanted by those of a generation that does not even remember that war.[28] Though some data of the most recent Chicago Council on Foreign Relations opinion poll suggest that Russett's conclusions, drawn in 1975, concerning general attitudes toward security issues should perhaps be further qualified, the underlying argument about generational attitudinal changes is well taken. Moreover, for those of us who have had occasion to observe the arrival of the Vietnam War generation to adulthood, there is clear evidence of the imprinting of that complex experience on their consciousness.

At any rate, as Tillema's study reminds us, there are a number of interrelated factors that constrain decision to intervene. Opinions and moods are probably contextual but not central concerns of the major policy makers. Once they perceive a situation as requiring at least the consideration of an option to employ force, they are most likely to be concerned about two directly interrelated things: the nature of the problem and the capabilities at hand. Because uncertainty of consequences and a heightened sense of risk is likely under most circumstances of this type, the motivation to try something short of direct military intervention will be paramount. In this instance, the international constraints are reinforced by domestic ones. External factors may make the problem seem intractable and/or susceptible of escalation and deeper, more prolonged involvement. Internal factors militate against actions that do not "solve" the problem within an acceptable time frame and cost. On the other hand, the proclivity for incremental actions to avoid "biting the bullet" may lead into the very quagmire that no one wanted to enter.

Concluding remarks

Although I have touched upon a number of factors that constrain American participation in low-intensity conflicts, I have placed most emphasis on underlying values, as these appear to have endured, shifting perhaps in emphasis as the mood of the nation changed, but within the framework of the same basic principles. These values appear to "channel" responses to international events rather than to present gates that open or shut in particular contexts. An international crisis acts as a stimulus to an American response. Political leaders usually define the nature of the crisis with reference to these values. If the crisis is severe, there is a good chance that initial support for any decision will be a consequence of the rally-around-the-flag effect. Unless the issue is perceived and defined in terms of American liberal values, intervention is not likely to occur or to receive sustained public support.

Perhaps the most important issue-defining symbol of the past several decades has been represented by the phrase "communist threat." Tillema's thesis held that the existence of that condition was necessary for American military intervention. However, the analysis presented here suggests that changes in mood and embittered experience have eroded the legitimizing effect of this type of assertion.

This does not mean that Americans will be insensitive to an alleged *"Soviet* threat," for there is already clear evidence of growing concern on that issue, and broadening support for defense measures to counter it. But as far as *low*-intensity conflicts are concerned—those in which Soviet direct participation in hostilities is, almost by definition, not a likely contingency (e.g., were we to consider intervening in hostilities in which Soviet armed forces were already involved, we would almost certainly face the prospect of *high*-intensity conflict)—experience suggests that the identity of the sources of instability and violence is likely to be perceived in more complex but less ideological terms. The dangers of communism per se are not as likely to trigger American military intervention in the 1980s as was the case in the 1950s and 60s. It is not an irrelevant issue, but it is less salient.

This does not mean that the American political leadership will be unable, in the years ahead, to legitimize military intervention in terms acceptable to the constraining values to which we have alluded. Public concern for strategic interest in petroleum resources in the Middle East, for example, suggests a context in which American intervention might be initiated regardless of the putative role of communist governments or parties. But one would surmise that such an undertaking would still have to be consonant with American national values. The use of force for undisguised economic or strategic interests is thus highly unlikely.

In short, the intervention of American armed forces in future low-intensity conflicts is still subject to traditional constraints to include a perception of prior armed intervention by a third party (aggression, violation of the principle of peaceful change), and American involvement is most likely to be preceded by a request for assistance from local authorities (legal and defensive).

The major exception to these rules is the prospect for rescue operations against acts of terrorists. Such missions are in any case easily legitimized in terms of basic humanitarian principles and international legal norms. And even in this category, unless *American* lives are involved, terrorist actions are more likely to be dealt with by lesser powers or through the United Nations, but usually by the aggrieved party.

Thus, for the most likely context in which low-intensity conflicts might stimulate an American consideration of intervention—the Third-World political arena—the traditional values of opposition to aggression and preference for peaceful change and legal action are likely to limit, restrain, and in most cases proscribe direct American military involvement.

Notes

1. The first draft of this chapter was presented at the Workshop on Low-Intensity Conflict, Loyola University of Chicago, November 15–17, 1979. A shortened version appears in *Parameters* 10 (September 1980).
2. See, for example, F. H. Hinsley, *Power and the Pursuit of Peace* (Cambridge: Cambridge University Press, 1963.)
3. *On the Uses of Military Power in the Nuclear Age* (Princeton: Princeton University Press, 1966.) See especially chap. 3.
4. Ibid., p. 50.
5. Ibid., p. 51.
6. Ibid., pp. 51–2.
7. "On the International Uses of Military Forces in the Contemporary World," *Orbis* 21 (Spring 1977): 5–27.
8. Ibid., p. 18; emphasis added.
9. Ibid.
10. Knorr, "Uses," p. 54.
11. Ibid.
12. Incorporation of the phrase "wars of national liberation" into the lexicon of Western nations has unfortunate implications in terms of the specific distinction between that concept and the Western one of "self-determination."
13. American media journalists are the most numerous in the world. Moreover, as a superpower and as an open society the United States takes actions more closely observed and reported than those of any other society.
14. Klaus Knorr also addresses this topic but in a different context. See Knorr, "Uses," pp. 74–79.
15. The leading exponent of this view is Hans J. Morgenthau.
16. *The Imperial Republic: The United States and the World, 1945–1973* (Englewood Cliffs, N.J.: Prentice–Hall, 1974), p. xxxi.
17. *American Foreign Policy Since World War II*, 7th ed. (New York: Praeger, 1977).
18. Ibid., p. 19.
19. *Gulliver's Troubles, or the Setting of American Foreign Policy* (New York: McGraw-Hill, 1968), p. 118.
20. *Appeal to Force: American Intervention in the Era of Containment* (New York: Crowell Company, 1973). Tillema presents his theory in chapter 1, which is summarized here.
21. John E. Rielly, ed., *American Public Opinion and U.S. Foreign Policy 1979* (Chicago: Chicago Council on Foreign Relations, 1979), p. 27.
22. Ibid., p. 4.
23. See an interesting discussion on this subject entitled "Why statesmen must sometimes lie in order to tell the truth," in James L. Payne, *The American Threat* (Chicago: Markham Publishing Company, 1970), pp. 83–90.

24. For example, see Bernard C. Cohen, *The Public's Impact on Foreign Policy* (Boston: Little, Brown, & Co., 1973).
25. Rielly, *American Public Opinion*, p. 26.
26. *War, Presidents and Public Opinion* (New York: John Wiley & Sons, 1973).
27. "The Americans' Retreat From World Power," *Political Science Quarterly* 90 (Spring 1975): 11.
28. Ibid.

CHAPTER 3

U.S. Capabilities for Military Intervention

Howard D. Graves

U.S. Defense Capabilities

The United States is concerned about the employment of military force across the entire spectrum of conflict. At the upper end of the spectrum of conflict is nuclear war with the Soviet Union. Because strategic nuclear war represents the only level of conflict that would immediately threaten the survival of the United States, our major security concern is deterrence of strategic nuclear conflict. The cost of failing to deter nuclear war is such that the highest priority must go to precise management of forces to insure strategic deterrence.

Below strategic nuclear conflict on the spectrum lies a major conflict between the superpowers, either conventional or involving tactical nuclear weapons. This kind of conflict is most critical in Europe, where both the Warsaw Pact and NATO maintain large conventional forces ready for deployment. Major conventional conflict involving the superpowers could also occur elsewhere, such as Northeast Asia or the Middle East, but forces are not deployed there on the scale that they are in Europe.

If restricted to Europe, a conventional conflict would be less destructive to the United States than a strategic nuclear exchange. There is, however, considerable doubt that such a conflict could be so restricted. Even if it were, the cost to both sides and their allies would be enormous. Because of the tremendous potential for destruction and the cost of failure to deter a major conflict in Europe, the U.S. commitment to NATO defense receives similar priority to deterring strategic nuclear conflict. In response to recent Warsaw Pact conventional force improvements, the United States and its allies are improving the capability for defense and timely reinforcement of NATO. The Department of Defense Annual Report for Fiscal Year 1979 reported the equivalent of 5⅔ U.S. Army divisions and 28 tactical air squadrons stationed in Western Europe. These forces can be augmented by one additional division and 40 tactical air squadrons within ten days of notification. Through additional prepositioning of equipment in Europe to reduce the amount to be moved in any reinforcement, current objectives are to increase that augmentation by 1983 to five divisions and 60 tactical air squadrons in the same ten-day time frame.[1]

The tremendous capacity that both sides have for destruction in major conflict and the resultant cost to both superpowers and their allies reduce the likelihood of such wars occurring. The least likely military contingency we face is a strategic nuclear war, and only slightly more likely is a major conflict in Europe. However, the cost of failure to deter either type of conflict necessitates that priority be given to those forces perceived as essential to deterrence.

Although the tremendous destructive capacity of the superpowers reduces the probability of major conflict, that same emphasis on deterrence appears to have increased the probability of conflict at levels of much lower intensity, particularly the use of force by smaller nations or insurgent organizations. Superpower involvement in these low-intensity conflicts has not been totally absent. The United States, for example, has used armed forces of varying sizes in specific contingency operations more than 200 times since World War II.[2] On the other hand, most of this involvement has been indirect and has been dominated by the desire to preclude escalation to a direct Soviet-American confrontation.

Two major considerations will affect the employment of U.S. military forces in any contingency in the near future. The first will be the continuing desire to avoid a direct confrontation with Soviet military forces. The second will be the difficulty of moving and supporting large forces. As the size of force to be employed increases, so does the difficulty of deploying the force rapidly, sustaining it during the operation, and then withdrawing it expeditiously once the objective has been attained. The effect of both of these considerations on any future decision to employ a military force will be to constrain the force to the smallest size possible to conduct the intervention successfully. The greater possibility of low-level intervention and the consequent requirement for the capability to deploy forces rapidly could well require a different priority for planning and allocation of resources.

It is with these two major considerations and other constraints on the use of force that are discussed in other chapters in mind, that the use of military forces in low-level conflict must be evaluated. Numerous possible options are available for evaluation. The lowest current employment of military forces is in the Security Assistance Teams. These teams, formed on an *ad hoc* basis when needed, include Technical Assistance Teams or Military Training Teams as part of a routine security assistance program, or advisory teams that may be provided to friendly nations resisting active external or internal threats.

Actual involvement of U.S. conventional forces in a conflict would most likely first include noncombat missions, such as a show of force to demonstrate American concern. Naval or air forces are suited for such employment because of their capability for rapid deployment, particularly in the case or air forces, and the flexibility of indicating concern without becoming directly involved—a flexibility that is, for the most part, foregone once ground forces are employed. Other possible low-level conflict missions that do not directly involve United States combat forces include support for allied forces engaged in combat or peacekeeping missions, such as the strategic airlift of French, Belgian, Senegalese and Moroccan forces to Shaba Province in Zaire in 1978. Numerous other combat support and combat-service support missions are also more probable than actual employment of U.S. forces in combat.

If combat forces were employed, the most probable commitment would involve small forces on missions clearly defined in geographical area, objective and time, followed by rapid withdrawal of the forces once the objective was attained. Yet, given the increasing levels of arms transfers around the world, these operations might well be conducted against forces that are small in number but armed with relatively sophisticated weapons. Objectives of U.S. forces on such limited operations would be to accomplish a well-defined, limited mission and to withdraw from the area, not to defeat or destroy the opposing forces. Likely missions at this level of intensity include rescue, evacuation, protection, and counterterrorist missions.

Beyond these limited missions lie much more extensive objectives of seizing and holding terrain and defeating enemy attacks. In addition to the difficulty of keeping the conflict limited, the nature of the military commitment changes dramatically at this level, particularly the ability to deploy forces in a timely manner and to define feasible military objectives that can be clearly attained with limited forces.

In the discussion that follows, we will address current capabilities of United States forces to deploy and participate in low-intensity conflict as well as to provide military assistance to other nations. We will consider the forces available, competing demands for those forces, the capability to deploy military forces, adequacy and priority of training, command and control, organization and equipment, and the quality and sufficiency of personnel.

Forces Available

No single U.S. military unit possesses all of the necessary capabilities required to conduct the wide range of operations appropriate to low-intensity conflicts. However, task forces composed of varied, specially trained forces can be formed for defined missions. The United States maintains numerous specially trained, elite units that are available in varying states of readiness for low-intensity contingencies. At the lowest level are advisory capabilities. In addition to Security Assistance Teams, which can be assembled to train allied armed forces in maneuver or equipment skills, Special Forces units are trained to organize and advise either resistance or host-government forces. Current capabilities of the Special Forces groups will be discussed below. Although Special Forces units are best utilized as advisors to friendly government forces or to resistance forces, the units are also capable of conducting quick-response clandestine or overt operations in remote areas against lightly defended targets. The Army also maintains an active-duty psychological-operations group and civil-affairs battalion, elements of which can be employed to assist both advisory or direct-action operations.

The Army maintains two Ranger battalions, assigned to Forces Command in the United States. From squad to battalion, these Ranger units provide a conventional force for conducting raids and attacks. They may be inserted by helicopter, parachute, or foot, or over the beach. Ranger units are also specially trained in rescue and urban-warfare operations.

Larger Army units specifically available for low-intensity conflict will be discussed below. These units have been selected from an active Army force that consists of airborne, airmobile, light-infantry, mechanized-infantry and armor divisions and separate brigades, as well as organic and attached support units.

Air Force resources that would likely be considered for employment include aircraft of varying numbers and types, such as fighter, reconnaissance, tactical air support, medical transport and tactical airlift. A small number of aircraft might well be deployed to demonstrate concern in a situation. Larger numbers and units can be rapidly deployed, depending on other commitments, their state of readiness, and availability of logistical support, particularly fuel. Also available are Air Force Special Operations squadrons, equipped with sophisticated aircraft capable of all-weather aerial delivery of troops and supplies, electronic warfare and countermeasures, and aerial supporting fires.

Naval forces include ships and aircraft of varying capabilities, which may be deployed offshore to indicate concern or on more specific missions. Naval forces could range from one ship, such as a destroyer, or a few P-3 reconnaissance aircraft up to several carrier task forces. The Navy also has special-operations teams that may be deployed by sea, air, or land techniques. These teams, known as SEAL teams, are capable of conducting small demolition raids, reconnaissance, intelligence collection, and other similar operations.

Fleet Marine Forces are also capable of many likely low-intensity missions. Elements of two Marine Amphibious Forces are forward deployed (i.e., close to anticipated combat area) in the Mediterranean Sea and Pacific Ocean. Marine units, from a squad to a Marine Amphibious Force (built around a division/wing team), may be deployed by air, amphibious shipping, or a combination thereof, depending on availability of aircraft and ships.

Rangers, Special Forces, and Security Assistance Teams

The most probable employment of U.S. ground forces in low-intensity contingencies in the near future will not be in large formations, but may rather be in small detachments committed to accomplish a designated direct mission or to assist indigenous forces against an internal or external threat. Organized units especially suited to these tasks are the Rangers and the Special Forces.

Rangers are best suited for direct-action missions of short duration. Two Ranger battalions are located in the United States, and may be employed in elements ranging from squad to battalion. The strength of Ranger units is their ability to respond rapidly to a variety of time-sensitive contingencies worldwide. They are a small, elite, highly trained, well-disciplined force whose training emphasizes meticulous planning, deception, and secrecy in preparation, and surprise, speed, and precision in execution. Special skills maintained within the Ranger battalions are high-altitude parachuting, water-borne infiltration, sniping, demolitions, and military operations in built-up areas. The battalions' annual environmental training includes jungle, desert, cold-weather, mountain, and amphibious training. These capabilities make them ideally suited for small independent contingency operations of a politically sensitive, military nature.

The Ranger battalions enjoy very high priority in the Army for people and supplies, as well as for training funds and facilities. Their small size permits training priorities and flexibility that larger units cannot afford, both financially and because of operational limitations. There are, however, several areas where improved management and support for the Ranger battalions are needed. A clearer doctrine is needed for employing and supporting Rangers to insure that their unique skills and flexibility are used properly. As the concept for employment of forces in low-intensity contingencies is clarified, the Rangers will need better training guidance and management to relate training priorities to probable missions. Current battalion training programs are based on the unit commander's assessment of the needs of his unit and probable missions. This decentralized training responsibility has clear advantages, but the unit commander should also be provided with assessments of probable missions from several levels of command.[3]

Whereas Ranger units are trained for direct-action combat or rescue missions, Special Forces units possess unique capabilities to train, work with, and direct indigenous forces. Special Forces units maintain skills that make them readily available for assistance missions. Units are, for example, required to maintain specific area, cultural, and language proficiency for their area of responsibility.

Special Forces may be employed in detachments ranging from a 12-soldier "A" team to a 1,400-soldier group. The nucleus of Special Forces employment is the "A" team, composed of two officers and ten senior enlisted people, cross-trained in a variety of skills. The flexible cellular organization, multiplicity of skills, and high densities of officers and noncommisssioned officers enhance the utility of Special Forces in advisory missions. The Special Forces group can provide command-and-control personnel for any number of its assigned "A" teams or be employed in its entirety as the nucleus of a Security Assistance Force (SAF) with a tailored augmentation. The augmentation can include military police, psychological operations, civil affairs and medical and engineering elements. Although their primary employment should be for training and assistance missions, Special Forces units also receive training for direct-action tasks such as reconnaissance, strategic-target destruction, and counterterrorist and rescue missions.

The United States currently has approximately 4,000 soldiers assigned to Special Forces units worldwide. The majority are in three 1,400-soldier Special Forces groups stationed in the United States. Although the state of readiness of Special Forces units fell to an extremely low level after the Vietnam withdrawal, it has been improved. Units are now operating at approximately 95% of authorized strength. There remain serious shortages, however, particularly in officers, communications personnel, and medical specialists. First-term enlisted personnel are filling noncommissioned officer positions and many positions are filled one or two grades below authorizations. As a result, although this low-intensity capability is easily deployable, some skill levels are below those desired. Language capabilities are particularly lacking—around 50%—due to the presence of many first-term enlistees, loss of Lodge Act personnel, and rotation of trained soldiers to conventional units. Intensive training programs at unit level would improve the level of proficiency somewhat, but the overall level of qualified personnel will remain lower than desired in the near future. However, detachments of skilled advisors can be assembled for advisory missions if required. In fact, 33 Special Forces Security Assistance Teams have been deployed in the past four years to various countries around the world.

Two additional limitations on the capabilities of Special Forces deserve note. The first is the present difficulty of attracting trained officers for second or third Special Forces assignments. Recent promotion and service-school-selection boards have consistently given priority for selection to officers who have varied assignments or repeated conventional unit assignments, and have failed to select those with repeated assignments to Special Forces, either during or after the Vietnam conflict. As a result of this lack of career incentive, there is a reluctance on the part of trained leaders to return to Special Forces assignments. The designation of Special Forces and psychological operations battalion and group command positions as centrally selected commands should draw some trained officers back for repeated assignments, but the reluctance continues.

The second limitation concerns training priorities in Special Forces units. Current training places top priority on the employment of Special Forces teams in unconventional warfare in a general war environment. Second priority is given to training for the direct-action tasks described above. Third priority is given to training to assist friendly countries in foreign internal defense. Those responsible for establishing these priorities contend that the skills necessary for unconventional warfare are transferable to the foreign internal-defense mission. These missions appear to be in reverse priority. The orientation of teams advising allied forces in foreign internal defense will be different from the orientation of teams advising resistance forces in a general war environment. Given the limitations in personnel skills and experience, a change in training priorities would enhance Special Forces capabilities to respond to low-intensity contingencies, and would be more consistent with their probable employment in the next decade.

At the lowest end of the spectrum of military force employment are the *ad hoc* Security Assistance Teams. As the number and size of Military Assistance Advisory Groups around the world has decreased, the United States has provided small Military Training Teams and Technical Assistance Teams in response to requests from other nations. The program is funded entirely by Foreign Military Sales and International Military Education and Training Program funds. In the Army alone, some 150 teams have been provided to 33 countries in the past four years. Army missions in the past year have included providing a Technical Assistance Team to the Yemeni forces to conduct training in the use of the Vulcan antiaircraft gun, and the deployment of a 12-man Special Forces training team to the Liberian Army to assist in conducting light-infantry tactical training.

Teams vary in size and are deployed for a maximum of six months. Individuals selected for the teams are drawn from service-school staffs, arsenals and depots, as well as from active-duty conventional and Special Forces units. Approximately one-fourth of all Army teams provided in the past four years have been Special Forces teams.

Limitations in this capability, like those of other small-unit requirements, center around identifying available individuals with the proper skills for the particular training mission. The primary limitation is, of course, language skills.

Rangers, Special Forces, and Security Assistance Teams offer two advantages for employment in low-intensity conflict. First, they are currently available and, within the limitations described above, trained for contingencies appropriate to their size and mission. Second, because of their size and light equipment, the units or teams are deployable with current strategic-lift capabilities. These forces are constrained, however, in the missions that they can be expected to accomplish. Though these forces are appropriate for instruction, advice and assistance, reconnaissance, rescue of small groups, strategic-target destruction, or counterterrorist missions, they are not capable of conducting larger or sustained operations. Operations requiring brigade-sized or larger force must be accomplished by conventional forces.

Conventional Capabilities

U.S. general-purpose forces are organized to provide the capability to deal with a major conventional conflict in Europe as well as with a lesser conflict in another area of the world. Secretary of Defense Harold Brown summarized what has become known as the "One and One-Half War" capability in his Fiscal Year (FY) 1980 Annual Report to Congress as follows:

> For planning purposes, it seems appropriate to have the size of our general purpose combat forces on the assumption of having to halt more or less simultaneously one major attack (with Europe as the most plausible and demanding locale for its occurrence), and one lesser attack elsewhere.[4]

Earlier, in his FY 1979 Annual Report, Secretary Brown emphasized the need for forces other than those programmed for a major war in Europe, stating:

> Accordingly, we must continue to maintain a defense posture that permits us to respond effectively and simultaneously to a relatively minor as well as to a major contingency. We currently estimate the needs of such a posture—over and above the forces we program for a major war with the Soviet Union—as a limited number of land combat forces, in large part relatively light (though their

actual configuration will depend on the nature of the forces they might be expected to encounter), consisting of both Marine and Army combat divisions with their support; naval, amphibious lift, and tactical air forces; and strategic mobility forces with the range and payload to minimize our dependence on overseas staging and logistical support bases.[5]

More recently, on 30 July 1979, Secretary Brown spoke specifically of forces received for relatively minor contingencies. Brown told the Commonwealth Club in San Francisco:

> Mobile and capable conventional forces are essential not only to support our allies in Europe, but also to execute contingency plans to assist friends outside of the NATO area, should conditions so dictate and should those friends or allies request it. For this latter purpose, we continue to maintain ready general purpose forces—we have called these "Rapid Deployment Forces"—distinct from those forces earmarked or assigned to NATO. Naturally, as their name suggests, these forces are available for use wherever required, even in the NATO area should that become necessary.[6]

The terms "over and above the forces we program for a major war with the Soviet Union" and "distinct from those forces earmarked for or assigned to NATO" have a specific meaning in force programming. Members of the NATO alliance annually identify specific forces in their structure that they are willing to commit to the various NATO commands for force planning. In the Annual Defense Planning Questionnaire, designated national forces are committed to European defense in one of three categories. *Assigned forces* are national forces in being that have been placed under the operational command or operational control of a NATO commander. *Earmarked forces* are forces nations have agreed to assign to the operational command or operational control of a NATO commander at some future date. Nations specify when these forces will be available. Finally, *other forces* are those forces not assigned or earmarked for assignment to a NATO command, which may, at some future date, cooperate with NATO forces or be placed under the operational command or operational control of a NATO commander in certain specified circumstances.[7]

An attempt to identify the large conventional forces referred to by Secretary Brown as being available for a minor contingency, however, immediately brings to light the traditional problem of constrained forces programmed to cover competing requirements. Most military units programmed for the minor contingencies are also programmed for employment in a NATO conflict. This approach has both risks and costs. The primary risk is that the two contingencies will occur simultaneously. The principal cost is that units are being structured, equipped and trained with emphasis on the NATO mission, and secondary missions do not receive a high priority. The cost is particularly notable when the primary mission is a high-technology conflict in Europe, where host nations are projected to provide much of the combat service support not available elsewhere in the world. Decisions to pre-position equipment in Europe, to orient training primarily toward high-technology warfare, and to delete combat service support units from the force structure reduce the capabilities to deal with contingencies of a nature different from war in Europe.

The trend in U.S. military force planning since the Vietnam conflict has clearly been toward more emphasis on European defense. The Army Posture Statement for FY 1979 reported that "U.S. Army support to NATO is the capstone of the Army's FY 79 budget. NATO priority permeates all Army programs."[8] Some Army units that were oriented toward low-intensity contingencies have been reoriented toward NATO. For example, in June 1978, then Lieutenant General E. C. Meyer, Army Deputy Chief of Staff for Operations and Plans, told members of the House Armed Services Committee that the "Army is currently studying ways of reorganizing the 101st [Air Assault Division] so that it can better meet its NATO mission as well as retain the capability to move rapidly to meet other contingencies worldwide."[9]

Although the Marine Corps has continued to pursue a global perspective, its orientation has also reflected emphasis toward NATO commitments. General Alexander Haig, then Supreme Allied Commander in Europe, reported to the same subcommittee that the two Marine Amphibious Forces in the United States "are important elements in our [NATO] planning."[10] General Haig assured the members that he had "talked to the Chief of the Marine Corps, General Wilson, and he has reoriented the US Marine Corps to place European deployment at top priority."[11]

If Secretary Brown's statement in San Francisco can be interpreted precisely as policy, measures may be underway to make exceptions to the prevailing trend toward NATO orientation, and designated Rapid Deployment Forces from all services may be identified for low-intensity contingencies and fenced from immediate commitment to NATO. Departing Army Chief of Staff General Bernard Rogers, also raised this possibility in his final press conference on 21 June 1979. General Rogers described the Army commitment to the Rapid Deployment Force as a corps-sized force of approximately 100,000 troops, including support forces, which

> when finally designed, will not include forces which are earmarked for initial deployment from this country to NATO, so that we could deploy that force of up to 100,000 or any part thereof to a non-NATO contingency, such as the Persian Gulf or the Middle East or Northeast Asia, and have it fight in that contingency and not have to reach in and pull out forces from it, if we go, shortly thereafter, into a NATO contingency.[12]

When questioned about the separation of the force from NATO commitments, General Rogers stated that "it will have its own equipment and it will be fenced." He specifically noted that units of the corps and supporting forces will not suffer equipment drawdown to offset pre-positioned sets of equipment in Europe. He also indicated that

> what we're working towards is a self-contained corps, one that will have sufficient combat service support units in it that it can maintain itself for X number of days, X being classified. So that we will not have to depend upon host nations for support, because it may not be available in some of the areas in which we go. And so that we will not have to mobilize, even under the option of the President to call up 50,000, we wouldn't have to mobilize initially even at 50,000 in order to be successful in maintaining ourselves for X number of days.[13]

It is unclear at this time exactly what the NATO commitment of such a Rapid Deployment Force will be. Indications are that it would not be earmarked for a specific deployment. It is almost certain that no new units will be activated for inclusion in the Rapid Deployment Force. Therefore, the risk of inadequate forces for simultaneous conflicts is not resolved, although training priorities for the selected units will be clarified.

The Rapid Deployment Force is obviously still in the planning stages. Identification of the size of force and specific units is still premature. The largest force described in public sources has been four or five Army and Marine divisions, five or six Air Force and Marine air wings, and one or two carrier task groups.[14] Timely deployment of a force this large to any overseas area, even in a situation that did not involve or that did not escalate to involve Soviet forces, would be extremely difficult given current strategic-lift capabilities. A more probable concept for employing such a force would be that the total force would not be employed, but that the various components of the force—from a Ranger company to a large joint task force—could be made available to a Unified Commander to respond to a specific contingency in his area of responsibility.[15]

The primary Army combat forces for inclusion in the Rapid Deployment Force are fairly readily identifiable. General Rogers has stated that the 82d Airborne Division at Fort Bragg, North Carolina, will be included. This 15,000-soldier airborne division is a light-infantry force, without tanks or heavy artillery, and is restricted in ground mobility once it is deployed. Designed for fast-strike operations rather than sustained combat, the division would have to be reinforced or supplemented for any mission requiring tactical ground mobility or for missions against large armored or mechanized forces. The division receives high priority within the Army on personnel and logistical fill. Even so, it currently has many noncommissioned officer positions filled by personnel one or more grades below authorized levels.[16]

For missions requiring armor and mechanized Army forces, the Fourth Mechanized Division at Fort Carson, Colorado, has been mentioned.[17] The Army command-and-control element would likely be the XVIII Airborne Corps headquarters, which trains regularly for rapid deployment. These forces, along with supporting elements, were previously included in the Army's heavy/light corps, a non-NATO contingency planning force. There was, however, considerable overlap between forces programmed for the heavy/light corps and forces earmarked for committed for NATO.[18] If the overlap is to be eliminated, specific units, including combat support and combat-service support units, will have to be fenced. Stockage levels will also have to be improved if the units are to attain their deployment objective for sustained operations without major resupply and reinforcement.

There will be a greater flexibility in assigning specific Navy, Marine, and Air Force units for the Rapid Deployment Force than Army forces. Many Navy and Marine forces are already allocated to the Unified Commanders. For example, of the three Marine Amphibious Forces (MAF), one MAF is assigned to the Atlantic and two MAF's to the Pacific. One Marine Amphibious Unit (a Battalion Landing Team and a Composite Helicopter Squadron) is continuously afloat in the Mediterranean Sea. Another Marine Amphibious Unit and an additional Battalion Landing Team are also continuously afloat in the Pacific, one from the First Marine Amphibious Force in California and one from the Third Marine Amphibious Force on Okinawa. The Marines will desire to retain a global orientation, maintaining all units available for contingencies, rather than committing a single unit to a Rapid Deployment Force. Their argument is that they can achieve high proficiency and suitable training better through this arrangement than by attempting special training of one unit.

The same position is held by the Air Force. Designated tactical fighter squadrons emphasize specialized missions, so the Air Force desires to tailor its response to the requirements of contingencies rather than to identify units in advance. The Air Force prefers to maintain a designated number of units at a high state of readiness for deployment, but to retain the freedom to select the unit to be committed.

Although the specific method for designating Air Force and Marine units is not clear, it is apparent that all services are now identifying forces for commitment to low-intensity contingencies. Most elements of such a Rapid Deployment Force will probably continue to be committed to NATO in some way; however, there are strong indications that training priorities for selected units will be directed more toward low-intensity conflict. Components of the Rapid Deployment Force—from a Ranger company to a large joint task force—should, therefore, be available to respond to contingencies as readily as deployment capabilities will permit.

Deployment Capabilities

The speed with which we can deploy units to an overseas contingency area depends, of course, on the type and size of unit to be deployed. The most rapid deployment would be a small group of tactical fighters that would signal an American presence by their arrival. A small element of aircraft, from Air Force units in the United States or currently stationed in Europe and the Far East, could be deployed to most areas of the world in a few hours. Sustaining the aircraft and crews is another question, however. For example, the 12 F-15s that were deployed from Langley Air Force Base, Virginia to Saudi Arabia early in 1979 required a support fleet of 42 planes, including refueling tankers, C5A and C141 transports, and other support aircraft.[19] Even so, tactical aircraft present the most responsive forces for deployment to an area with secure air-landing facilities. A land-based Air Force tactical air squadron could deploy from the United States to most areas of the world within 48 hours, with supporting forces following at appropriate times.

On the other hand, the United States has limited capability to deploy large military forces overseas by air in a timely manner. Missions requiring the element of surprise will have to be tailored to those appropriate for battalion-sized or smaller units. For example, the 82nd Airborne Division can assemble its initial battalion for deployment by air in a matter of hours. The initial battalion can also be readily deployed using available strategic transports. However, the last support elements of the division would not arrive in an overseas area until some weeks after notification, depending on distance and aircraft availability. Combat force buildup would be continuous, of course, with the combat elements of a light airborne brigade being available in an overseas area within several days.

The total active aircraft fleet available for airlifting forces over extended distances is the Military Airlift Command's 234 C141 "Starlifter" and 70 C5A "Galaxy" transports. The C141 can lift payloads of over 32 tons but is limited by the size of its fuselage to cargo loads of between 16 and 20 tons. It can lift most of the equipment in an infantry division and almost all of the equipment in an airborne division. The larger types of Army equipment that the C141 will carry—M113 armored personnel carriers, 2½-ton trucks, and M551 light tanks—are categorized as oversize cargo. Outsize cargo— equipment which, by its size and weight, is too large for the C141, such as the M60 tank and self-propelled howitzer—must be air lifted by the C5A, which has a capability in excess of 100 tons. Because of the deterioration of the C5A wings before their full-service life, the Air Force has embarked on a program to reinforce the wings so a full-service life of 30,000 flying hours can be fulfilled. Until completion of the wing-improvement program in 1987, C5As with unreinforced wings will be flown with a maximum of 50-ton loads to slow the deterioration process. At this time, the C5A has an aerial-refueling capability, but the C141 does not. The C141 "Stretch" program, currently in progress, will increase the capacity of the C141 by about one-third by adding sections to the fuselage and will add an aerial-refueling capability. All C141s are programmed to be "stretched" by the end of FY 1982.[20]

In any large airlift operation, crew availability would be a constraint. The personnel increase required to maintain a surge rate for strategic airlift will have to be obtained by augmenting active crews and maintenance personnel with Air Reservists.

In addition to the primary force of military aircraft, the Civil Reserve Air Fleet (CRAF) serves as another source of strategic airlift. The CRAF, which is based on contractual commitments with the U.S. commercial airlines, can be called up in stages to provide equipment, aircrews, and maintenance support in the event of a national emergency. There are presently over 300 wide-bodied aircraft in the U.S. commercial air fleet. Though the majority of these can be available to carry military passengers, they could also be modified to provide the capability to carry military cargo and equipment in time of war or mobilization. Negotiations are currently being conducted with commercial carriers to provide 55 wide-bodied cargo or convertible aircraft in the CRAF by the end of FY 1982.[21]

U.S. strategic airlift capabilities are programmed to increase by some 60% in the next five years. However, other constraints may well neutralize the improvement as it applies to moving large forces to low-intensity contingencies. Because of their nature, low-intensity contingencies are most likely to occur where reception facilities are very limited. Staging bases will also be required en route in most instances. The availability of modern air bases at the destination and at crucial staging locations and their ability to handle the surge rates of aircraft flow will be major factors in any decision to deploy large forces by air. The declining U.S. base structure overseas requires increased reliance on foreign-controlled bases. In 1958, for example, the U.S. Air Force maintained 107 airbases overseas. By 1975, the number had declined to 29.[22] Bases at the destination, if they exist, will probably be available if the mission is at the request of, and in support of, a friendly government. On the other hand, existing staging bases, as well as overflight rights, might well be denied the United States for political reasons, particularly in contingencies not involving Soviet forces. Assured access to staging bases for limited contingencies is a major uncertainty in current contingency planning.

An even more serious constraint may well be the availability of adequate fuel supplies at the destination and staging facilities. In the 1973 aerial resupply to Israel, Military Airlift Command required one ton of fuel from Israeli reserves for every ton of cargo delivered. More fuel was required to support the C5As than to support the entire Israeli Air Force.[23] Informed planning for future contingencies, therefore, will require up-to-date and accurate intelligence on the availability and capacity of overseas bases, as well as on fuel stockage levels and fuel transfer capabilities.

If only a few aircarft are required for a contingency, the absence of a convenient base can be partially offset by aerial refueling tankers. Strategic Air Command has over 600 KC-135 tanker aircraft for refueling B-52 bombers as part of the strategic triad. A portion of the tanker force can be made available to support a contingency operation. The KC-135 is limited, however, in the amount of fuel which it can dispense at extended distances. Strategic Air Command is currently procuring a small number of Advanced Tanker Cargo Aircraft, which will have twice the offload capability of the KC-135 at 2,000 miles' range, and will offload five times as much at 3,000 miles. Total procurement will be 20 new tankers—six by FY 1982—so the effect on deployment of a large force will be minimal.[24]

Any movement of large land forces will require sea transport. Resources for movement by sea would come first from the 25-30 ships owned or chartered by Military Sealift Command, which can provide for a small but rapid surge capability above normal peacetime operations. Other ships available with mobilization are those of the Ready Reserve Force of the National Defense Reserve Fleet. These are Maritime Administration-owned, inactive, dry-cargo ships, maintained at a state of readiness so that they are supposed to be available on berth for loading within five to ten days after call-up. Nine of these ships are currently available, but the number is programmed to increase by seven more this year. These ships are in varying states of readiness, however, with only small maintenance crews. Crews for the Ready Reserve Force must be commercially hired after the decision to employ the force and before the force will be ready for use.

The Sealift Readiness Program provides a source of strategic lift similar to the Civil Reserve Air Fleet. Commercial ships are made available by shippers for call-up by the Secretaries of Defense and Commerce in the event of an emergency requirement. A constraint on available civilian ships, as on civil aircraft, is that in cases of limited contingencies the administration might be less willing to declare the emergency of sufficient magnitude to divert civil ships and aircraft to military use.

Even with these large numbers of ships available, adequate port facilities in the contingency area may not be available. And movement by sea is slow. A mechanized division could not be expected to assemble at its home station and move by sea to overseas location outside the Western Hemisphere more rapidly than several weeks after initial notification. Certainly if a heavy force were required portions of the force would be moved by air. However, given the air- and sealift limitations described above, brigade- or division-sized mechanized or armor units would not complete their move until several weeks after notification.

If the Fourth Mechanized Division at Fort Carson, Colorado is the Army's heavy division in the Rapid Deployment Force, response will be further delayed by the movement of the division by rail to seaports for loading. A more likely candidate for a mechanized force to be deployed by sea would be the Fifth Mechanized Division at Fort Polk, Louisiana. Light infantry units that are near ports and that could be mechanized are the Ninth Infantry Division at Fort Lewis, Washington, the Seventh Infantry Division at Fort Ord, California, and the 24th Infantry Division at Fort Stewart, Georgia. The 24th Division is currently being converted to mechanized infantry. However, it has only two active-duty brigades, so it would have to be supplemented or brought up to strength for it to be rapidly deployable as a full division.

The Marines also have limited capability for rapid deployment. A small force can be made available in a relatively short time, by sea or by air, but rapid buildup and deployment of a larger force is constrained by the limited number of amphibious ships. If some advance notice of their necessity is available, battalion-sized forces currently embarked in both the Mediterranean and Western Pacific can be moved toward an area of possible need without actually being committed, and can be readily available at the time of decision. Prior movement of the force could be a valuable signal in itself, but would reduce any surprise to be gained from rapid insertion. Initial movement will be relatively slow: the Marine Amphibious Unit embarked in the Mediterranean would take 3-10 days to move through the Suez Canal to the Persian Gulf or East Africa, depending on its location at the time of notification. Nevertheless, a battalion-sized force can be available in most areas of the world in less than ten days, and a brigade-sized force in less than three weeks.

Lack of amphibious-ship availability limits the ability to deploy a complete Marine Amphibious Force in a timely manner. Sufficient ships are available to lift one MAF, but they are deployed in both the Atlantic and Pacific Oceans. U.S. Marine Corps doctrine requires some 52 amphibious assault ships for the assault echelon and about 27 commercial ships for the follow-on echelon to support a Marine Amphibious Force in a high-threat over-the-beach assault operation. Most limited contingency requirements, however, will be in a low-threat environment for offshore forces and, in some cases, assault forces, so that some of the ships may not be necessary in every case. The Navy and Marine Corps are examining requirements of low-intensity operations, as well as the potential for commercial ships to augment programmed amphibious ships. Currently, however, an entire Marine Amphibious Force cannot be expected at any contingency location until 30-60 days after initial notification.

Current U.S. capabilities for deploying a force larger than a brigade in a timely manner are, therefore, critically limited. Battalion-sized or smaller forces can be readily deployed, and the combat elements of a light airborne brigade can be deployed to most overseas areas in a matter of days. However, timely airlift of a complete airborne division with elements to support and sustain the force is not possible with current strategic-airlift assets. Marine forces face similiar limitations. A Marine Amphibious Brigade could not be expected to arrive in some areas of the world until almost three weeks after the decision to deploy the force, depending on the location of ships and units at the time of notification. An Army mechanized division deploying by sea would not close at overseas locations until several weeks after notification. These deployment limitations seriously constrain U.S. capability to respond to contingencies requiring a force larger than a brigade. Furthermore, the uncertain availability of overseas bases, ports and fuel will complicate any deployment of forces, regardless of size and mission.

Command, Control, and Intelligence

Command and control for contingency operations is currently being reviewed for both operational and training requirements. Unified Commands have authority over all military operations, including security assistance, within their areas of responsibility. The concept for command and control of contingency forces is under review to identify areas for training emphasis.

The command environment for forces employed in any contingency operation will require flexibility and responsiveness. Because of the complexity of most situations that will require military force, all levels of command would hope to receive clear and timely guidance as to the objective to be accomplished, the limitations on the use of force, options open to the commander at each level, current intelligence regarding the local situation, and a defined chain of command. The nature of such contingencies, however, is such that most of these essentials will either not be available or will change as the operation develops. Moreover, diffuse reporting channels and current technology preclude a clear-cut chain of command.

There are numerous sources from which information and possibly instructions will be issued to commanders of air, sea or ground forces employed. The current concept for control of contingency forces is that the

Unified Commander will control forces in his area of responsibility. If the forces are already assigned, he will do so with the existing joint chain of command, appointing a Joint Task Force Commander to command the deployment, employment and sustainment of forces, whatever the size. If contingency forces are deployed from the United States, a Joint Task Force headquarters from Readiness Command at MacDill Air Force Base, Florida could deploy to command the force, under the overall command of the respective Unified Command. The chain of command for forces employed, therefore, would be from the President through the Secretary of Defense, the Unified Commander, and the Joint Task Force Commander to the deployed air, naval or ground units. Current technology allows all levels of command to maintain real-time direct communications with maneuver units on the ground and tactical aircraft in the air. The Mayagüez operation clearly showed that directives may be issued from each level of command directly to the man on the ground or in the ship or plane.

In addition to the military chain of command, there is a political chain that plays a part. The United States ambassador to the country involved leads the country team, composed of representatives of all agencies involved in relations with the local government. Military operations may well be influenced by the ambassador's instructions, which can be introduced at any level in the chain of command. Further complicating the situation will be coordination, at some or all levels of command, with allied forces being assisted or participating in a combined operation.

Training at all levels, including the National Command Authority, will reduce the confusion somewhat. There are established procedures for deploying and controlling contingency forces. Training will familiarize participants with the procedures and planning times for types of missions, as well as the confusion resulting from changed instructions in a rapidly developing environment. Of equal importance, however, is the training in flexibility and responsiveness that unit leaders gain through repeated exercises and regular unit training, as well as through instruction on the nature of low-intensity operations. Improvement is particularly needed in the quality and quantity of instruction on low-intensity operations in all the services.

Communications should not pose a problem at long distances, regardless of the size of force employed. Satellite and airborne communications relays will be available, as will long-range tactical radios deployed with small maneuver units. However, effective command and control of small units in urban areas are reduced by the limited range of the current family of FM tactical radios in built-up urban areas. Given the need for precise maneuver of small units in likely contingencies, the tactical communications limitation is serious.

Current intelligence, both technical and tactical, will be essential to a successful low-level contingency. Tactical intelligence available in Washington through radio and television reporting may be more reliable than local reports. Current technology permits real-time passing of such information to the committed force. Sorely lacking in many countries, however, is current information of a technical nature on road and airfield capabilities, fuel shortage capacity and stockage levels, and expedient air landing sites. This information is usually obtained through human sources, an intelligence area which needs drastic improvement. Attaché staffs would also be likely sources of information, if such staffs were available in the country and if they had access to the desired information.

Training Priorities

Although there are many common skills applicable to all types of military operations, low-intensity conflict situations will require skills and orientation considerably different from a large-scale conflict in Europe. Units oriented toward non-NATO contingencies will need regional and environmental training in cold-weather, mountain, jungle, and desert warfare. Combined exercises with forces from many different nations will enhance proficiency in multilateral operations. Training should emphasize flexibility in command relationships, in unit sizes, and in rules of engagement. Commanders and troops need to practice constraint and should be given training that simulates missions under varying political circumstances. Such training should emphasize civic action programs, for the psychological effect of the military presence may well be more important than the tactical objective. Target discrimination should be emphasized, particularly in insurgency situations, where the battlefield is not clearly defined. Small-unit and individual initiative also needs emphasis, perhaps more than controlled movement of larger forces. Finally, units should be trained in urban warfare, because many probable contingencies will call for operations in cities.

Environmental training is currently being conducted in all services. If and when specific units are designated for contingency operations, this training can be intensified for those units. At this time, the Marine Corps, for example, conducts battalion and regimental exercises regularly in the desert near Twenty-Nine Palms, California. They have also recently reopened the cold-weather training center at Pickle Meadows, near Barstow, California, and plan to rotate battalions through that center. The same type of training is available to Army units. The XVIII Airborne Corps sends battalions to the Jungle Warfare School in Panama and the Arctic Warfare School in Alaska. The XVIII Corps also conducts periodic Emergency Deployment Readiness

Exercises in special environments. Recently, exercises have been conducted in the snow at Fort Drum, New York; in the mountains of Yakima National Forest, Washington; and in the desert near Fort Bliss, Texas. Battalions have also conducted cold-weather training as part of an exchange program with the Canadian Armed Forces. Similar environmental training is being conducted by Air Force squadrons as well. The training will need more specific focus for selected units in all services and should be extended to cover sustained operations in an austere environment, but the program for such expansion is available.

U.S. military forces also participate in numerous multilateral training exercises, ranging from small exercises coordinated by the various Unified Commands to large joint and combined exercises coordinated by the Joint Staff in Washington. Most of the exercises involve forward-deployed forces in the Unified Commands. These forces may well be the Marine, Navy and Air Force units that would be committed in a contingency operation. Army contingency forces in the United States—the 82d Airborne Division, for example—have not participated in a combined exercise recently. Any effort in this direction will be financially constrained. The best use of funds may well be toward Command Post Exercises to familiarize commanders and staffs with the unique challenges of combined operations.

Some imaginative training is being conducted to emphasize flexibility in command relationships and unit sizes at the maneuver-unit level. Perhaps the best example is the periodic joint Emergency Deployment Readiness Exercise conducted by the XVIII Airborne Corps. The corps tailors the force and mission for each exercise to match aircraft and funds available. Emphasis is on flexibility of mission and command. A recent exercise, DRAGON TEAM X, conducted August 26–31, 1979, for example, deployed a force for a disaster-relief mission. Forces deployed were a military-police group, a medical brigade, an engineer company, and pyschological-operations and civil-affairs teams. Physicians from Walter Reed Army Hospital were deployed to fill shortages in the medical brigade. The forces were employed by parachute, as well as air-landed, at Camp Robinson, Arkansas, where they assisted a "friendly government" in recovering from a recent earthquake and in coping with looting and demonstrations. The situation was further complicated by a local group of marauding bandits, who were not clearly determined to be insurgents. The exercise demonstrated how units can train in flexible unit sizes and relationships to meet specific mission requirements, and how small-unit commanders can be placed in training situations where the political environment is constrained and uncertain.[25] As combat support and combat-service support units are identified and included in the Rapid Deployment Forces, exercises dealing wtih low-intensity situations will include numerous flexible force combinations to accomplish low-intensity missions.

Much less encouraging is the amount of instruction given by all services to leaders, particularly junior officers, in the special political and tactical environment of low-intensity conflict. After the withdrawal from Vietnam, service-school instruction was directed almost entirely to major conflict in Europe. For example, by 1975 no instruction in low-intensity conflict was presented at the U.S. Army Armor or Field Artillery Schools. The Infantry School offers no instruction on the topic to future platoon leaders in its Officer Basic Course and limited instruction to captains in the Officer Advanced Course.[26] Instruction on low-intensity conflict has doubled since 1975 at the Command and General Staff College at Fort Leavenworth, Kansas, and now encompasses 49 hours of the 726-hour course. Instruction on low-intensity conflict may increase as the Vietnam experience fades. The prevailing view at this time, however, is that low-intensity conflict is another type of special operation, like desert and mountain warfare, which may require special tactics and equipment, but which should not distract from training for high-technology war in Europe. The 1976 U.S. Army Field Manual 100-5, *Operations*, which sets forth current Army doctrine, places almost total emphasis on high-intensity war in Europe. The manual states in the introductory chapter:

> Battle in Central Europe against forces of the Warsaw Pact is the most demanding mission the US Army could be assigned. Because the US Army is structured primarily for that contingency and has large forces deployed in that area, this manual is designed mainly to deal with the realities of such operations. The principles set forth in this manual, however, apply also to military operations anywhere in the world. Furthermore, the US Army retains substantial capabilities in its airborne, airmobile, and infantry divisions for successful operations in other theaters of war against other forces.[27]

Instruction, unit training, and doctrine for low-intensity conflict will require new emphasis on restraint, flexibility, precise maneuver by small units, operations in built-up areas, and the psychological and civil-affairs responsibilities of conventional forces. The Army is preparing a new field manual on low-intensity conflict. The manual is expected to place special emphasis on employing only necessary force. It will also include lessons shared by British forces in Northern Ireland on urban operations. Procedures for low-intensity conflict will be presented amid repeated cautions that each contingency operation is unique and must be tailored to match the political and military objectives of the commitment. The manual will include instruction on U.S. conventional-force employment; however, its primary thrust will be advice and assistance to host-government forces in internal defense and development.

Equipment Shortfalls

Most of the identifiable equipment requires at this time call for improvements in, or greater numbers of, current items, rather than for new equipment unique to contingency forces. Most pressing is the need to improve the ability to deploy forces rapidly. If mechanized forces are to be deployed rapidly, more reinforced wide-bodied civil aircraft capable of transporting oversize equipment are needed. For sea movement or sustainment of large forces, more and faster breakbulk cargo ships with integral cargo-handling gear, as well as roll-on-roll-off ships, would reduce dependence on existing port facilities. The Marines need improved landing craft for over-the-beach operations. Air-cushioned landing craft are under development which, through increased speed, will reduce troop-exposure time in any ship-to-shore movement.

The Army and Air Force have made good progress in developing tactical delivery and resupply capabilities. Improved aerial-delivery platforms and development of the Low-Altitude Parachute-Ejection System make possible aerial delivery and resupply of such heavy items as armored personnel carriers, light tanks, and towed 155 mm howitzers.

The most notable shortfall in equipment designed for unique environments is that for desert operations. A major logistics problem is the supply of potable water. Planners project a requirement for six gallons of potable water for consumption by each person per day. The current portable water-desalinization unit is unreliable. A new 600-gallon-per-hour reverse-osmosis desalinization unit has been tested and should be available to high-priority units by FY 1981.

As more consideration is given to specific contingencies, identification of special equipment needs will develop. Many of the sophisticated weapons systems in the inventory will not be useful because of their size and weight. Opposing forces may have heavy weapons and sophisticated equipment in limited quantities, so lightweight antiarmor capability will be required for some U.S. contingency forces. Current tactical radios used by the Army and Marines are unsuitable for built-up areas. Radios capable of operating in an urban environment are available commercially and should be purchased for all high-priority contingency forces. Army Ranger battalions have been issued these radios. Reliable tactical communications will be essential in contingency environments, where the emphasis will be on precise maneuver, controlled use of firepower, rapid insertion and rapid withdrawal. The emphasis for research should be on light, easily transportable equipment, capable of sustained operations in an austere environment.

Manpower Levels and Quality

As the services struggle with numerous manpower issues, the major manpower problems should have less effect on high-priority contingency forces than on lower-priority units. Nevertheless, as the services attempt to maintain force levels with fewer personnel, the capabilities of even the high-priority units may well be seriously affected.

The most serious personnel problems affecting low-intensity contingency forces in the near future will result from overall personnel shortages and shortages of personnel with selected critical skills. For example, the Army failed to meet its FY 1979 recruiting objectives by over 16,000 recruits. Army Chief of Staff General E. C. Meyer stated on 17 September 1979 that overseas units will be maintained at 100% strength in spite of the shortages and that rapid deployment units will be maintained "as close to 100 percent as we can."[28] Also, the Marine Corps may reduce its manpower levels by 10,000 personnel in FY 1980, as a result of a 4,000-Marine shortfall in recruiting and a need for funds elsewhere.[29] This reduction will certainly affect the divisions and their embarked battalions.

The most dramatic effect of these personnel shortages will be increased turbulence as the services attempt to maintain existing force structure with reduced numbers. The turbulence will have its most serious effect on unit cohesion and training proficiency. The effect will be pronounced in all units, but will be particularly acute in small teams with specialized skills, such as the Special Forces. There is no reason to expect that contingency forces will be able to escape this turbulence.

Shortages in specific skills continue to plague all the services. The Air Force and Navy are suffering from shortages in pilots and technical engineers, and all services are seriously short of medical personnel. These shortages are acute and would be felt clearly in any contingency operation involving a large force.

There are serious doubts that the active-force manpower shortages and the much greater shortages in the Reserve Forces will improve in the near future. The size of the youth population will begin to decline in 1980. By 1985, the number of eighteen-year-old males will be about 15% below the FY 1977 level. Particularly in a healthy economic environment, competition for high-school graduates among colleges, vocational schools, private employers, and the military will be keen. Though the shortage will be partially offset by increased numbers of older people and women in the work force, competition for male high-school graduates will still be strong.

It is not evident that the other manpower trends which may cause concern in the long term have reached the point that they will seriously affect capabilities for contingency operations in the next few years. The proportion of high-school graduates—a key indicator for stability, discipline and retention—remains relatively high at this time. In FY 1978, 77% of all non-prior-service acquisitions to the services were high-school graduates.[30] The proportion of high-school graduates will remain an item for attention in the future as overall shortages continue. First-term attritions are a problem. Over one-third of those who entered active duty in FY 1974 did not complete their initial enlistment.[31] The problem deserves attention and is a matter of concern at this time. The ethnic and geographical representation of the services may be the beginning of a trend that deserves discussion, but there is no indication that these factors should seriously affect U.S. capability to participate in low-intensity conflict at this time or in the near future.

Summary and Conclusions

The capability of the United States to employ military forces in low-intensity contingencies varies greatly with the size and kind of forces involved. The primary constraint is the limited capacity for strategic airlift and sealift. Rapid deployment of battalion-sized forces is possible, but prompt deployment of forces larger than a light brigade is not possible with current resources.

The services maintain several small, highly trained elite units that could be deployed rapidly and employed in both direct-action and advisory missions. The Army's Ranger battalions and the Navy's SEAL teams are capable of limited contingency operations, such as reconnaissance, rescue of small groups, strategic target destruction, or counterterrorist operations. Special Forces teams provide the capability to train, advise, and direct indigenous forces. Security Assistance Teams have also been organized and deployed to advise and assist friendly government forces.

Both the Army and the Marine Corps maintain divisions and larger units that can assemble rapidly and prepare for deployment to overseas contingencies. Both the Army and Marine divisions are engaged in active training programs for low-intensity missions. The principal limitation on their utility is the inability to deploy either type of division rapidly to an overseas area of operations.

The most rapidly deployable forces for minor show-of-force operations are tactical aircraft already deployed overseas. Small number of aircraft can be deployed to most parts of the world within hours of notification, given a secure airbase and adequate fuel. Sustainment of even a small force over a period of time, however, is complex and cumbersone. When time is available, naval vessels are able to perform the same function, without the requirement for secure landing facilities.

Several limitations in our capabilities deserve analysis regarding priority for planning and resources. The most readily identifiable is strategic airlift and sealift, particularly the capability to move oversize equipment. Along with this limitation is the lack of assured staging bases, fuel supplies, and overflight rights in many parts of the world. Training priorities for low-intensity conflict also deserve evaluation, particularly the quality and quantity of instruction given to junior officers and noncommissioned officers on the nature of low-intensity operations. The effect of personnel turbulence on small units with specialized skills needed for low-level contingencies needs study, as does the effect of personnel shortages on Rapid Deployment Forces from all Services. Among other remaining issues, the priority to be given to the development and procurement of special equipment for contingency forces should be considered.

The United States, therefore, has the capability to deploy and employ military forces rapidly for selected low-intensity contingencies requiring small, elite forces for direct-action or advisory missions. There are, however, serious limitations in U.S. capability to deploy larger forces rapidly to any overseas area. Other limitations concerning the effectiveness of forces to be employed deserve attention, but none are so pressing as the limitation in strategic transport.

Notes

*The views and conclusions expressed in this paper are solely those of the author and do not purport to represent those of any agency of the United States Government.
1. Harold Brown, *Department of Defense Annual Report, Fiscal Year 1979*, p. 7.
2. Barry M. Blechman et al., *Force Without War: U.S. Armed Forces as a Political Instrument* (Washington, D.C., The Brookings Institution, 1978), p. 23.
3. Strategic Studies Institute, *Organization, Missions and Command and Control for Special Forces and Ranger Units in the 1980's* (Carlisle Barracks, Pa.: U.S. Army War College, 1979), SECRET-NO FOREIGN DISSEM (Review by ODCSOPS, DA on April 18, 1979), Unclassified Paragraph 4-VII-4, p. 60.
4. Harold Brown, *Department of Defense Annual Report, Fiscal Year 1980*, p. 13.
5. Brown, *Defense Report, Fiscal Year 1979*, p. 9.
6. Harold Brown, *Speech before the Commonwealth Club*, San Francisco, 30 July 1979.
7. Joint Chiefs of Staff Publication No. 1, *Department of Defense Dictionary of Military and Associated Terms* (Washington, D.C., Joint Chiefs of Staff, 1979), pp. 37, 119, 249.
8. Army Posture Statement, Fiscal Year 1979, p. 60.
9. United States Congress, House of Representatives, Committee on Armed Services, Special Subcommittee on NATO Standardization, Interoperability and Readiness, *NATO Standardization, Interoperability and Readiness*, hearings held 6 June 1978, p. 258.
10. Ibid., p. 322.
11. Ibid., p. 304.

12. U.S. Department of Defense, *Press Briefing by General Bernard Rogers, Army Chief of Staff,* 21 June 1979 (Washington, D.C.: Acme Reporting Company, 1979), p. 24.
13. Ibid., p. 25.
14. Juan Cameron, "Our What-If Strategy for Mideast Trouble Spots," *Fortune,* 7 May 1979, pp. 157–58.
15. U.S. Office of the Assistant Secretary of Defense, Public Affairs Information Paper, *Unilateral Corps,* Department of Defense, Washington, D.C., undated.
16. Cameron, p. 158.
17. Mike Jansen, "The Force," *NBC News,* 26, July 1979.
18. U.S. Department of Defense, *Press Briefing by General Bernard Rogers,* 21 June 1979, p. 28.
19. Cameron, p. 158.
20. Brown, *Defense Report, Fiscal Year 1979,* p. 199.
21. Ibid., pp. 199, 203–4.
22. John R. Pickett, "Airlift and Military Intervention," in Ellen P. Stern, ed., *The Limits of Military Intervention* (Beverly Hills, Sage, 1977), p. 139.
23. Ibid., pp. 143–44.
24. Air Force Posture Statement, Fiscal Year 1979, p. 24.
25. Bill Branley, "Corps Checks Disaster Plan," *The Paraglide,* Fort Bragg, N.C., 6 September 1979, pp. 1–3.
26. Donald B. Vought, "Preparing for the Wrong War?" *Military Review 57* (May 1977): 29–30.
27. United States Army, Field Manual 100-5, *Operations,* 1976, pp. 1–2.
28. Larry Carney, "Meyer: Low-Priority Units Face Shortages," *Army Times,* 1 October 1979, p. 4.
29. "Are the Marines Obsolete? Their Chief Speaks Out," *U.S. News and World Report,* 10 September 1979, p. 29.
30. Brown, *Defense Report, Fiscal Year 1979,* p. 280.
31. Ibid., p. 297.

CHAPTER 4

Lessons of Modern History: The British Experience

Dennis Duncanson

The country with the most low-intensity conflicts in its history, both modern and ancient, is undoubtedly China. In the modern period, Britain has been a creditable runner-up, having fought several score "small wars" in the nineteenth century and taken part in more than a score since 1945 alone, without counting two under the United Nations' flag. Not even during the twenty years of relative world peace between the world wars was Britain's Temple of Janus quite shut. Like China's, some of Britain's conflicts have lasted a long time: the Northwest Frontier conflict went on for seventy years or so, that in Ireland has been with us on and off since about 1800 and still shows no prospect of resolution. In some conflicts that have broken out more than once after interludes of peace, Britain has been involved in earlier stages but not in later ones: such as Palestine in 1917, 1937 and 1946 but not thereafter, or Cyprus in 1931 and 1954-60 but not from 1963 onwards. In Malaya, Britain saw the "emergency" through to its end in 1960, made the expanded Malaysia secure in Borneo against the guerrilla "Konfrontasi" with Sukarno's Indonesia a few years later, but has taken no hand against communist resurgence in the 1970s. The disengagement can be explained in some cases by cold judgement that cost-effectiveness was declining as the successive phases of the conflict advanced across the spectrum of intensity—a less familiar manifestation of Clausewitzian *Steigerung* than the one for which we coined "escalation" the other day. Another class of conflict is that in which Britain has taken a leading diplomatic part while avoiding the

95

fighting—Indochina in its Geneva phase, or Rhodesia.¹ In Oman, a treaty ally of Britain since before 1800, ideas of, and training for, counterinsurgency have been British, but the foreign troops have been from the Iranian and friendly Arab armies.

Reasons for Involvement

The Gorchakov Doctrine

It is hard to think of conflicts whether long or short, with the exception of Oman (a particularly low-intensity *involvement*), Britain has joined in, resolved and then moved away from, as has been the pattern of American involvement; we have not been prompted by any policy equivalent to the Truman doctrine. Instead, British involvement in low-intensity conflicts has nearly always been incidental to other commitments in the same territory— commitments of one of two kinds. The first kind, smaller in number, has arisen from military occupation of former enemy territory at the end of a major war—certain Middle East conflicts in 1919, Eritrea, Java, and South Vietnam in 1945. The action of the Office of Strategic Services at Hanoi and Ta Khek, also in 1945, by way of intervention in local domestic conflicts— albeit in itself unauthorized by Washington and not understood by the agents themselves—provides something of an American example of this kind of involvement. The second and more numerous kind has arisen from commit- ments consequent on imperial policy, of which the most recent and serious have been in Malaya, Cyprus, and Aden, though not Kenya, for independence was not an issue in Mau Mau. During the nineteenth century, imperial policy favored expansion; in Asia especially, Britain became involved in the factional conflicts of native states under what I call the Gorchakov doctrine, after the Russian prince who, as Foreign Minister of Tsar Alexander II in the 1860s, explained Russian absorption of one Central Asian khanate after another as a *ragion-di-stato* imperative: keeping the peace on the frontier of the original metropolitan territory, he wrote to foreign ambassadors in Saint Petersburg, made intervention necessary in the struggles between factions fighting among themselves in the first khanate; resolution of that local conflict extended the frontier of Russia and forthwith necessitated intervention in the next khanate, which in turn "widened the bounds of civilization" another step. British power in the Indian subcontinent had been spreading by much the same "domino" process, at least down to the suppression of the Mughal monarchy in 1858: "Small wars," says a British War Office manual of 1896 (much studied in France as well), were "a heritage of extended empire, a certain epilogue to encroachments into lands beyond the confines of existing civilization inhabited by races with unconventional methods of warfare. ...

Out of the original compaign of conquest sprang further wars—all vexatious, desultory and harassing."[2] Britain's involvement in the struggle against the Mahdiya in the Sudan originated, not in British imperialism, but in that of the Egyptian *khedivate*, itself a British protected territory though nominally under the suzerainty of the Ottoman Empire.

Punitive Expeditions

Nevertheless, there was a substantial difference of standpoint between Britain and Russia (or Egypt) that is specially significant when we bring British experience in low-intensity conflict to bear on American policy in the contexts of today and tomorrow. For Russia, operation of the Gorchakov doctrine resulted in enlargement, at the expense of contiguous countries, of the metropolitan territory, and consequently the cost-effectiveness of the "small wars" it entailed was high; for Britain, as a maritime empire, victory or defeat was a question of indifference to strictly national defense, so that the cost-effectiveness was lower—and troop morale lower with it. The cost-effectiveness of America's recent involvement in Indochina might be said to be lower still because the United States is not even a *maritime* empire. All the same, where to draw the line was often difficult for Britain to decide: two-and-a-half centuries of our relations with Persia-Iran—now interventionist, now abstentionist—bear witness. Initial withdrawal from a punitive expedition against one faction in Afghanistan rebelling against the ruler we recognized in Kabul (1838–42) entailed a second costly war there for the sake of control over the Northwest Frontier (1878–81), but even after a British protectorate was set up in Kabul, disturbances on the frontier continued little checked. Indeed, to the chagrin today of the Soviet inheritors of British hegemony, the Pathans appear externally unsubduable, the low-intensity conflicts they generate unquenchable. A common experience of colonial powers was that they found themselves heirs to social tensions of a tribal, religious, or other nature, and became the butt of the aggrieved, not necessarily because they were alien, but because they were the government of the day. Such was the reason for endemic trouble in the Hadhramaut, and there is some consolation in the thought that troubles in Cyprus are traceable to the fall of Constantinople—to the Crusades even. No true conflict resolution was ever likely in these instances.

Involvement in Native Conflicts

Although maintenance of British imperial rule generally went un-disputed, so that, for example, no British troops saw service anywhere in sub-Saharan Africa between World War I and the outbreak of Mau Mau in Kenya in 1952, internal native conflicts sometimes engaged Britain in colonial wars fought with native security forces. I would cite the struggle against the

Dervishes in Somaliland, which went on from 1900 to 1920 and, surprisingly, was resolved in the end through recourse to bombing. However strongly the Mad Mullah also desired to chase the Christian infidels out of Beila and Berbera, that was incidental to his principal object of founding a Muslim dictatorship in the interior of the Horn of Africa under the revivalist banner of the Salihiya Order at Mecca—an object in which he was opposed by other tribal interests. In certain respects, the Dervishes stood for old-believer tradition against the encroaching modernism that followed from colonial dependence, as the Mau Mau were to do half a century later. The extension of British administration ultimately into the interior of Somaliland was the result, not the cause of the *jihad*.[3] Since World War II, Britain's colonial struggles—like those faced by Belgium and the Netherlands, and by France elsewhere than in Algeria (which France treated as inalienable metropolitan territory)—have not been over maintenance of imperial rule but over what, if any, single native faction was going to inherit British power and authority; for all the outgoing powers, the intention of decolonization was to leave behind a constitution of parliamentary democracy, not an oligarchy or a dictatorship. In many colonies there were factions that sought precisely that monopoly of power, and feared either that they could not procure it through the ballot box or that their rivals would seize it first; for them the surest road to power was to force the colonial power's hand in advance. Thus, in the Congo there was no fighting until independence had been proclaimed in Léopoldville by the King of the Belgians in person and the Belgian flag lowered, whereupon the Belgians became involved in a conflict of great violence and brutality, Congolese against Congolese. Likewise, in what turned out to be the most intractable, though not the most important, of Britain's recent conflicts, the one in Aden, the contending parties did not even constitute themselves until after Britain had announced the intention to end colonial rule.

National Interest and Troop Morale

That Britain never came face to face with united subject nations in wars for colonial succession has proved difficult for outsiders to comprehend, yet was inescapable for anybody involved closely enough to read the small print, as it were, on the back of the contenders' political manifestoes. The cost to Britain of the decolonization struggle in Malaya, Cyprus, and Aden was high; the potential benefit for Britain was low. The psychological consequence for the British forces can be appreciated; far from fighting for national territory like the Tsarist troops in central Asia, they were no longer even fighting for a minor imperial advantage comparable to that of the Northwest Frontier, but for abstract ideals that could have no direct consequence for their own society. Firmness of Tsarist purpose made the task easier for Russian troops than for British (or French), remarks Callwell, and inspired their high morale to "brilliant feats of arms."[4]

Validity of Experience

Rules of Conduct

Ever since the eighteenth century, besides an international lead in formulation of rules of the Congress of Vienna and the various Hague and Geneva Conventions, Britain has taken pride in elaborating bodies of doctrine for the execution of *national* policies overseas in both their practical and their legal aspects: from *Satow's Guide to Diplomatic Practice* to rules for conduct in war, rules for military occupation of enemy territory, for imperial government, for colonial emancipation and so on. The lessons that can be distilled from the long list of conflicts in which world trade and power have involved Britain fall under two heads. Under one head, we possess a corpus of both military and legal-political action, mainly tactical in scope, that has been recorded in the memoirs of administrators and officers who subsequently embodied it in the basic training of infantry formations and the technical training of specialized units with intelligence or administrative duties—to such an extent by 1914, it might be said, that the British army was overtrained for low-intensity conflict in the East and undertrained for conventional or trench warfare in Europe.[5] Under the other head come the less clearly defined—often disputed—lessons, largely strategic and almost entirely political, that successive generations of political leaders have handed down as a national policy, notwithstanding the occasional complaint that our statesmen do not learn from their predecessors' mistakes. An example of *not* learning from history was the Anglo-French intervention in Egypt in the Suez crisis of 1956: Britain had employed force at Alexandria in rather similar circumstances in 1882, France dissenting on that occasion out of fear of that very antiimperialist opposition that was to hit both governments in 1956. British leaders have been blamed more frequently in recent years for the opposite fault of transferring, together with the generals and colonels in command, the tactics learnt from one conflict to another where either the nature of the challenge to authority or the social environment, or both, were so different as to invalidate reapplication of the earlier measures. The criticism has become one of those finger-wagging incidents where the people echoing it rarely possess the experience to judge for themselves. More than that, the principal culprits in drawing false analogies have often been the critics themselves, in press, parliament, and church.

A Guerrilla Lore

If we acknowledge the universal validity of the theories enunciated by the social sciences, we should not be surprised to discover, in practice, that parallels of circumstance do arise between one low-intensity conflict and another in different times and climes, that rebels embarking on the road to seizure of power by force profit from parallel opportunities, and that the assisting authorities resort to parallel instrumentalities or find themselves confronted by parallel constraints. Where formerly such parallels were coincidental, in recent times they have often been the result of the deliberate study of the tactics of struggle by the contenders. It is therefore no futile endeavor if we try to identify the salient points in common and bring them to the attention of a wider segment of the public, which, under democratic constitutions, is going to pass judgement on the merits of the two protagonists in any future conflict. The record of the Sun Yat-sen and Toilers-of-the-East Universities in Moscow in the days of the Comintern, what is known about the Hòa Bình Guerrilla School in Tonkin (evidently still open as recently as December 1978),[6] and the facilities for training South American revolutionaries in North Korea are all evidence of Leninist belief in the universality of communist tactics; Colonel Qaddafi's guerrilla training camps, though non- and even anticommunist in purpose, apply the same methods to the society of the Middle East.[7] In some conflicts one cannot readily separate the effects of ideology or training from those of tradition, or either from mere force of circumstances. On the side of the defense, a similar exchange of tactical experience and of guerrilla training has developed between the military establishments of NATO, CENTO and SEATO, certain members of the British Commonwealth, and two or three Arab states with whom we have bilateral defense agreements.

Victory and Defeat

The test for validity of experience in armed conflict ought to be victory or defeat. However, victory or defeat are not always easy to measure under conditions of decolonization, the end result of which was, by definition, surrender of the colonial power's mandate sooner or later. The British army would not like to think it was defeated in Aden, which it evacuated in its own time and without having to fight any rearguard actions; and yet it left behind political chaos that was resolved among the rivals for power by more of the very bloodshed the army had been trying to stamp out. At the opposite pole of decolonization, that of peaceful transition to independence, where no armed conflict broke out before or at the time, the aim of British policy, namely establishment of a native parliamentary democracy, has failed sooner or later in colony after colony, more or less universally in Africa. Apart from India, Singapore is all but unique in having preserved the original constitution, after a protracted conflict on the margin of the Malayan Emergency and without military action, and in having upheld British ideals and standards in government. Achievement of the policy aim in the short term is therefore an ambiguous criterion for judging the outcome of the armed conflicts over decolonization. In Kenya, Mau Mau ceased to exist as a consequence of

British action; that therefore was a victory. And yet, though some analysts would deny it, others maintain that it was Mau Mau that shook the hold of the white settlers over the Kenya highlands, spurred London's determination not to risk a struggle for independence, and a decade afterwards made of Jomo Kenyatta (sometime recipient of revolutionary training from the Comintern and convicted—despite the best legal assistance from International Red Aid, to which I shall refer again—of management in secret of Mau Mau), paradoxically, the most likely candidate to fulfil British aims in decolonization. The end result in this instance was that Kenyatta did uphold parliamentary democracy in Kenya whereas all his neighbors did away with it, that once in power he pursued a foreign policy antagonistic to the USSR, and that he became a pillar of the British Commonwealth and on one occasion invited British forces to return and put down a mutiny in his own army. Kenya *was* a victory.

Malaya and Cyprus

In Malaya, the insurgents were not crushed quite so decisively, but sufficiently to cease to be a political force. The Union Jack was lowered three years before the final skirmishes and surrenders; had the communist bid for power hastened independence, as is sometimes asserted? Despite close connection with these events, I do not find a judgement over Malaya easy to reach either, for if, instead of the decade of conflict, the country had enjoyed a decade of peace and prosperity, the likelihood was strong that other pressures would have tended just the same towards decolonization. Any hope that Britain ever entertained of effecting a final resolution of conflict in Cyprus was presumptuous: British occupation of the island in the first place, in 1870, was the result of Greek and Turkish rivalry for control of it and of its mixed population (as a result of Greece's emancipation, in part under Britain's influence). Insofar as the aim of EOKA was to bring about *enosis* with Greece, British achievement in crushing the insurrection and installing an independent joint Turko-Greek Cypriot regime was a victory; yet the inseparable condition for that achievement was that we left Cyprus so defenseless that it fell victim afterwards to an Athens-prompted coup d'état and consequent invasion by an army of occupation from the Turkish mainland, which turned Britain's earlier victory, perhaps not into defeat, but into failure, inasmuch as it took the political position back to that of 1870. A similar combination of strategic failure with tactical victory was a bitter feature of American experience in Indochina.

Northern Ireland

Yet another problem of judgement is afforded by the conflict in Ireland. There Britain has no definite aim: any formula whatever for resolution that brought about a permanent peace between the contenders for power would be welcomed in London. This is no place to analyze the issues that have defied several generations of drafters of constitutions for Ireland, but only the outcome of the last decade of violence there. Current hostilities between the longstanding factions—with Britain caught as peacekeeper as in Cyprus and Aden—broke out in the wake of the general escalation of civil violence round the world (the exaltation of "proletarian culture" and the vogue for Maoism) that followed the communist offensive against South Vietnam in 1968. British counteraction in Northern Ireland has not quelled the troublemakers; has it therefore failed? Various tactical measures (e.g. detention without trial) have been introduced and later dropped; persumably they must be judged failures. On the other hand, the violence has not gotten worse; although both factions resort to terrorism and assassination, if in unequal measure, and the threat of disorder keeps army and police standing by (expensively for the exchequer), danger of civil war has receded and life has, since the early peak of atrocities, become much safer again for travelers, shoppers, and families asleep in their homes. The tactical measures that have continued in effect must, to the extent of achieving containment, be judged successful.

Ethics, Causes, Realpolitik

Victory and Virtue

Thus, to contemplate the vagaries of Machiavelli's *fortuna* in British experience of less-than-wars is salutary as a warning against the Providential view of politics—the assumption that when revolution succeeds the old condition must have been worse than the new, and conversely that where counteraction has been frustrated, the frustration is a priori evidence that the counteraction was in a bad cause. British public philosophy ranges through the same Comtean stages of interpretation of public fortunes as does American, and is equally impervious to experience: in contrast to the jingoism of an earlier era, some of our churchmen have been swift to interpret the inability of our troops in recent conflicts to forestall terrorism, and even more the setback of ambushes in which they have sustained heavy casualties, as signs of the immorality of our engagement in the struggle. The same defeatism (play on which is the crux of Leninist tactics) underlies the argument of certain American political scientists after 1954 that, because the Vietnamese communists won the battle of Dien Bien Phu so dramatically, it was wrong (wicked) for the Bao Dai Government not to surrender the entire country to them and wrong (imprudent) for Britain, France and America to help them avoid doing so. If the argument be sound, then it was wrong for Britain not to surrender to Germany after Dunkirk in 1940, but right for Germany to surrender to Britain in 1945—a conclusion inconsistent and absurd. That there can be no Providential correlation between virtue and victory can be shown wherever systems of ethics as well as factional interests are in conflict, and where the exponents of both systems claim that they are divinely inspired: to choose another *reductio ad absurdum*, it was immoral in Muslim eyes, but not Hindu, for Britain, during the conflicts on the Northwest Frontier, to victual her troops with pork, but the judgments were reversed if the victuals were of beef. More than once in that part of the world, and again in Somaliland and during the Mahdiya, the mauling of British patrols was explained by triumphant chiefs to their warriors as due to the ritual uncleanness of the vanquished.

Victory and Popularity

If we move from "theological" explanations into Comte's second stage of etiology, the "metaphysical," there is hardly less ground for rejecting the correlation between victory and "popular causes"—the belief that ferocity is an accurate gauge of grievance. I can recall no example from British experience of quite such blatant reversals of declaratory cause as the Vietnamese communists practiced, but their ruthless extermination of rivals declaring the same cause could be matched in all recent conflicts and should be enough to disprove theories of correlation between ferocity and grievance on the strategic plane. There have, however, been plenty of examples in the experience of all of us of a correlation of a kind on the tactical plane. It is a deliberate policy on the part of Communists not to stress their "maximum program"—that is, establishment of "dictatorship of the proletariat" exercised by the Party alone (their strategic cause); instead, agitation is concentrated on "minimum programs"—that is, on demands whose fulfilment will weaken authority, and whose nonfulfilment will provide a general grievance and a pretext for extremist action (their tactical causes). The place of Marxism in a Leninist program is not to prescribe postrevolutionary constitutions or policies, but to urge a political theory that justifies the overthrow by violent means of any existing government, without reference to what is to follow; it purports to prove that noncommunist governments are guilty of original sin till proved innocent. Lenin pointed out that, during the Fenian phase of the conflict inside Britain over the Irish question, Marx had demanded the separation of Ireland from Britain, definitely not for the sake of "justice for Ireland" (Marx's words), but as a means of weakening the British government at home and facilitating a "proletarian" revolution throughout the British Isles, after which the program would be to reunite Ireland to Britain.[8]

Persuasion or Coercion?

It is reasonable to question the tactical force even of "minimum programs" in cases where they are allied to terrorism—"persuasion combined with ... ruthless forms of coercion" in Lenin's words.[9] In the practice by guerrillas of "armed propaganda," the gun is obviously more persuasive than the tongue, whose function is to advance a justification for use of force. If within well-safeguarded industrial societies at peace, trade unions are able nowadays to put pressures on workers and nonworkers to conform to union action whether or not individual union members concur in the action, the predominance of intimidation over argument must be all the more marked under conditions of armed conflict. In many low-intensity conflicts round the world, in British experience just as in everybody else's, terrorism against markets has succeeded in establishing rebels' social control over shopkeepers, and in procuring clandestine subscriptions to insurgent funds that would not have been forthcoming on what an impartial judge would rate a voluntary basis—even though the victims of the intimidation might, out of fear of their persecutors, maintain that they were paying up spontaneously. In Malaya, Britain had to deal with a Chinese political culture that had a tradition of mafia-type extortion; communist recruiters and collectors of money stepped into the shoes of the Triad Society, fortified with such unconvincing pretexts that Professor Pye could find only seven out of 60 of their cadres he interviewed who actually believed in the Party's good faith.[10] In Cyprus, the declaratory cause of *enosis* might seem calculated to appeal strongly by itself to members of the Greek-speaking community; and yet coercion across a wide spectrum of severity was employed—from patriotic shaming of known, suspected, or merely expected dissenters, through to kidnapping and cautionary murders—and can therefore be assumed to have been necessary. In Aden, a city created by colonial rule whose hinterland had never been anything but a spear- and gun-toting society of feud and vendetta, the cause of Arabism was shared by all the contenders, that of "national liberation" *known* by the whole population to have been conceded by Britain before the first shot was fired: so that the conflict there belies the theory that all guerrilla movements have to have a good cause. In Kenya, the Mau Mau cause was one of tribal superstition and confined to the Kikuyu; even so, the use of terror and force was so widespread that it must have accounted for the majority of adherents— another example of a truth Britain learned in the days of press-ganging by the Navy, and which has been repeated in the kidnapping of Greek children to become guerrillas in Yugoslavia against their own homes or of Rhodesian Africans to be so embodied in Mozambique: namely that fighters who have been forced to join up often fight neither more nor less loyally and bravely than true volunteers. This truth is no novelty in China either: mythology there has it that the tiger, symbol of the swashbuckler, will attack its victims up to three times till it subdues them, and that, thereafter, the victims' souls will spur it on to prey on ever more and more of their own kind.

Fronts and Terrorism

Terror invariably achieves its tactical purposes, either of destroying installations like bridges or railways, or of deterring people in the vicinity of the victims from continuing to do the things that victims were doing when they got hurt. At the same time, however, it can be strategically counterproductive both at home and abroad. In Malaya, Asian workers were at first obliged by the communists to sabotage rubber estates and tin mines from whose product they earned their living; thereafter the workers no longer disposed of any "surplus value" to hand over to the collectors. Although the policy was in due course reversed, numbers of workers profited from the high degree of mobility in the Malayan labor market to remove to other districts and change their employment, so that the Party's long and patient initial work of organization to establish social control over them was lost for good. The Irish Republic Army is much more dependent than the Malayan communists on external support, and it has been disadvantaged to some extent in a different way by the terrorist image it inherited from the Fenians and yet has done so much to enhance for itself. It has tried to overcome its ethical problem by recourse to the front of Sinn Fein, and its dissident wing in Ulster, the "Provisional" IRA, has similarly given out that there is a "Provisional" Sinn Fein as well. In the Sinn Fein guise, the IRA leaders save the face of the church bodies they desire should collaborate with them and keep their own hands clean, in the eyes of the wider world, from the stain of the IRA action which is their chief instrument for commanding popular support. Both Makarios and Kenyatta used a "front" strategy—the Orthodox Church and the Kenya African Union respectively—but to more opportunistic effect than the IRA. Conveniently interned while the British were annihilating the clandestine operatives they had intended at first should carry them to power, the Cypriot and Kenyan leaders subsequently accepted office from British hands; both of them thereafter pursued policies sufficiently at variance with their initial declaratory cause to invalidate the citing of their triumph as proof of the idealism and moral force with which they embarked on their struggle. Instead they confirm the other evidence, support August Comte's third stage of causation, the "Positivist," and demonstrate that victory or defeat is at bottom a question of *efficiency* in the conduct of the struggle. Challengers to authority in the low-intensity conflicts of British experience, especially in this century, have all had "materialist" realpolitik aims and realpolitik tactics; unfortunately, large sections of the opinion-forming classes in Britain have been unwilling to grasp the truth that, however loftily Byronic the idealism of slogans and propaganda may sound, every one of these challengers has in reality been fired by ambition for power over his fellow countrymen. Whenever Britain has had success in resisting them, it has been thanks to a clearheaded realpolitik in defense; cunning, not gallantry, is the decisive quality in low-intensity conflict.

Leninist Strategy

Multipolarity and Collaboration

The cold war produced two opposite strategic tendencies in low-intensity conflicts: on one hand the development of "multipolarity" in the communist block, on the other the capture for Marxism-Leninism, one after another, of a variety of extraneous struggles for power round the world whose origins in many instances are much older than Marxism-Leninism—most notably for British experience, the accession to that ideology of the Irish Republican Army. Sooner or later *every* low-intensity conflict has, consequently, become a length of trench in the cold war. The second of the two developments is more apparent on the tactical than the strategic plane and has been furthered, paradoxically, by multipolarity: the Russian schools that have taken the place of the Toilers-of-the-East have furnished training for potential revolutionaries of very varied strategic ambitions (sometimes actually opposed to Marxism-Leninism's "maximum program"), directly or through branches in East Germany, Ghana-Congo or Cuba; while China, North Korea, and the Democratic (now Socialist) Republic of Vietnam have offered separate facilities, sometimes in opposition to, sometimes in collaboration with, Moscow.[11] All these exponents of revolutionary tactics appear to have acted on the idea of a common strategic interest in upsetting the established order in the world at large—an idea of Leninist conception—leaving to a later stage the sharing of the spoils in Southeast Asia, the Middle East, Africa, or Latin America—sharing, as the world has had cause to lament, by proxy combat between clients of the USSR and the Chinese People's Republic in Burma, Angola, and the Horn of Africa. Libya devotes a generous proportion of its oil revenues to the same "destabilizing" strategy, not only in pursuit of its declaratory policy as a Muslim state, of *jihad*—for example in the Philippines and Uganda—but also by supplying arms to the infidel IRA in the days before the IRA built up its present sources of supply in the USA and the international cannabis market.

National Liberation

Although Lenin's strategy before he came to power had no Russian-national focus, he was separated in time from Prince Gorchakov by no longer than we are from *him*, and resumption of the Tsarist forward policy at the expense of Turkey, Persia, Afghanistan, and India was the first foundation stone he laid for Soviet external relations—"stretching a friendly hand" (from

Gorchakov's Muslim khanates) to class revolutionaries in those countries.[12] The aftermath of the Russian Civil War enabled him to extend the range of the policy eastwards into Chinese Turkestan, Mongolia and China itself. Lenin's second foundation stone was "national liberation"—a slogan for transferring the British and other European empires to his own state system, and, most immediately, challenging British succession to influence, after the Treaty of Versailles, in the Arab possessions of the Ottoman Empire. While condemning nationalism as "irreconcilable with Marxism"—which aimed at "ending the division of mankind into tiny states . . . and integrating them . . . into a Socialist United States of the World"[13]—he realized that movements for "national liberation" in dependent territories could become an instrument for undermining the social order in metropolitan countries and overthrowing the governments there. Europe and America were the real objects of communist revolution, destined for absorption into his world socialist state. He did not envisage national liberation as the work of communist parties relying on their unaided efforts in colonies any more than revolution would be in industrial societies, but similarly as a formula for tactical alliance with better-supported "bourgeois" parties, on condition that the end result was Socialism—that is, the maximum program of concentration of power in communist hands.[14]

Communist Nation-States

The factor Lenin seems never to have allowed for is the ambition of the leaders to whom the Comintern would have to entrust national liberation: with time, men who have devoted themselves to a long and arduous struggle have aspired to wield Lenin's power themselves, although that could but be within the confines of the very nation-states the master execrated as embodiments of "chauvinism." Indeed, it was the ambition of potential leaders, rather than mass movements for emancipation, which forced the pace for dissolution of the French and British Empires. The same factor that prevented evolution of those empires into an Union Française or a British Commonwealth, bound together by formal constitutional ties, has worked to preclude formal bonds between communist states today, unless by conquest and military occupation, and has made multipolarity inevitable, on the Party as well as the state level: the Comintern could not be revived in the postwar world, and even its pale successor, the Cominform, lasted less than ten years. During the Malayan conflict, communist forces sometimes sported Chinese Red Army uniforms and thereby aroused Malay, as well as British, fears that, if victorious, they would turn the country over to Mao Tse-tung; but although China has its own traditional version of the Gorchakov doctrine, that eventuality would have depended on the lands lying in between getting incorporated into the People's Republic first.

Effects of decolonization

Nevertheless, for all Lenin's early hopes from the work of Borodin on the Clyde and M. N. Roy in Bombay, Britain has not come face to face with direct challenges over territory from the Russian state or party. Admittedly, Russia has got possession of several former colonial bases—from Britain only Aden and for a few years Berbera—but by means of some subsequent political change, not by direct usurpation from imperial rule. There is in this order of events an important political lesson: after 1945, the view was widely—nay, officially—held in the United States that delay in colonial emancipation would hasten the spread of communist rule, whereas the opposite expectation was implicit in the writings of Lenin and was maintained by the colonial powers (unheeded at the time), whom events immediately proved right in Indochina. The reason has nothing to do with patriotism or any other sentimental impulse among the masses: it is simply that radical changes of personnel in government, especially when accompanied by constitutional changes, render public administraton and security forces specially vulnerable to subversion because decision makers and commanders lack confidence about what to do and how to work together. Emancipation of British colonies did not lead to exact fulfilment of Lenin's plan in any instance, although the Chinese communists did make a bid for power in Singapore. Because emancipation was so swift, few parties in British colonies were ready enough and organized in time, and, although the circumstances usually militated against orderly fulfilment of *British* hopes as well, the leaders to whom power was handed over or the military or political rivals who unseated them set up authoritarian regimes of their own, and by curtailing personal freedom, protected themselves from supersession by clients of Moscow or Peking.

Russia and Britain in the Middle East

In the end, the Malayan Emergency was the only conflict the British army was drawn into by the "national-liberation" policy at a distance from Russia's frontiers; we have had more to contend with in the Arab lands from the Islamic policy of the Soviet Union, or from the two combined, as in South Arabia. The French sociologist, Jules Monnerot, pointed out years ago that Leninism owes more to Islam than to native traditions of Orthodox Christianity in its aims, its organization, and its hold over the masses. The Soviet Union has encountered no insuperable difficulty in getting itself accepted as a friend, if not actually a patron, of Islam against "imperialism" at two levels: government-to-government, and by support for both reformist and revolutionary movements, especially among the modernizing middle classes, in Iran, Turkey, and the Arab countries. As a result, Britain has faced conflicts in

Muslim Asia (though not Turkey) almost ceaselessly for 60 years, of an intensity too low on the spectrum to be more than mentioned in this paper (because conducted almost entirely through competitive diplomacy and technical assistance), but of rather more serious national consequence for us—because in all of them we have been slowly losing ground, moral, territorial, or economic (for example, over Iraqi and Iranian oil)—than the more spectacular conflicts in Palestine or Aden. Some lessons can be drawn from British experience in this context. First, ideological alignment is irrelevant to Leninist strategy. Second, there is a psychological value for that strategy in geographical proximity, because, paradoxically, the latter enables the USSR to pose as nonimperialist by identifying "empire" with sea instead of land power and, by coining concepts like "neocolonialism," persuade Arab pressmen and politicians that, for all Britain's lowering of military and diplomatic postures, we shall forever be an "aggressive imperialist" power and fair game for abuse and spoliation. Third, retreat and withdrawal from empire or zones of influence, far from being an escape from vilification and further attack, tend to be followed by intensification of both, the numerous new members of the United Nations General Assembly responding eagerly to the Moscow or Peking lead and joining in the vilification as a pretext for still demanding aid and technical assistance by way, as it were, of unending conscience money even after they have seized all our local investments.

Guerrilla Diplomacy

The expansion of Soviet power into both the Middle East and the former colonial empires has been much slower than Lenin predicted. The keynote of Soviet strategy has been gradualness and irreversibility of communist take-overs. The "progressive forces" of revolution earn that epithet two ways: in Marxist theory, they are harbingers of a more advanced social system, but they are also advancing all the time in the sense of going forward against the existing social order in retreat. Before World War II, except for Mongolia-Tannu Tuva, the Russians made no progress in expanding their territory until the pact with Hitler; but since then they have given the Gorchakov doctrine a dimension of guerrilla diplomacy, of some subtlety, for which my phrase is "Progress piece by peace"; *Hoa, de tien*, the Vietnamese Communist say— "Peace is the springboard for advance." The strategem is to demoralize the defense's resistance to communist attack through guerrilla warfare, and then to offer a cease-fire in exchange for cession of territory and recognition of the advance achieved by communist power in an international agreement. The process is repeated a few years later, and a second agreement lays the ground for a third round of armed struggle, and so on indefinitely. Britain has not been attacked in any part of the world quite by this process, but became involved through the Geneva cochairmanship on Indochina.

Britain and the Vietnam War

In 1954, Anthony Eden presided over the drafting of a set of capitulations which opened three doors for extension of communist rule to take in the rump of the Vietnamese state within a few years: the elections (weighted in favor of the Communists by balance of population), subversion by free movement across the demarcation line, and mass onslaught. On the face of it, the terms were the same for both sides, but in practice the openness of the South to inspection ensured its compliance, whereas totalitarian social control over the North made inspection impossible and enabled mobilization by the Communists of the resources newly assigned them for any purpose they liked without detection. The problem of inspection that has delayed nuclear disarmament arises equally on the humbler scale of low-intensity conflict. In 1962, after the Vietnamese Communists had profited from this advantage, Malcolm MacDonald presided over negotiations for a second set of capitulations, the effect of which was to evict U.S. and Royal Lao forces and administration from the districts of Laos through which ran the Ho Chi Minh Trail. The U.S. press was safeguard enough for compliance on that side, but there was nobody to watch while the Vietnamese Communists consolidated their hold over this extra territory, adjacent to what they were given in 1954. In February 1973, British Foreign Secretary Lord Home followed in the suite of the dozen other foreign delegates Kissinger bade to Paris to give their blessing to a new ceasefire promising the Communists eventual absorption of the South, meanwhile leaving their expeditionary force camped thirty miles from the Southern capital, on the understanding that if they moved aggressively the United States would oppose them militarily. The understanding rested on the false belief (not credited in Hanoi) that in Thomas Jefferson's republic the president's word is the nation's bond.[15] If the "peace with honor" *could* be broken—and Nixon called it "fragile"—realpolitik left no doubt that it *would* be; the willingness of many Western commentators to believe that permanent compromise was possible in the Indochina conflict was born of faith in the Providential view of politics and depended on ignorance of Lenin's repeated condemnations of any "strategic" compromise that did not constitute one more step forward to absolute Communist rule. It is hard to say how far Eden, MacDonald, or Home were taken in at the time they underwrote the compromises.[16] Every time, British statesmen were responding, in a conflict that was not Britain's, to the wishes of an ally on the run—France in 1954, the USA in 1962 and 1973. How to get the other side's allies on the run is the essence of Leninist tactics.

Leninist Tactics

Psychological Object of Tactics

All warfare is largely psychological in its tactics, but in the "piece-by-peace" strategy it is so in high degree: the *sub*version of the "people" the leaders intend to recruit comes before, their *con*version after; the important thing is what they can be made to do, not what they believe. The practitioner of "agitprop" leads those he mobilizes only by stages towards indoctrination in the "maximum program"—a last step only necessary for stilling doubts, ethical or practical, they may, with time, begin to harbor. The Mau Mau administered their horrible oaths—a savage act of conversion calculated to inspire awe through disgust—only after they were assured of the men's loyalty. What then is Lenin's key to recruitment? Apart from the industrial scene at home, Britain felt the effects of his doctrine of "conspiracy" (*zagovor*)—expounded in *What is to be Done?* (1902) and tantamount to harnessing workers' greed to the Party's ambition—chiefly in Malaya-Singapore. There, during World War II, the interests of China ruled out strict adherence to Lenin's 1916 slogan "turn imperialist war into civil war by revolutionary defeatism" (that is, sabotage the war effort of your own side), and a delay of nearly three years, in Stalin's as well as their own interests, occurred after 1945 before it was opportune for Malayan communists belatedly to act on it. The Leninist handbook of tactics of widest application has been *Left-Wing Communism—an Infantile Disorder* of 1920. The key tactic of "conspiracy" *here* is "zigzag," by which Lenin sums up exploitation of fronts, minimum programs, and any and every other kind of strength, as well as weakness or tension, within the target society or government—none with more constant attention than those of the free press. By such statecraft, Lenin could have brought revolution to Utopia.[17] The candid package of tricks for action outside the Soviet frontiers is set down at the end of the Civil War with laudable candor: "The fact that the powers that took up arms against us because of our terror and our entire system have been compelled, against their will, to enter into trade relations with us in the knowledge that by so doing they are strengthening us."[18] Although Lenin tried to deflect the charge of opportunism by giving the word a disarmingly narrow meaning in his own writings (that of acquiescence by communists in "strategic compromises" with "temporary allies" so loyally that they could not subsequently turn on those allies and seize a monopoly of power),[19] the implication is borne out by his condemnation of "terror" when it meant the assassination of statesmen in office practiced by the Anarchists, solely because it had proved inexpedient, while insisting that it *must* be used for such purposes as intimidating the press of a foreign state.[20]

Tactics of Guerrilla Combat

Whether it be that "people's war" (a term going back to Clausewitz) is today the extension of Leninism to the battlefield, or Leninism is an adaptation of guerrilla action to the field of "peaceful" politics, what the French generals called pirates, the Indian Army marauders, the Scots mosstroopers, and the New Left freedom fighters are identical in their tactics; a dacoit is the same as a bandit, a *sicario* a terrorist, and so is a thug, irrespective of the different structures of society they have flourished in. Like Lenin condemning a narrowly defined terror or opportunism, Mao Tse-tung condemns banditry only when it "lacks clear political direction"; his explicitly Leninist Sixteen-Word Formula for *attrition* ("Enemy advances, we retreat; enemy camps, we harass; enemy tires, we attack; enemy retreats, we pursue") is identical with Grivas's "process of attrition by harassing, confusing and finally exasperating the enemy forces with the effect of achieving our main aim," or again with Mazzini's pre-Leninist (and forthrightly anti-Marxist) "planting spies in every village, attacking the enemy in flank or rear, seizing convoys of provisions or ammunition or money, destroying roads and bridges, and continually breaking in on hours of refreshment and sleep, ... and above all exacting contributions for the guerrilla's own subsistence and their central command's."[21] Ambush tactics and blowing up bridges are studied in army schools throughout the world, and need no recital here. In all the postwar guerrilla conflicts Britain has had experience of, except Kenya, the objective has not been the conquest of territory, still less acceptance by the guerrillas of the consequential responsibility for defense (and feeding) of population, but the demoralization envisaged by Mazzini; in the Irish conflict, the sabotage side of the tactics has been carried from the target area of Northern Ireland into our heartland in Great Britain—a detail that emphasizes the essentially psychological "attrition" purpose of guerrilla operations. The difference in Kenya arose from the identity of Mau Mau with a tribal territory, outside which it was generally, though not quite always, difficult for them to move about undetected; on the other hand, it was precisely in Kikuyu territory that most white settlers had their farms, and consequently sabotage within that territory could have serious consequences for the colony's development economy, centered as that was on European enterprise.

Outrages Against Civilians

Guerrilla attacks are often directed against the security forces, native or foreign, but the true target is *civilian* morale and maintenance of a steady supply of *money*. The actual victims of terrorist attacks in British experience have been predominantly civilian—members of the community on whose behalf the guerrillas claim to be fighting but their true interest in whom is cash flow or similar services. Single attacks are often planned to provoke overreaction by the security forces in the form of general restrictions on civilian life. On the whole, the masses' cowed obedience is less fickle than voluntary support: whereas victims in Cyprus were mostly known opponents of Grivas, killings in both Aden and Malaya tended to be indiscriminate as well as cautionary—designed, it would seem as a kind of decimation to drive home the point that, if submission to guerrilla demands were to fall off, the backsliders risked "revolutionary violence." It is easy to ambush and murder civilians, and the psychological effect can actually be greater when the blows fall at random, according to opportunity, because that appears to prove that the guerrilla hand is capable of striking anywhere unpredictably. Although the use of terror in this way in Malaya never attained the sophistication shown by the Vietnamese communists, the Malayan communists had notable success in isolating community leaders and, by wearing them down, forced then either to come to terms in secret or to leave their rural homes for the safety of towns. In both Cyprus and Ireland, where the British role was to hold the ring between hostile ethnic groups, the guerrillas have, of course, made attacks on the other group—IRA against Protestants, EOKA against Turks—but in order to provoke revenge against their own side and (by a sort of "revolutionary defeatism") oblige conciliatory members of the Catholic or the Greek community respectively to acquiesce in the protection of the guerrillas, therefore enabling them to operate closer to their homes than the security forces could.

Guerrilla Sanctuaries

One tactical dimension of the domino principle has been very marked in recent British experience—use of cross-frontier sanctuaries. The national liberation of Aden, fostered from Moscow, only became possible after Nasser—a conscious proxy in the matter out of gratitude for the new Aswan Dam—had procured the coup d'état in the Yemen, with his eye on long-range vengeance against Britain over Suez. Hardly had British forces evacuated Aden and given up protection of the Hadhramaut than their officers—now in an advisory and training capacity—found themselves up against the same guerrillas moving eastwards into Dhofar and Oman. Cyprus is an island, but close enough to Greek islands for movement to be easy for Grivas in person and for his importation of arms. The Malayan Emergency was fought to a victory by Britain at a time when the Royal Navy could still patrol the South China Sea and before the Vietnamese, with Maoist help, had reorganized the Thai Communist Party as a backup guerrilla force in South Thailand, as is the position today. There is a spectrum of utility in sanctuaries as there is of intensity of conflict. It is in Ireland that the asset is at its most valuable for

Britain's challengers: the Republic of Ireland condemns IRA methods in its declaratory policy, but declines to sign the European Convention on Suppression of Terrorism and insists that outrages committed in the United Kingdom by hit-and-run from the Republic are "political crimes" and therefore excluded from the scope of extradition. There is here another lesson of wide applicability: partition of a territory by way of political solution, even though the successor state, not being Communist, is willing to enter into a "strategic compromise" and renounce further irredentist claims, may, by foreshortening the defense's range of pursuit, make resumption of armed conflict more, not less, likely: real peace requires that the guerrillas be liquidated first. Sanctuaries are also essential for preservation of the illusion of Robin Hood-like "self-reliance" to cover gunrunning by outside powers concerned to avoid jeopardizing peace campaigns and disarmament talks on a higher plane. Connected in turn with self-reliance is the use of sanctuaries to cover infiltration by "patriotic forces"—that is, aliens recruited to fight in a "national liberation," whether as adventurers like the Guevarists in Bolivia and Chile, as mercenaries like the Africans from the Ghana-Congo guerrilla schools in the former Portuguese colonies, or as tribal conscripts like the Vietnamese Meo in the Laotian Patriotic Forces—Britain has to negotiate with, though not fight, "patriotic forces" of mixed origin, operating in Rhodesia from bases in five neighboring countries.

Double Standards

Although British governments have never, in any conflict, had to contend with quite the hostility from public opinion that United States presidents have been up against over Indochina, or with mobilization of trade unions for sabotage of fighting men at the front ("revolutionary defeatism") on the scale that dogged the Quatrième République, the international communist movement has exploited the British market economy and open society tactically; in no sphere have they been more skillful than in double-standard conduct (Charles de Montalembert's "When you are in power, I demand freedom from you because that is your principle; when I am in power, I withhold freedom from you because it is not *my* principle"). A double standard is implicit in Marxism-Leninsim—Marxism as the "proof" that old regimes are tyrannical and ought, by liberal standards, to be overthrown, Leninism as the method for substituting another tyranny. There are two tactical fields in which British experience is relevant. The first is the treatment of prisoners: because of their mobility, guerrillas cannot hold prisoners let alone care for enemy wounded; they must therefore kill them on the spot, and throughout history have done it with studied cruelty and mutilation in order to frighten the victims' fellow soldiers into shirking combat in future. British soldiers repeatedly suffered that fate at the hands of the Pathans, and again in the 1940s in support of Haile Selassie against guerrillas in eastern Ethiopia. Although mutilation tactics have not occurred in the more recent of Britain's conflicts, Leninists have organized the exposure as "inhuman" of the security forces' practice in Malaya of burying dead communists in the jungle but cutting off their heads first to fly or carry back for identification—not because they were personally affected by its gruesomeness, but because it was so useful to government intelligence.

"Class Justice"

The second field of double-standard tactics—one reaching into the arena of "peaceful struggle"—is that of "class justice." One issue of *International Press Correspondence* (edited for the Comintern by Willi Münzenberg, discoverer of "fellow travelers") in the 1920s reported Andrei Vishinsky, Stalin's Chief Prosecutor in the 1930s purges, as laying down that in the Soviet Union the courts were "an organ of class justice," whereas another issue a few weeks later told its readers that the purpose of International Red Aid (the lawyer face of the Comintern's organization, also managed by Münzenberg, for rescuing comrades in trouble with the authorities of their countries, the politician face being the League against Imperialism) was to provoke "political trials" under "imperialist" jurisdiction and then stir up the intellectual classes in the metropolitan country "to agitate against class justice."[22] The London panel of International Red Aid was headed by a barrister, the late D. N. Pritt, who was the leading light, at Münzenberg's invitation, in the Reichstag Fire Countertrial at The Hague in 1933. Pritt specialized in defense of communists on trial in India or one of the other British possessions scheduled for national liberation. In 1932 he was briefed by Red Aid's Hong Kong solicitor to appeal to the Privy Council against a Hong Kong High Court ruling that a deportation order against Ho Chi-Minh—who at the time was one of Münzenberg's reporters—specifying his destination as his home country (where there was a warrant out for his arrest on a capital charge), was lawful. The Hong Kong Government's London solicitors unthinkingly included this brief with others on more routine colonial questions in a heap sent to Sir Stafford Cripps, a fellow-traveling collaborator with Pritt (for example, in the Countertrial). When Pritt threatened to publicize the case as tantamount to extradition to stand trial for a "political crime," Cripps made a settlement on behalf of his principals, without consulting them, under which Ho was set at liberty—having profited in effect from swearing affidavits, first that he was, and second that he was not, Nguyen ai Quoc.[23]

The Kenyatta Trial

Twenty years later, Pritt defended Kenyatta, former student at the Toilers-of-the-East, who was charged with management of Mau Mau; he lost this case—a defeat which redounded, as I said above, to Kenyatta's political advantage—but must have been specially riled when Kenyatta, elevated to the presidency of Kenya, appointed the magistrate who had convicted him to be his Chief Justice. Pritt summed up his court practice thus: "The primary object of a good political defense is not to win the case, although that in itself may be very useful, but to maintain and propagate one's political point of view, and never to sacrifice or compromise principles for the sake of trying to win. ... The essential thing is to justify politically the defendant's action, and the policy and conduct of his party too, and to turn the defense into a counterattack by denouncing and discrediting the Government both for prosecuting for political motives and for following the bad policies which led the defendant to react as he did; and, moreoever, to do all this with as much publicity as possible."[24] In other words, the outlaw uses the rule of law to overturn the rule of law. Kenyatta was unwilling in the end to be turned to political account by the international communist movement. On its side, dodging the Pritts and Crippses has been one of the dominant preoccupations of Britain's response to Leninist tactics.

The British Tactical Response

Fighting tactics for small wars are a technical question for the soldier. Besides the manuals I have mentioned before, the instruction given in British combat schools is as proficient as it can well become, and the whole of the infantry gets some of it; in his day, Callwell was already noting that advances in guerrilla tactics were more often a result of improvements in the arms available to either or both sides in conflict than the fruit of novel ideas, and that remains true in the age of electronics. I propose to dwell in the following paragraphs on the psychological and political measures that have been tried in British experience and that appear to have succeeded or failed.

Maintenance of Morale

British planners have had an eye to maintenance of morale at three levels: that of their fighting men, that of the population whose fate is in the balance, and that of the public at home. The principal danger for the first of these is the feeling that, whatever effort they make, they cannot win and that the battles they fight are purely incidental to political decisions that will be made without much regard to the fortunes of war. (We have generally been lucky in not having to deploy men in fortresses quadrating the countryside, where they would sit and wait to be assaulted without equivalent targets to strike back at for themselves and whose loss in battle, were it to occur, would have an adverse effect on the morale of the local people.) The remedy has been, first, short tours of duty that permitted frequent patrols, and second, representation of the experience as part of the general professional life of the infantryman and just as honorable as action in a major war. The difficulty in regard to the local population is to inspire confidence that the guerrillas are not going win, and take it out on any "collaborators" after the British Army has gone away; we have found no easy solution either to this problem or to the third one, of convincing the people at home that struggles in far places are worthwhile even though the men are coming home in the near future anyway. So anxious was the Governor of Cyprus to disarm the anti-British ferocity of EOKA by assuring Greek leaders of his personal distaste for the idea of colonial rule that, it is said, he spread fresh hope in the ranks of EOKA, despair among his subordinates, and active hostility among the Turks who felt doomed if *enosis* came about.[25] Public reaction in the United Kingdom was to want to abandon even faster the duty not to lay down responsibility until an equitable settlement had been reached between rival interests.

Army and Police

The governor of Kenya dismayed *his* subordinates by refusing to recognize the gravity of the Mau-Mau troubles when they started.[26] The fact that Britain's involvement in low-intensity conflicts has arisen from being already on the spot as administrator has led to a preference for dealing with them at as low a level of intensity as possible and for bringing the army in as a last resort—especially in a colony like Kenya where the governor had, till then, no white troops; the posting of army units to Northern Ireland in 1969 was a reluctant decision taken at the request of the Catholic community, whose leaders complained (with well-authenticated justification) that the predominantly Protestant police were persecuting them, on the excuse of IRA violence (even better authenticated), to the advantage of the Protestant community—a case in point of Leninist provocation. Only under circumstances like those of 1919 or 1945, when Britain already had a military administration established for other reasons, has the army been allowed to exercise legal powers; the tradition is that it does not act except in aid of the police. General Templer, while still a serving officer, was appointed high commissioner in Malaya, but there was a separate director of operations under him; the arrangement was repeated with General Harding in Cyprus. Elsewhere, directors of operations have always served under civilian governors—in the case of Aden at the end, a career diplomat instead of a colonial administrator. It is no mere coincidence that Britain has faced insurgency in just those dependencies where the police, temporarily or all the time, have not policed the areas chosen by the guerrillas as a "popular base"; even in Northern Ireland, the police had accepted that Catholic streets were "no-go areas." Reorganization of the police has been a first task in Ireland, and was so in Malaya and Kenya, before the army could be fed the intelligence vital to *its* operations.

Indirect Methods

Counterinsurgency is always taxing and disheartening, for its remedial measures are invariably slow to take effect when they do at all: there is consequently a temptation to turn to indirect methods leading to "political solutions," especially social betterment and meeting the guerrillas' propaganda grievances, in the hope of depriving them of the popular support security measures seem ineffectual against. Yet it is logical that, if the guerrillas aim uncompromisingly at absolute power, there is no halfway house that can content them, and, if they hold the masses in fee with terror, a rise in local resources increases also the money they can extort; Leninists, because they turn their back on "strategic compromise," cannot be appeased—they have to be outwitted. It is right for governments always to do their utmost for the welfare of the people, but there is no evidence from British experience for the Providential expectation that a government's virtue in that respect will affect either the occurrence or the outcome of the struggle. Satisfaction of grievances—"minimum programs"—only leads to the framing of new ones, even though that is no reason for neglecting them. Indirect methods were not applicable in Cyprus or Aden; but in Kenya and Malaya, and more recently under British advice in Oman, care has been taken to avoid *bribing* the people—even if, often enough in the past, we have bribed guerrilla leaders— but to make special welfare efforts as soon as security has returned to a district, and thereby *reward* the ending (at some risk for individuals) of support for guerrillas. In Malaya especially, where different parts of the country suffered different degrees of insecurity, news of welfare in one district acted as an incentive in others. But the policy would not have been workable without other measures for the security forces to "pacify" the district—to get the better of the guerrillas first. The essence of the matter is to protect the people against coercion and, by convincing them that the guerrillas are the losing side, irrespective of their popularity, make the risks of collaboration with the government a sound calculation: the *minds* of the people are worth more, as Machiavelli pointed out, than their hearts if you cannot command both.

Pacification

Although the word "pacification" is of great antiquity in both English and French history, as in that of China and most other empires, it connotes no consistent basket of tactical measures; the exponent of it Callwell singled out for admiration was General Bugeaud of Algeria, who had learnt many of his lessons fighting under Napoleon against Britain's Peninsular War guerrillas. The object of pacification must be to create a barrier, physical or moral, between the guerrillas and the people they prey on. At one extreme, a *zariba* of barbed wire of huge dimensions was erected five or six years ago in the west of Dhofar; at the other extreme, in Ireland, the most that has been possible has been checkpoints on roads to hinder fast movement by terrorists and searches of handbags for bombs at shops and markets and cinemas. In Malaya, sections of the rural population were required to pull down their scattered huts and rebuild them closer together behind barbed wire; they were then subjected temporarily to a strict regime of food control, prohibited from taking food to work in field, plantation, or mine (lest, out of sight, it be appropriated by guerrillas), and even in the village there would be a communal kitchen and a ban on cooking at home. However, such oppressive rigor, which we were lucky never to get recorded on the television screens in the outside world, could not be maintained for long, and its success depended on intelligence work to enable the turning of passive defense into pursuit of the guerrillas and their arrest; as soon as the latter ceased to be a threat to the masses, the restrictions were lifted.[27] Advantage was taken of the "new village" regime to "win hearts" as well by accustoming the inmates to use of electric light and other amenities, so that few if any ever returned to the discomforts of their earlier way of living, with perpetuation of which the "liberation forces" became linked psychologically through their necessarily hostile propaganda. It must be admitted that the windfall effect on the rubber and tin markets of the communist aggression in Korea unexpectedly contributed to the happy result. The same system was adapted to conditions in Kenya, but has not been possible in other countries, least of all among nomads, although an effect analogous to that of the Korean War in Malaya has operated behind the *zariba* in Oman in consequence of oil exploration in the *jabal* districts the Adeni guerrillas have tried to liberate. The Malayan government made a gesture of confidence in victory by arming the masses, under the control regime, as part-time militia and thereupon entrusting the first line of defense to themselves. The same measure has a long history in many countries of the world, most notoriously in nineteenth-century China; there the militias sometimes turned brigands themselves, but rosters of not-too-frequent duty, coupled with close supervision of weapons in a central armory, prevented abuse in Malaya.

Law and Justice

What to do with terrorists when caught has been an acute problem in every conflict. When Britain's part has been auxiliary to a foreign government, the problem is transferred to it, although undue leniency on the latter's part could redound to the detriment of the auxiliary forces; fortunately, the foreign governments Britain has had to do with have generally been Muslim, and any mishandling has erred by severity and eye-for-eye. The liberal inclination is only to deprive miscreants of their liberty after due process of law; some of the difficulties are well known, others encountered by British commanders less so. The law may need tightening in illiberal directions: for example, by making the mere carriage of arms a capital offense where the law in peaceful times would be satisfied with a fine or failure to register a firearm; prevalent intimidation of witnesses—practiced on a vast scale in Malaya, in Cyprus, and in Ireland—may require relaxation of the rules of evidence; and regimes like the residence and food control described above, with punishment for terrorist-supporters who contravene it, cannot be left to arbitrary administrative action, but must be incorporated in legal regulations made known to the public at large, with the penalties, and to the security forces whom it is desired to prevent from exceeding the provisions. The device of temporary Emergency Regulations, mentioned in note 5 above, is traceable to British domestic history—invariably in the teeth, even in wartime, of vociferous opposition—and has been applied in all conflicts where Britain has been in authority. But long experience has taught that the guerrilla cannot be handled satisfactorily by trial, conviction, and imprisonment, for reasons even more taxing than intimidation of witnesses or, in Ireland, of juries and (occasionally) judges.

Detention and Intelligence

There is substance in the argument that political work for national liberation, as distinct from participation in terrorism, as well as guerrilla combat, is legitimate warfare, entitling the captive to prisoner-of-war status: if that opinion, urged by both the International Red Cross and what remains of International Red Aid, is correct, captives ought not to be put on trial. What then can be done with them? Only two alternatives are available: to detain them without trial or to shoot them—as they shoot *their* captives in many instances. Trial-and-imprisonment has practical snags as well: the government's victory is not advanced by punishment of the convict—what is needed is to keep him out of circulation for the duration of the conflict, which may be longer or shorter than one individual's sentence: he may have valuable intelligence to communicate, but cannot fairly be interrogated if he is to be put on trial for the same *res gestae*. The ideal outcome of his arrest or capture is to "turn" him, perhaps use him to guide the security forces to his comrades' hideouts, and certainly rehabilitate him, whether he is a local resident or a "patriot" from a neighboring country.[28] Many liberally disposed people find the idea of turning "national liberators" into "collaborators" distasteful, even though they find no fault with the converse process. In fact, it is of hoary antiquity in political practice, favorable response to it the natural consequence of the individual's finding himself suddenly in another social setting with no road back; the miserable truth is that causes are immaterial to most combatants. This psychological reaction is anticipated by Leninists, so that they rarely trust a comrade again if he has been in enemy hands; that fact of realpolitik is known to the captives too, and adds to their willingness to change sides—and perhaps "get" their comrades before their comrades can "get" them. One of the aims of interrogation has usually been to extract information that can be used for psychological action against the morale of individual guerrillas still in the field, and lead them to surrender—a procedure carried out with great success in both Malaya and Kenya, where money rewards were paid to civilians who could persuade a guerrilla to surrender and to men who, having surrendered, needed funds with which to start life again in a new place. Bribing tribal leaders was much practiced on the Northwest Frontier, as it has been by many empires when that seemed a more cost-effecitve safeguard for the frontier than the Gorchakov policy.

Enemy and Opposition

The British Army overseas has never been caught quite so miserably between the enemy in front and homeside opposition behind as the French and American armies were in Indochina, but most of our governments have had to keep one eye on the baneful influence against our public policy worked by the World Peace Council (successor to Münzenberg's League against Imperialism) and (in more recent years) the revived Fourth International on fellow-travelers, theirs on pacifists (especially university students), and theirs again on liberal opinion influential in all three political parties and every newspaper office. No easy remedy against malicious propaganda has been discovered in London any more than in Paris or Washington; but luckily *pragmatic* considerations have helped us avoid incurring criticism from our own side, above all in two specially sensitive fields— "scorched earth" and misbehavior by security forces.

Scorched Earth

The fact that Britain has been the governing authority in almost every low-intensity conflict we have become involved in has added an important cost factor to the cost-effectiveness of any battle tactic that smacked of scorched earth; Somaliland was an almost unique example—a great many years ago—where use of the blunt instrument of aerial bombardment destroyed a guerrilla force on thinly peopled and completely undeveloped terrain. Bombing was resorted to at one time in Malaya, but to little ascertainable effect; as a scare tactic it proved useless, and no communist casualties ever came to light—which, I would judge, was on balance a good thing for us. Thenceforward, aircraft were confined to observation, supply, evacuation of wounded, and the strictly controlled spraying of defoliants. Scorched earth has been avoided primarily because it would have amounted to destruction of our own installations on a scale exceeding the enemy's capability, and we would have had to pay for rebuilding—a Leninist trap there is no question but was set for the Pentagon in South Vietnam. But there were other considerations as well, unless a guerrilla enemy employing Leninist tactics from a cross-frontier sanctuary can be wiped out in his base area, he cannot be deterred by losses to his fully expendable front-line forces. Once territory has passed under Communist Party rule, the world at large acknowledges that the process must not be reversed; it would be futile to argue otherwise in the U.N. General Assembly. That, I venture to suggest, is why bombing of North Vietnam did not deter the aggression against South Vietnam: whereas it had been politically possible to annihilate—not merely deter—Hitler's regime in German in 1945 and that of the Dervishes in 1920, in Tonkin the bombing had to stop short of the destruction of the communist regime. One cannot bomb the IRA and their façade of stone-throwing ragamuffins out of their squalid streets in Belfast; even if one could, and got away with it against a hundred other objections, the leaders would lie up and reform in the Republic of Ireland.

Troop Behavior

Thus, pragmatic considerations restrained British planners from scorched earth before the factor of opposition at home had to be taken into account. The United States, on the other hand, through insufficiently discriminating use of defoliants and napalm,[29] earned obloquy for resorting to chemical warfare—even though the enemy boasted in its own (strictly domestic) press of also using napalm "on most battlefields."[30] Troop behavior has, if anything, provided more promising material for international communist propaganda. In the days of the Northwest Frontier, some shocking reprisals were taken by the British Indian army for the kind of atrocities I mentioned earlier, and there were occasional outcries in the narrower circle of public opinion of those days, much of which was at all times ideologically antiimperialist. In recent years, the risk of outcry has increased in inverse proportion to the risk of misbehavior by troops; although Army policy was very circumspect and troop discipline high, a few cases did come to light in Malaya, Aden, Cyprus and Kenya of commanding officers covering up offenses in order to avoid the press scandal inseparable from a modern court-martial—disclosure through unofficial channels then leading to worse scandal: in the words of Saint Gregory, "*melius est ut scandalum oriatur quam ut veritas relinquatur."* Kenya was the biggest source of trouble on this score: every British solider fighting there was a newcomer for the duration of the emergency, and all contact with Africans was through African troops or paramilitary units. Mau Mau prisoners under African guards from other tribes were exposed to neglect and brutality, on the excuse of the unspeakable savagery they undoubtedly practiced among themselves and visited on the African population, and detention camps were sullied from the prisoners' own dirty habits when at home. But a British commander in chief was held responsible by public opinion in London, and the old argument, "We're no better than them," had free run for a time.[31] Had television been more developed in 1953 and Mau Mau been in touch with the World Peace Council, there is no doubt that the double-standard Leninist line would have been brought into play ("Our side has one flaw, so the whole enterprise should be abandoned; their side is bad throughout, but we expect no better, so nothing's wrong"), with incalculable consequences for the Government of Kenya.[32] In Northern Ireland, convicted terrorists have run a campaign in 1978–79 for moving round their prison naked rather than wear prison clothes—on the grounds that being "political" they are not "criminal"—and for committing nuisances all over the place in the manner of the Mau Mau; they have then had the satisfaction of hearing the Primate of Ireland blame prison and authorities for the disgusting conditions.

The Future for British Involvement

Some of the contenders for power who challenged London's arrangements for emancipation of the British Empire have lost their lives in vain, and for none was there any certainty of victory when they took up arms; yet all of them knew that Britain was withdrawing, so that the gamble was worthwhile. Their haste was not to bring the withdrawal about, but to get the better of their rivals at home before it occurred. Conversely, British forces knew they could never win anything tangible for themselves or their nation and might get hurt, even killed, in another people's power struggle. As the world balance has continued to move adversely (from our point of view), British obligations have been curtailed further and further both in geographical range and in function. Training in the tactics of internal security and organization of logistic and intelligence services are about the limit of commitment, and then only in countries of the Middle East or the Commonwealth that ask us for them—there is no question from now on of British initiative to take a hand in conflicts outside Europe or the Commonwealth merely to uphold civilized standards of government. The international community as a whole regards it as more prudent to keep the peace by holding back the policeman than by holding back the cutthroat: in 1950, the more blatant an aggression, the easier it was to get a Korea Resolution through the General Assembly, but today, ironically, the more blatant the aggression, the harder it is. Henceforward, there is no need for the deceptions and cunning and hard slog of the guerrilla in low-intensity conflict—big guns offer an "economy of scale." In Britain, more and more public decisions depend on public opinion, and public opinion reaches lower down the educational scale; education in world affairs cannot keep pace with their deepening complexity. I anticipate that in future Britain will only send soldiers to fight distant aggression after some kind of referendum; it is impossible to say in advance whether potential conscripts, and their parents, in an affluent society, will vote yes. It is improbable anyway that the national economy will be able to pay for it.

Notes

1. The British diplomatic involvement in Indochina as Geneva Cochairman (with the USSR) lasted from 1954 to 1973. Under the aegis of SEATO, Britain joined Australia and New Zealand in helping the U.S. garrison northeast Thailand for a few weeks in 1962 during the Nam-Tha thrust by the People's Army of Vietnam (ostensibly by the Laotian Patriotic Forces), but in the event there was no fighting.
2. Sir Charles E. Callwell, *Small Wars: Their Principles and Practice* (London: Harrison & Sons, 1899), p. 22.
3. The opinion of I. M. Lewis (whose sympathies lie rather with Sayyid Muhammad), *Modern History of Somaliland* (London: Weidenfeld & Nicolson, 1965), p. 85.
4. Callwell, pp. 16–17.
5. See, again, the work of Callwell (based on broader military experience than that of Britain alone, including North American), and also Frank Kitson, *Low-Intensity Operations* (London: Faber, 1971)—a counterinsurgency manual based on the author's service in the Kenyan, Malayan, Cypriot, and Adeni conflicts. In Malaya, the security forces (whose general staff also took the trouble to study the methods of De Lattre de Tassigny in Indochina) were provided with a tactical handbook known as *The Atom Book* (mimeographed) because it "atomized" every detail of procedure for them to follow, not only in combat but also in handling prisoners, evacuating casualties, calling on government services, and dealing with the populace; senior civil administrators and army officers, as well as the police, also had on hand Lee Tian-huat, *The Emergency Regulations* (Kuala Lumpur 1948) (with revisions), which legislated for just about every eventuality and specified the extent and the limitations within which they could act. In the context of military government, a similar though less comprehensive effect was achieved during World War II by issue to British officers (myself among them) of copies of sections 8–10 of Chapter IV of the 1936 *Manual of Military Law*. A recent analyst of U.S. experience in Vietnam (not hostile) has pointed out the disadvantages that accrued from the Pentagon's neglect of such precautions (Guenter Lewy, *America in Vietnam* (New York: Oxford University Press, 1978), pp. 336 ff.
6. According to the Bangkok weekly, *Thai Nakorn*, the Vietnamese still had Thai trainees whom they sent home on the eve of their conquest of Cambodia (reported in *Business Times*, Kuala Lumpur, 9 May 1979).

7. For North Korea, see Institute for the Study of Conflict (London), *Conflict Study* no. 41 (1973), p. 6; for Libya, no. 28 (1972), p. 8.

8. V.I. Lenin, *Collected Works* (Moscow: Progress Publishers, 1960–), vol. 21, p. 410.

9. Lenin, vol. 31, pp. 496–97.

10. Lucian Pye, *Guerrilla Communism in Malaya* (Princeton: Princeton University Press, 1956), pp. 226–27.

11. For references, see notes 6 and 7 above and also Duncanson, *The Peacetime Strategy of the Chinese People's Republic* (London: Institute for the Study of Conflict, 1977), pp. 25-7. A conference of the IRA with other European, African, and Latin American subversive movements was held at the Instituto Stensen at Florence in October 1971 (*Daily Express*, London, 18 April 1971).

12. Quotation from K. Eudin & R. North, *Soviet Russia and the East, 1920-1927* (Stanford: Stanford University Press, 1957) p. 96.

13. Lenin, vol. 20, p. 34; vol. 21, p. 33; vol. 22, p. 146.

14. Lenin, vol. 21, p. 409.

15. For an outright admission that the "progressive steps" in this Leninist strategy were no more than temporary "tactical compromises," see (*inter alia loca*) Ode Le Duan in *Hoc Tap* (Hanoi, October 1975).

16. Eden cast doubt on Geneva 1954 almost immediately (*Hansard* 8 November 1954, Commons, col. 929); but Home had no doubts about the genuineness of communist intentions in 1962 (*Hansard* 25 July 1962, Lords, col. 1030).

17. Lenin, vol. 5, p. 167, and vol. 31, pp. 96. Political scientists who pour scorn on "the conspirational theories about Lenin" are thus on even weaker ground than those who dispute the domino concept.

18. Lenin, vol. 31, p. 414.

19. Lenin, vol. 21, pp. 438–53.

20. Lenin, vol. 31, pp. 33 and 249. When Earl Mountbatten was assassinated by the IRA, the Russian Government—possibly apprehensive that a supreme act of extremism might occur during the Pope's forthcoming visit to Ireland and turn the whole Catholic world against revolutionary movements everywhere—repeated Lenin's condemnation, at the same time approving the declaratory cause in which the outrage had been committed, namely to bring about separation of Northern Ireland from the rest of the United Kingdom. Cf. p. 12 above.

21. Mao Tse-tung, *Selected Works* (Peking: Foreign Language Press, 1965–), vol. 1, pp. 200 and 213; George Grivas, *Guerrilla Warfare* (London: Longmans, 1964), p. 6; Giuseppe Mazzini, *Life and Writings* (London: Smith, Elder, & Co., 1891), vol. 1, pp. 369–78.

22. *Inprecor*, Berlin, vol. 7, no. 63 (1927), and vol. 8, no. 13 (1928).

23. For the full story, see Duncanson, "Ho Chi Minh in Hong Kong 1931–32," *China Quarterly* no. 57 (1974): 84–100.

24. D.N. Pritt, *Autobiography* (London: Lawrence & Wishart, 1965), vol. 1, p. 129. Between the Stalin-Hitler Treaty of Amity in September 1939 and Hitler's invasion of Russia in June 1941, Pritt organized a "revolutionary-defeatist" Peace Convention in London, taking advantage of his being a Member of Parliament (Labour, not Communist, Party although a declared Marxist) to keep out of trouble for treason (Pritt, especially pp. 245 ff.).

25. See H.D. Purcell, *Cyprus* (New York: Praeger, 1969), p. 291.

26. Anthony Clayton, *Counter Insurgency in Kenya 1952–60* (Nairobi: Transafrica, 1976), p. 4.

27. For the evolution of these tactics, see R. Clutterbuck, *Riot and Revolution in Singapore and Malaya 1945–1963* (London: Faber, 1973), pp. 211–50.
28. On the use of stool-pigeon methods to this end, see Douglas Hyde, *The Rehabilitation of Detainees* (London: Inst. for the Study of Conflict, 1972).
29. Not that all the charges were true: more than once, ignorant pressmen flying over rubber estates during the months of January or February assumed they had been defoliated when they were merely wintering, like rubber trees anywhere else (personal experience from conversations in Vietnam).
30. Maj. Gen. Vuong Thua Vu commemorating fifteen years of the People's Army's chemical-warfare units in Quan-doi Nhan-dan (People's Army Daily, Hanoi), 18 April 1973.
31. Clayton, *Counterinsurgency in Kenya*, is devoted almost entirely to this side of the conflict.
32. Pritt was in touch with the World Peace Council at the time over other "issues," but he seems to have kept clear of sticking up for Mau Mau, preferring to concentrate (in vain) on "proving" that Kenyatta was not its manager. Mau Mau was not Communist, Kenyatta at least *had* been–perhaps still was.

CHAPTER 5

Lessons of Modern History: The French Experience

Jacques L. Pons

Tradition and Evolution

It is not necessary to go back as far as the French and Indian wars to find that France has persistently demonstrated a talent for overseas interventions, thus accumulating a wide scope of valuable experience if not large profits.

The achievement of the national unity of France relatively early in the history of Europe, her wealth and strength as compared with her neighbors' situations, and the adventurous trends of the Gallic character can explain such a continuous tendency to explore the seven seas of the world, to help or fight people, to build or lose empires.

In opposition, however, to France's worldwide ambition are the traditional prudence of her peasants, the stay-at-home mentality of her bourgeois, and the immoderate taste for abstractions and legality of her intellectuals.

On the other hand, the much too frequent necessity to defend the home country, "la Patrie," against European invaders or rivals has often interrupted the course of external expansion, but at the same time has made France's interest obvious—to rely on a worldwide establishment capable of providing men and resources in case of emergency.

The durable characteristics of the French involvements in the world can be summarized as follows:

- Though colonial in essence, they have not been motivated by sheer profit but have always integrated altruistic or humanitarian considerations in variable proportions.
- Seldom planned as large-scale enterprises, they were mostly triggered by the unavoidable enlargement of local crises or minor conflicts.
- In most cases initially confined to a "low-intensity" mode, they too often resulted in dramatic issues leading to drastic, painful and costly solutions for the nation.
- Despite some bitter fights, they were never purely military operations, and, in accordance with Mao Tse-tung's principles for subversive warfare, they had to combine repressive, psychological and political actions.
- With the exception of the 1954–62 operations in Algeria, where conscription units had to bear the brunt of law-and-order activities, conquest or pacification have been normally carried out by professional troops—French regulars or Foreign Legion, supplemented by native soldiers and local militia.

In fact, the long story of the French experience in low-intensity conflicts can be divided into three different periods:

"Colonial expansion" started with the first European settlements in America, developed with the conquest of Algeria in 1830, and came to an end in 1945 after a prestigious climax at the beginning of the twentieth century.

"Decolonization," dispersal of the French possessions, sometimes through a friendly process of autonomy but more often through protracted, ruinous, and unpopular military involvements such as the wars in Indochina and Algeria. Termination of these wars in 1962 marked the end of a long dream.

"Cooperation," a new concept for overseas policies, currently effective and reasonably successful, mostly consisting in a peaceful stabilization process, though punctuated by fits of violence necessitating the use of force under various and flexible aspects.

The following pages will try to analyze those three periods in a pragmatic mode, primarily aiming at defining concepts and modes of action that might be used in today's changing world.

Colonial Expansion

The New World and India

The first French explorers, traders and trappers needed no more than minimum force for their protection, and they had a greater ability to infiltrate or negotiate than their Spanish or British counterparts.

Later on, the settlers in "New France," as well as the merchants in India, did not like the Royal Army or Navy to interfere with their business; such was the reputation of the old time King's Regulars. Unfortunately, as the wars in Europe dragged on indecisively, the kings of France and England were tempted to export their disputes overseas, where the intensity of the fighting was lower and the expected profits higher. Active offshore operations were carried out by regular units utilizing the equipment and tactics then prevailing in the Old Countries. It is also interesting to note that on the French side it was already a common practice to rely on native allies for intelligence, reconnaissance, and covering actions, whereas static security tasks were carried out by unofficial militia units recruited and paid by such powerful trading corporations as "La Compagnie des Indes." In the long run, the cost-efficiency balance proved to be negative, inasmuch as France had lost practically everything overseas at the end of the monarchy. However, a special tribute must be paid to the brilliant achievements of the French troops and vessels during the American Revolutionary War, but such campaigns are out of the framework of this study; major confrontations such as the battle of Yorktown cannot be described as "low-intensity" warfare. Nevertheless, the American example was instrumental in preparing the French people for the dramatic events of the 1789 Revolution.

The First Republic and Napoleon were too busy in Europe to give any consideration to overseas actions, with the exception of Bonaparte's expedition to Egypt, which was at the same time scientific, artistic and military in purpose. In May 1798, a French fleet carrying 40,000 men and a selection of 150 talented civilian experts set sail from Toulon. Malta was stormed on the way, Cairo was occupied, and the famous Mamelouks plus a rescuing Turkish army were defeated. Unfortunately, the destruction of their fleet by Nelson at Aboukir trapped the French in Egypt. Without losing impetus, Bonaparte took control over the whole country, established a democratic system of government, developed farming and irrigation (with the use of windmills, a locally unknown device) and considered digging a canal linking the Mediterranean and the Red Sea! Dramatic events in Paris prevented him from giving dimension to his projects, but a valuable amount of scientific and artistic information was brought back to France, and the influence of French culture remained vivid for quite a long time along the Nile.

The Conquest of Algeria

In fact, the French colonial adventure really started with the conquest of Algeria in 1830, which primed an unprecedented overseas expansion, and which influenced the history of France in such a lasting way that it deserves a more detailed discussion.

The official purpose of the expedition was to punish, and if possible suppress, the corsairs of Algiers, then a Turkish possession, who caused much damage to the Mediterranean commercial traffic and held a few hundred Christians in captivity. Among other motivations was the necessity to divert French public opinion from somber domestic issues, to offer some glory to the inactive military, and to avenge an insult to the French Ambassador—not to mention the sordid question of unpaid Turkish debts.

The whole operation was designed as a "hit-and-go" action, but it was nevertheless carefully prepared for months. A regular force of a few thousand men including infantry, cavalry, artillery, and support units was assembled at Toulon and sailed to the Algerian coast under the protection of the Navy.

It was assumed that the mere appearance of the French fleet would incite the corsairs and the official Turkish representative to surrender. On the contrary, Algiers displayed a firm will to fight, and it was decided to conduct a full scale landing some 30 miles west of the city to be followed by an artillery-supported assault. Both succeeded, the fortress was blown up, the privateer ships burned, and the town occupied. The only question left was what to do next?

The answer was a dangerous process of ever-increasing involvement that was to become more and more frequent in the history of low-intensity conflicts, known as pacification.

Pacification

As the military leaders of the expeditionary force were not in a hurry to sail back to dull garrison life in France, they thought that it would be a good thing to continue the occupation of Algiers until complete suppression of the aggressiveness of its citizens. Paris accepted, and "pacification" started. The city was divided into military districts held by battalion-size garrisons, intervention units were positioned as a reserve force, and a network of intelligence collectors was organized. The Turkish administration quickly turned into chaos, and French Army officers were appointed to run the city. Then the news came that Arab forces were approaching, and the French commander decided to dispatch patrols. A few men were killed in ambushes, and punitive raids were launched by the French. As skirmishes became more frequent, a security perimeter was established, and brigade-sized, long-range forces penetrated deeper and deeper into the Algerian territory. Though sporadic and frontless, the fighting was bitter, and the high command had no difficulty persuading Paris that the termination of the expedition would mean a disastrous loss of prestige. Large-scale operations were successfully carried out, a few tribes asked for French protection, while rebels had to submit to the power of arms. Year after year, "pacification" sprawled all over the country like an oil stain, reaching such remote cities as Constantine and Oran, hundres of miles away from Algiers. It was too late for a withdrawal.

In 1852, Napoleon III took power in France after a successful coup d'état, and a new concept for Algeria was developed. The idea was to complete pacification, and to transform the new conquest into a friendly "Arab kingdom." At the same time, the new regime in Paris was embarrassed with hundreds of "Republican" opponents, very active throughout France, and Napoleon III decided to get rid of them by deportation into Algeria, where they were offered free land and a new career. Such was the actual origin of "colonization," which was to expand successfully for the next decades as a constant flow of families came and settled in accordance with an ambitious plan designed by the French authorities in Algiers. Algeria, however, was not a safe place until the end of the century; settlers were murdered, villages were burned, and from time to time entire Arab tribes revolted, thus triggering painful "law-and-order" military operations.

The tactics then developed by the French troops are interesting enough to be briefly described, for they have set a pattern for similar situations around the world. Basically, they consisted in establishing a network of strong points on carefully selected sites in order to control the activities of the most turbulent tribes, to offer logistical support to mobile troops, and to permit the safe implantation of prosperous colonial villages. At the same time, mobile task forces were to move across the country to show the flag, deter or fight rebellion, and contact remote tribes, in order to pave the way for further expansion. Such forces were brigade-sized units mainly composed of light infantry, covered by fast cavalry detachments and supported by minimized artillery. Their equipment was alleviated, and they were supposed to rely on local resources for their logistics. Engineers and medical aides were key personnel; the former had to open roads, dig wells, build bridges and structures, and the latter offered their help to the settlers but also to the Arabs. Such demonstrations of good will, in association with a "big stick" policy, laid a base for a successful psychological action that resulted in total pacification at the beginning of the twentieth century.

Algeria was not the only field of expansion for France, whose officers, politicians, businessmen, and missionaries endeavored to reproduce and enlarge the Algerian model everywhere possible in a world which seemed open to bold enterprises. Tunisia and Morocco became protectorates, thus giving some substance to the expression "the western Mediterranean is a French lake." Senegal, Congo, Niger, Guinea, Chad, and Sudan became colonies; and when the Sahara desert was employed linking up "Afrique Occidentale Française" and "Afrique du Nord Française," more than half of the map of Africa could be printed in pink, the color of the French Empire in school textbooks. Asia was not neglected. A few daring navy officers, acting without official orders, began to penetrate the Indochinese rivers, sailing upstream as far as possible with their gunboats, triggering the famous "pacification" involvement, and adding Tonkin, Annam, Cochin China, Laos, and Cambodia to a long list of overseas possessions.

That, of course, was not accomplished without conflicts. Native populations often opposed violently the French expansion, but their fighting was incoherent and clumsy and their lack of equipment, unity, and political determination doomed their rebellion. Rivalry between colonial nations was also a source of trouble, and major crises occurred; with England at Fashoda over Central Africa, and with Germany over Morocco. Active diplomacy and the wise idea that there was enough room for everybody fortunately avoided escalation.

Imperial Policies

During such a long period and across such a large empire, the French courses of action were various and flexible. For instance, no effort was made to implant French settlers in unsuitable climates or environment. In Indochina, Tunisia, and Morocco, traditional monarchs were left in power under the tight control of a French representative, whereas in Central Africa the tribal groups were organized into large federations. However, in order to manage and, if possible, to prevent armed conflicts, the following concepts were developed in a uniform way throughout the Empire.

- Native units were recruited, equipped, and trained as regular forces. Their soldiers came, through enlistment or conscription (as was the case in Algeria), from specific tribes considered warlike. The officers were French, but the door was left open for the promotion of natives who held the majority of NCO positions and a few junior officer commissions. Tough training on the job, active field operations, and long term service contributed to maximize the combat effectiveness of such units, whose prestige and esprit de corps were considerable. A hierarchy of value existed. "Tirailleurs Marocains" were at the top and considered as "lions," whereas their Algerian equivalents only deserved the title of "men." Much hope was invested in all-black units such as "Tirailleurs Sénégalais," because of their athletic appearance and reputation as warriors. The native units were organized in divisions on a territorial basis, and they normally served in their province of recruitment, where their popularity and knowledge of the environment offered both deterrence and intelligence. In case of emergency, however, they were to be committed preferably into other territories where their liberty of action was larger. The arrival of one Senegalese battalion in Syria, for instance, was equivalent to the engagement of a white brigade in terms of deterring power. During World War I and World War II colonial troops behaved with unmatched gallantry on the European battlefield in such hot places as Verdun or Cassino. Strangely enough, Vietnamese troops did not enjoy a good reputation, and the rare "annamite" units were mostly considered as providers of good cooks and orderlies.
- Auxiliary forces were also locally organized as police forces with the task of maintaining law and order under the control of the territorial authorities, French or native. Those "moghazenis" or "harkis" patrolled the country night and day on horseback or afoot and were instrumental in preventing trouble or supplementing regular forces in more serious cases.
- French forces were of course deployed overseas, but they mostly consisted of professional units—either all white, as in the Foreign Legion, or with various proportions of natives in "Infanterie Coloniale" formations. Artillery, engineers, and other support units were mostly all French. Normally stationed at strategic locations, they were considered and trained as reserve forces, only to be committed when the situation was too serious or too delicate to be handled by native or auxiliary

troops. Major operations, such as the pacification of the Rif mountains in Morocco or the reduction of the Druze rebellion in Syria shortly after the end of World War I, were their normal combat tasks, which they successfully carried out without the intervention of Metropolitan draftee regiments.

• Direct administration was the rule wherever the mere transposition of the French organization was not possible or not desirable. It was the case in most rural areas, where a "civilian administrator" was appointed to run every aspect of a territorial community's life with the assistance of a native chieftain and a traditional assembly of distinguished citizens. Such positions were often held by Army officers whose dedication and efficiency became so obvious that they were organized into a special corps called "Affaires Indigènes" (or A.I.). A.I. officers were carefully selected and properly trained in order to acquire proficiency in local dialects, law, farming, and medicine. In charge of a "circle" adapted to geographic and tribal constraints, they were responsible for practically everything within its limits including security, development, health, and education. Protected by auxiliary police they lived in a fort or "bordj," grouping various facilities and offering a refuge or a base for military operations. Though medieval in nature, the A.I. system, originally designed for Morocco, responded well to the needs of the population and was successfully exported to other territories.

The combination of native regulars, auxiliary forces, French units, and direct administration was able to complete pacification, ensure security, and develop health, education, and welfare throughout the empire for more than a century. Only two low-intensity conflicts occurred in Morocco and Syria, both in the late 1920s, and usual "search and kill" operations sufficed to deal with them but many others were avoided through timely action at appropriate levels. It is remarkable that during both world wars, colonial populations loyally contributed to France's war effort, particularly after the occupation of the home country in 1940, instead of seizing this opportunity to revolt and be rid of French rule. The empire remained united and made every effort to contribute militarily to the liberation of "la Patrie." In 1945, however, the world had changed, new forces were emerging and good old methods were no longer instrumental in checking the tide of modern nationalism. France was to experience it in a painful way.

Decolonization

When World War II came to an end, France was exhausted by German occupation and allied destruction, but the empire remained unscathed and even more prosperous because of profitable wartime trade. If France was ranking among the victorious nations, it was partly owing to the war effort of her colonies who expected something in return. Native elites had traveled through many countries, and were particularly receptive to such ideologies as Marxism or the American theory of self-government. Though basically loyal to the mother country, every colonial nation made it quite clear that things could not simply revert to the *status quo ante*. Paris realized this, and developed the concept of a large federation of autonomous states called "The French Union," as a substitute for the former colonial order. The word "independence," however, was never mentioned, and "decolonization," if accepted, was envisioned as a long-term evolution in direct opposition to the impatience displayed by most indigenous political leaders. Such a fundamental contradiction generated conflicting situations, which France was unable to handle without using military strength, thus triggering the uncontrollable process of escalation in violence, as highlighted by the Indochina war and the operations in Algeria; two typical examples to be discussed now.

The Indochina War (1945–53)

In September 1940, profiting by the weakened position of defeated France, the Japanese government demanded bases and facilities for their troops in Indochina, and the French governor had no other choice but to accept. During four years, French, Vietnamese and Japanese coexisted without much trouble but on March 9, 1945, the Japanese forces attacked the French by surprise, killing or arresting every public servant, military person, or civilian and replacing the French rule by puppet governments in Annam, Laos, and Cambodia. As early as 1940, the leaders of the Indochinese Communist Party had found refuge in China and had developed a strong underground organization called "Vietminh" in Tonkin, under the control of Nguyen Ai Quoc, who was to become famous under the name "Ho Chi Minh." On August 19, 1945, immediately following the Japanese capitulation, the Vietminh staged a countrywide revolution and established a provisional government with Ho at the top. The Allies were not in a position to send forces into Vietnam; the Japanese forces were left in charge of maintaining order pending the arrival of Chinese and British units north and south, respectively, of the Sixteenth Parallel as it had been decided at the Potsdam Conference. During this time, the Vietminh found it safer to keep the French prisoners in their camps under the custody of the defeated Japanese.

Such a situation was unacceptable for General de Gaulle, head of the provisional government of France, who decided to restore French supremacy in Indochina by combining a military expedition and the establishment of a favorable political regime in Saigon. On 24 March 1945, a formal declaration was made in Paris, recognizing the autonomy of the five Indochinese states within the French Union, while an expeditionary force of 70,000 men was assembled and trained. The British government supported the idea for various reasons, and the Truman administration did not follow the Roosevelt line and did not oppose the French comeback. It took place on 5 September 1945, when a small force of British Gurkhas and French Marines was airlifted to

Saigon just in time to be involved in the difficult process of restoring order, since the Vietminh had decided to meet the French with fire. The British withdrew as the main French expeditionary force arrived and occupied strategic positions around the city. An eight-year war was beginning which can be divided into three periods: the "phony war" (1945–46), the "colonial war" (1947–50) and the "international war" (1951–54), not to mention subsequent developments.

The "phony war" had a good start on the French side, as the Commander in Chief General Leclerc, one of the most famous leaders of World War II, dispatched light armored columns in every direction in connection with amphibious raids in order to reoccupy the main cities of South Vietnam. Very little opposition was met, and after some bitter fighting in Saigon, the Vietminh decided to disappear into the jungle. Quite often the French were welcomed by the populace, particularly in Cambodia and the Central High Region. By the end of the year, the main cities and the main highways south of the Sixteenth Parallel were under control, and the whole operation could be considered a success.

In Tonkin things rapidly became disconcerting with the legal invasion of the country by poorly disciplined Chinese Nationalist troops who behaved as in occupied territory. Ho Chi Minh realized the danger and decided to accept the return of French troops so as to avoid Chinese domination. On 6 March, a French naval force landed at Haiphong after some fighting with the Chinese, and a few days later General Leclerc, leading an armored force, was warmly greeted in Hanoi by the Vietminh authorities. It took quite a long time to persuade the Chinese to go home but satisfactory relations were established with the Vietminh leaders. Ho Chi Minh was officially invited to France and a *modus vivendi* was signed in Fontainebleau on 14 September 1946, recognizing the existence of a Republic of Vietnam associated with the French Union and ordering a total cease-fire throughout the country.

Guerrilla warfare started again in Cochin China, and the French authorities were quickly convinced of Ho's duplicity as the Vietminh almost openly prepared for the next phase of their strategy: the elimination of France. On 20 November, three days of bitter fighting in Haiphong confirmed that strategy, and on 19 December, a general attack was launched against the French garrisons throughout Vietnam, with the main effort in Hanoi. Thanks to good intelligence and superior equipment the French troops defeated their attackers, and the Vietminh had to withdraw to jungle and hills. The "phony war" was over, but the French had already lost 3,500 men—killed or missing in action—including 232 officers. The Vietminh had overrated the support they could get from the population and underrated the determination and firepower of their opponents. The French had suffered from a complex of superiority as an elite all-professional force. Their losses were mainly due to mob-control operations and combat in built-up areas where they were outnumbered and could not make adequate use of their heavy weapons.

The "colonial war" was the predictable consequence of the general uprising of 19 December. The French, realizing that they had been cheated and that no further agreement would be respected, decided to follow a hard line to enforce law and order in Indochina, and to prevent contagious influence throughout the newly established French Union.

The Vietminh, after a broad "autocriticism" campaign, abandoned open action and reverted to guerrilla tactics in accordance with Mao's principles, which defined three necessary phases. In chronological order, they are:

- "strategic-defensive" or general guerrilla war with total support by the population;
- "movement warfare," progressively developed by regular units armed and trained abroad;
- "general offensive," combining all-out operations to annihilate the shattered imperialistic enemy.

The first phase was implemented with drastic methods: a large sanctuary was established in the densely wooded "High Region" of Tonkin, beyond the reach of French routine actions. Every form of opposition was eliminated, and the entire population was mobilized on the village base under the leadership of fanatic cadres or "Can Bo." The terrain also was organized to help guerrilla tactics, each village being fortified and equipped with concealed depots and shelters. Partisans were grouped in teams of three men always on the move, who could concentrate into company-sized units to deliver easy blows from strong to weak, and then disappear.

The French plan was simple in theory: (1) isolate and destroy the Vietminh sanctuary in Tonkin; (2) pacify the "useful" part of the country; (3) utilize the friendly population to fight the communists. In order to implement this new policy, the French forces had to be reinforced to a strength of 115,000 men, and restructured into territorial units in charge of pacification tasks and brigade-sized "mobile groups" to carry out large-scale operations. A two-year time frame was considered necessary to complete the whole program.

In early fall 1947, the Vietminh sanctuary in Tonkin was attacked by two division-sized French task forces combining a land and riverine approach into a double envelopment. Considerable time was spent breaking through the protective belt of fortified villages, and a few weeks later, when the vital areas could be approached, the communists had had every opportunity to move away their command and control organization. By the end of the year, however, the sanctuary had been disrupted, the support infrastructure destroyed, and significant losses inflicted. But the core of the Viet-Minh remained intact, while the French forces had to return to their bases in the delta, not to overextend their deployment and increase their vulnerability. In the following years the same strategy was to be repeated in the north along different tactical approaches, with the same frustrating results.

In the south, by contrast, the Vietminh implantation was much weaker. There were only a few refuge zones and no large sanctuary, but the politico-military organization was represented everywhere, dispatching guerrilla commandos and committing the population to sabotage action. The French tactic there was to control large areas of the country through a dense network of some 500 small forts. Each fort was mostly triangular in shape, with a central main tower and makeshift bulwarks and bunkers. The garrison consisted of a platoon of French regulars, supplemented by local auxiliaries whose families lived within the protective perimeter of the fort, which also sheltered a refugee village. The network was controlled at battalion level, each battalion being responsible for a sector. Pacification was carried out by crisscross patrolling and a friendly attitude. It worked well during the day, but at night the forts closed their gates and the Vietminh took advantage. Despite intervention companies and flexible artillery support, many a fort was stormed by carefully prepared attacks. The main highways were also controlled by a chain of observation towers erected every five miles and held by a handful of auxiliaries who were supposed to report any suspect activity, thus triggering artillery and armored action. Moreover, the influence of such original sects as the Cao Dais, the Binh Xuens, and the Hoa Haos was utilized to check the Vietminh. Contracts were made with the sects who guaranteed security and order within the limits of their area of obedience in exchange for certain privileges and better equipment for their partisans. The security of western Saigon, for instance, was contracted with the Binh Xuens, who received exclusive control of gambling in Cholon as a reward.

After three longs years of that colonial type of warfare, neither the Vietminh nor the French had won a decisive advantage, but the former had considerably developed their organization while the latter had suffered a steady attrition. The strength of the expeditionary force had dropped to some 87,000 men (70 battalions), half of them dispersed in pacification (static deployment), and their morale was affected by the indifference or even hostility of French public opinion.

In 1950, however, things were to take a significant turn: the defeat of Chiang Kai-shek's armies in mainland China allowed the linking up of Mao's and Ho Chi Minh's forces along the Tonkin border, and the implementation of a considerable military aid program by Red China and the Soviets. After the Soviet-Chinese treaty a monolithic communist block occupied most of Asia, and with the beginning of the Korean War the western nations realized that, after all, the French were also fighting communism and deserved some support. Internationalization was on its way.

The international war started when the first Vietminh battalions, equipped and trained in China, appeared in Tonkin during the spring of 1950. According to the aid plan, unarmed Vietminh units would walk across the border into Chinese training camps, get brand new equipment and clothing, and go back home after three months of tough training with combat capabilities equivalent to those of the French units, including heavy mortars plus antitank and antiaircraft weapons. More than 30 battalions (half of the Vietminh total strength) were modernized in China that year, while thousands of coolies poured ammunition and supplies into the Vietminh secret depots.

The French high command analyzed the threat correctly and concluded that Ho Chi Minh was ready to release orders for the second strategic phase of his plan: "movement war." General De Lattre, former commander of the First Army during World War II, a charismatic and capable leader, was appointed as the commander in chief with full civil and military powers. He redeployed the French units, built a fortified perimeter to cover the delta, boosted the morale of the troops by spectacular measures, and instead of waiting for a Vietminh attack took the offensive. Several defeats were inflicted on the enemy in pitched battles at Vinh Yenh, Hoa Binh and Nghia Lo. At the same time, General De Lattre developed the national Vietnamese Army up to 35 battalions. A draft law was passed, and a national Vietnamese high command was established. Anticommunist "maquis" were organized by the French Special Forces along the Vietminh communications lines, and Operational Administrative Detachments were created to take the populations in charge in combat areas. Moreover, he personally conducted a propaganda campaign in the United States to explain the French positions and obtain military aid. Unfortunately, General De Lattre died of cancer after one year in command, just when success was in sight.

After De Lattre, the situation quickly deteriorated, for his successors were unable to deploy the same leadership. American help reached a considerable level, and financed up to 40% of the war budget, but the successive unstable French governments of those times had only one strategy in mind: get out of Indochina under acceptable conditions. General Navarre, the new commander, thought he could modify the balance of forces by developing an offensive strategy of strong fortified operation bases to be established deep into the Vietminh-controlled territory. The concept was right, but the available troops and air power were not adapted to the magnitude of the task. While Nasan could be considered a success, Dien Bien Phu, though well engaged, resulted in a disaster, with the loss of 12 battalions literally submerged by the fanatic tide of Giap's elite divisions. Obviously the war had ceased to be a low-intensity conflict, and short of massive American intervention the only wise recourse was negotiation at the international level. Such was the purpose of the Geneva conference, and an honorable cease-fire was accepted by all parties with the exception of South Vietnam on 21 July 1954. The country was divided into two zones limited by the Seventeenth Parallel, free elections were to take place within two years, and the French forces agreed to evacuate the country before 1956.

The Indochina War was at the same time a revolutionary war as described by Mao Tse-tung opposing a professional force to a Marxist politico-military organization, a civil war between two halves of the same country, and an episode of the ideological East-West conflict. Such a dramatic combination resulted in more than 500,000 people killed in eight years, including 60,000 members of the French forces.

Could it have been avoided? Probably so, had the French government adopted and implemented a more realistic policy as early as 1945.

Could it have been won? Certainly not, considering the balance of forces, the distances, the impetus of a revolution, the attrition of morale, and the international environment. The most powerful nation in the world was to suffer from the same painful experience a few years later on the same battlefield, with no better results.

Algeria (1954–62)

Throughout the French Union, the termination of the Indochina War was the signal for nationalistic claims. A few countries peacefully expressed their desire for greater autonomy, or even independence, but in Algeria an open rebellion burst out on 1 November 1954 without too much political warning.

The status of Algeria was special because it was legally a part of France, where the French law guaranteed equal rights to every citizen, Christian, Moslem, or Jewish. The administrative organization, public services, and school system were the same as in France, and every effort was made to support the idea that Algeria *was* France.

In fact, many differences separated the European community (one million) from the Algerian masses (eight million): religion, culture, standard of living, employment, and so on; but because generations of Algerians did not know anything else, they accepted the French law without major problems. However, nationalistic unrest was initiated as early as 1940 by the Algerian Communist Party; the Allied landing in 1942 disseminated the image of another society, and Algerian soldiers, back from their two-year tours in Indochina, talked about what they had seen. With the development of education new Algerian elites emerged, clamored for more political responsibilities, and envied the autonomous status of Tunisia and Morocco.

The rebellion started in the hills of Aures, at the eastern end of the country, with the assassination of Christian and Moslem local authorities. This unexpected violence generated an outburst of rage in France as well as in

Algeria, and the reaction was to send troops as in the old days of the 1871 Khabylian rebellion. The province of Aures was isolated, and a large-scale "search and kill" operation was carried out by local forces. The general opinion was that nothing worse would follow.

The FLN or "Front de Libération Nationale," as the rebels called themselves, changed its tactics and started a countrywide campaign of bombing public buildings and killing selected personalities. The idea was to promote terror everywhere, in order to compel the police forces to disperse their action and the government to negotiate or accept the escalation. Moreover, the situation was complicated by two specific factors: (1) legally the events were happening in France and in peacetime: the law permitted only arrest by gendarmerie and a fair trial, a lengthy procedure not at all adapted to the magnitude of the threat; (2) the outraged Christian community was about to expedite justice by lynching every suspected Moslem. So the problem was how to check terrorism while preventing racial massacres.

In spite of all the lessons learned in Indochina, the worst solution was chosen. It simply consisted in multiplying police actions and granting military protection to every potential target. In order to meet the huge requirements in manpower, all units available were dispatched to Algeria, including draftees and recruits, while reservists were called to active duty. That mass of unskilled troops was scattered all over the country, and divided into small sections who were supposed to guard post offices or railway stations. Their morale was low and their discipline nonexistent, particularly with reserve units. The FLN quickly realized that such detachments were ideal targets, and multiplied assaults and ambushes—an easy way to procure weapons and spread panic. During this time the professional gendarmes and national policemen were submerged by routine investigations and paperwork.

After one year of such an aberration a series of energetic and sensible measures were taken:

- the reservists were sent back home;
- two active divisions were transferred from Germany;
- the withdrawal from Indochina was accelerated;
- the legal procedure was simplified;
- under the name of "territorial units," a sort of national guard was created and exclusively recruited among the Christian community;
- the famous corps of "Affaires Indigènes" was revitalized and reinforced with some 300 young and dedicated officers.

At the same time a new strategy was developed under the influence of a lobby of young colonels back from Indochina, where they had practiced anti-guerrilla warfare for years. Some of them had studied Mao Tse-tung's theories in the Vietminh's prisoner-of-war camps. Through an adequate use of the media, they conviced the public opinion and the high command that the ultimate goal was to gain the Algerian population's minds, not to protect structures or fight for terrain. Accordingly, the following plan was conceived:

- Algeria would be divided into "zones" held by divisions, "sectors" held by battalions, and "districts" held by companies. At each level the commander would be responsible for security, psychological action, and coordination of antiterrorist actions;
- "Sections Administratives Spécialisées" or SAS (a new term for the old AI "circles") would be established in remote rural areas;
- Elite battalions (parachutists, Foreign Legion, and commandos) would form a strategic reserve;
- Mobility and air power would be enhanced by massive purchases of helicopters and aircraft.

The process of "gaining the minds" consisted in being constantly on the move: of demonstrating night and day, in the cities as well as in the countryside, that the French were better, quicker, tougher, and more helpful than the FLN. The saying was that a new medical-aid station opened to the public was better than a dozen rebels killed. The plan was enthusiastically implemented, and in 1956 the rural areas were no longer safe for the FLN, who decided to revert to urban terrorism.

The city of Algiers was chosen as a target, and bombs or hand grenades were exploded everywhere, killing innocent people. The Tenth Parachute Division under General Massu was tasked to restore order and security at any cost. Without much noise, the red berets methodically smashed the FLN underground system, killing or arresting most of their leaders through instant exploitation of intelligence. A few months later the "Battle of Algiers" was won.

In Paris, however, the government continued to display the most regrettable weakness and seemed unable to take advantage of the encouraging results obtained. In Algeria, on the contrary, the entire Christian community and a significant part of the Moslems demanded the continuation of a firm line. On 13 May 1958 the French populace, outraged by the assassination of three French prisoners-of-war by the FLN, stormed the Government Building in Algiers and established a "Committee for Public Salvation" to take care of the Algerian affairs directly. In Paris, General de Gaulle was appointed as prime minister by the president, and things changed immediately. A new constitution established a strong presidential regime, and de Gaulle concentrated unprecedented powers in his hands. France was to be firmly ruled after years of instability.

A dynamic policy was defined during a triumphal visit of the new leader to Algeria. It combined three concepts: (1) equal rights and opportunities for everyone; (2) massive psychological action; (3) annihilation of the rebels. Consequently, military commanders in the field received full powers to achieve success. For the first time since 1954 a large consensus was found throughout both communities, as Moslem masses openly demonstrated their support for the new policy. Much to their surprise, the rebels were losing in the cities as well as in the mountains, and many of them surrendered, obtained pardon, and were immediately reutilized as "harkis" or auxiliaries against their former comrades. The dynamics of pacification were working, and the FLN had no other choice but to look for international support. A "Provisional Government of the Algerian Republic" was established in Cairo and a "National Liberation Army" was created in Tunisia and Eastern Morocco, with the active support of all Arab nations.

In 1959, however, de Gaulle, realizing that such a long-term policy was too heavy a burden for the French economy, significantly softened his line, and on 16 September he pronounced the magic word "autonomy." The effect was immediately devastating; the troops felt cheated, the pro-French community of Algeria was outraged, and the rebels recovered hope and aggressiveness. Within a few months, years of efforts were ruined: the French forces had to revert to defensive modes of action, particularly along the Moroccan and Tunisian borders, where huge protective lines had to be established so as to intercept rebel penetration into Algeria. Those tactics, combining electrified barbed-wire lines, mine fields, artillery, and armored intervention forces, proved efficient but too expensive in terms of manpower, and most damaging to the morale as a "Maginot line" complex began to develop.

Slowly but steadily the idea of a "disengagement" pervaded everybody's mind on both sides, with opposite effects. Fear, anger, and frustration pushed the French community of Algeria and part of the army into such adventures as the 1961 "Putsch" and the "Secret Armed Organization" (OAS). As 1962 began, the French forces had to fight two terrorist organizations in Algeria as well as at home (FLN and OAS), and the country was on the verge of a civil war. Public opinion in France no longer accepted protracted sacrifices and, with the exception of the "ultra" faction, favored any compromise to stop the bloodshed. De Gaulle decided on drastic surgery, and independence was granted to Algeria as the result of the Evian agreements on 18 March 1962. More than a million French settlers and faithful Moslems had to suffer an exodus and the loss of everything they had, but France retrieved her unity. The French withdrawal was not the result of a military defeat. It was a painful but necessary political decision made in order to avoid the worst and preserve the nation's future.

Suez

Before closing the discussion on decolonization, it is necessary to mention briefly the Franco-British intervention at Suez, hitherto owned and operated by a French-British corporation. In order to defend their economic interests as well as their national pride, and after the failure of a diplomatic action, both nations decided on the use of force. A binational joint task force was assembled in Cyprus, a combined staff was created, and contacts were established with the Israeli Department of Defense. On 29 October the Israeli forces invaded the Sinai, and on 4 November the French and British landing took place at the northern exit of the canal, preceded by devastating air strikes and naval gunfire. The official goal was to separate the Egyptian and Israeli belligerents, and to guarantee free navigation for all shipping along the canal. From a technical point of view the operation was perfect, and every military objective was conquered in less than two days with very few casualties. The Soviets, however, issued an ultimatum threatening both nations with nuclear weapons, and the United States used various means of pressure to stop the conflict. On 7 November the cease-fire was effected and the allies pulled out their forces progressively. From a political viewpoint, on the contrary, the whole operation amounted to a disastrous loss of prestige. It demonstrated the vanity of the use of force without real determination or an alternative plan, the fragility of alliances, the emergence of new powers, and the importance of an international consensus. There was no longer a place in the world for a gunboat policy, and the colonial era was definitely over.

Fortunately enough, decolonization was not as dramatic for France in the rest of the empire: the black African republics, for instance, acquired their independence through friendly negotiation. Far from being ruined by the loss of her overseas possessions, France was relieved of an unbearable financial burden and she recovered, at the same time, prosperity and freedom of action.

Cooperation

A New Look

The period following the independence of Algeria was marked by General de Gaulle's determination to build a strong France and to channel the nation's ambitions into a European destiny. Sick and tired of overseas commitments, the French people gave full support to that new concept and favored for a time the philosophy of the famous journalist Raymond Cartier, who claimed that French money and energy should be entirely invested at home to meet domestic needs.

It was, however, difficult to be rid of the past immediately. A few ancient French possessions, such as Martinique, Guadeloupe, New Caledonia, and Polynesia, preferred the status of French provinces to any other form of association, and most of the African republics wished to continue close cooperation with France. Consequently, a new overseas policy was defined by General de Gaulle and followed by his successors under the title of "cooperation." It is still valid today without much change.

Primarily focusing on Africa, the policy of cooperation aims at helping the friendly nations to consolidate their independence, develop their economy, and guarantee their security. In return, cooperation insures the protection of such vital French interests as raw-material sources, commercial sea or air routes, and safe working conditions for the more than 260,000 French nationals living abroad.

Accordingly, in addition to diplomatic, economic, and cultural ties, military assistance agreements have been concluded with the limited goal of providing advisors, equipment, and training, along with defense agreements that contain provisions for the permanent deployment of French units and the availability of port, airport, and overflight facilities. Such are the arrangements with Senegal, Ivory Coast, Gabon, and Djibouti.

Concept 67

French military strategy, mainly based on nuclear deterrence in Europe, had to be modified in order to meet the requirements of the assistance/defense agreements, to protect French establishments and lines of communication, and to maintain an adequate capability of intervention in other parts of the world. The new concept may be called "67" for convenience. Accordingly, the French forces were organized into four categories: strategic nuclear forces, maneuver forces, territorial defense forces, and intervention forces.

The intervention forces consisted of two parts of professional units: (1) home-based forces with one parachute division, one amphibious brigade, and the Foreign Legion operational task force, supported by tactical air units. Strategic transportation was to be provided by navy aircraft carriers and air force airlift squadrons supplemented by the reserve fleet of Air France; (2) overseas-stationed forces (13,500 men), including Foreign Legion and "Infanterie de Marine" battalions.

The concept for the employment of intervention forces considered three levels of action: (1) routine action by forces stationed overseas providing assistance to host-nation armies, collecting and updating information about the country, and maintaining transit facilities; (2) indirect action to support military operations carried out by friendly government forces, mostly consisting in air transport, command and control communications, and logistics; (3) direct action ranging from air strikes on request to helicopter or airborne assaults.

Emergency plans were drafted and updated in Paris, and annual joint exercises enabled the specialized troops to conduct adequate training for their missions and to become familiarized with their potential environment.

The system worked well for a few years, and it was successfully tested at Djibouti against Somali raids, in Mauritania to repel Polisario aggression, and in Chad to help the legal government in antiguerrilla operations. Experience proved, however, that the maintenance of overseas bases was a costly procedure, that permanent deployment of forces could lead to overcommitment and escalation in such cases as Chad, and finally that the principle of specialized intervention forces was damaging the "one army" concept; the whole system was often criticized as "neocolonialist."

Concept 77

Consequently, it was decided in 1977, within the framework of the Army divisions' reorganization, to conserve the general philosophy of military cooperation but to modify the force organization and modes of actions, in order to promote a more efficient, less expensive, and less conspicuous system. Discreet facilities would be preferred to overequipped bases, permanent deployment would be replaced by enhanced joint exercises and rotation of units, and general-purpose forces would develop an overseas-intervention capability. Moreover, direct intervention would only take place in case of vital necessity and would be staged directly from France.

Kolwezi

The best example of such a low-profile concept is the successful intervention of a French parachute battalion in Kolwezi (Zaire).

On 13 May 1979, a force of some 4,000 Katanguese rebels from Katanga who had taken refuge in Angola occupied the industrial city of Kolwezi, headquarters of the powerful mining corporation called "Gecamines." Surprise was total, and the regular Zairian units withdrew. Twenty-five hundred European technicians, mostly Belgian and French, were imprisoned in their homes with their families. Many of them appeared for trial before so-called people's Courts of Justice and were shot on the spot. Very quickly anarchy and looting spread all over the city, and it became clear that the Europeans were considered as hostages by the rebels and could be murdered at any time. With the agreement of General Mobutu, chief of state of Zaire, and after consultation with Washington, a rescue operation was decided upon in Paris, combining a French airborne assault on the city and a Zairian ground operation.

On 17 May at 11:00 A.M., the Second Foreign Legion Parachute Regiment (Second REP), stationed in Corsica, was alerted while strategic and tactical airlifts were organized with participation by the U.S. Air Force. On 18 May, in the afternoon, the parachute echelon of the regiment (650 men, including command post, four parachute companies with organic support weapons) was airlifted by French jets to a staging area near Lumumbashi; the heavy echelon (100 vehicles) was to be flown on the next day by U.S.A.F. The airborne assault itself was planned for 20 May, but the situation estimate concerning the chances of survival of the hostages was so pessimistic that the French operational staff in Lumumbashi decided to commence the operation as early as 19 May at dawn.

The Second REP Commander received the mission: (1) to rescue the Europeans; (2) to restore the security within the city; (3) to maintain law and order in the area. In order not to waste time he decided to jump directly over the city instead of using the airfield located four miles away. The assault was carried out as planned at 3:30 P.M., and the first wave occupied key positions throughout the city, inflicting severe losses to the rebels and rescuing 50 hostages.

On the next day the dropping of the second wave at dawn enabled the commander to take full control of the city, and to release the rest of the hostages. Unfortunately, the ground Zairian column was unable to reach Kolwezi, and the following days were utilized by the Second REP to mop up the area around Kolwezi; it advanced as far as 50 miles deep into the unknown environments. Belgian units, transported by air to Kolwezi on the 20th, took care of the rehabilitation and evacuation of the European population. When the Second REP left Zaire for France on 6 June, the balance of the operation was on the French side: 5 killed and 25 wounded, whereas on the rebels' side there were 250 killed and 1,000 modern weapons captured.

Lessons of Kolwezi

Many tactical lessons were learned at Kolwezi, but in terms of strategy the success of the operation proved that a long-range intervention is still possible today under the following conditions:

- first and foremost, accurate and constantly updated intelligence must be available;
- highly trained professional units only can be committed;
- strategic airlift capabilities must be assembled on short notice;
- adequate and protected long-range communications must be established;
- local sympathies and facilities must be utilized;
- a consensus must be obtained at local and international levels prior to the commitment of forces;
- the purpose of the operation must be acceptable for both national and international public opinion;
- the main politico-military decisions must be taken at presidential level, in order to avoid escalation by the military commanders involved.

The French System of intervention seems now to be reliable, and does not surpass the capabilities of France or the necessities of her policy. Flexible, discreet, and tailored to meet various needs, it has recently proved its efficiency by smoothly preventing any trouble or bloodshed during the elimination of Bokassa's regime by the people of Central Africa on 22 September 1979.

Conclusions

For centuries and all over the world, France has been confronted with a wide range of conflicts, some of them provoked by the country's ambitions, but quite a few imposed upon her by external constraints. Her strategy, sometimes wavering and often overconfident, was never purely aggressive or mercenary; her servants, civilian or military, have constantly and earnestly tried every possible mode of action in order to preserve a social order they considered the best suitable to time, place, and people.

In the near future, unfortunately, the threats to world peace are not likely to recede. A major conflagration in Europe, for instance, caused by a Soviet initiative following Marshal Tito's death, cannot be considered improbable. The situation in Africa, though seemingly cooling down with the Rhodesian cease-fire, is still far from stable. Recent events, such as the Iranian Revolution, the seizure of U.S. hostages, and the Soviet commitment in Afghanistan, indicate that the combination of Islamic fervor, oil shortage, and Soviet ambitions is apt to create explosive conditions in Southwest Asia. Although the role of the People's Republic of China is still to be determined, the United States, as well as its allies, has but little control over such situations, and it lacks adequate tools to defuse them early enough. Consequently, it is not unreasonable to predict that the 1980s might be dominated by the end of détente, the restoration of a cold war climate, and the potentiality of military interventions triggering low-intensity conflicts fraught with a lethal danger of escalation, particularly around the Persian Gulf. The French experience tends to support the following points:

- the use of large military forces as a means of coercion, even if technically possible, is seldom politically feasible;
- an excessive projection of power, such as massive airstrikes or large-scale airborne operations, might not be the appropriate answer to current challenges;
- even the deterring effect of military gesticulation can be seriously questioned;
- in contrast, "hit and go" type actions, involving only highly skilled professionals, based on accurate intelligence, and supported by local facilities, seem more capable of suppressing causes of trouble before a dangerous level is reached;
- other forms of covert or low-visibility interventions have to be preferred whenever and wherever possible, including the use of religious or political antagonism to generate counterforces;

- in no case should regional contingencies be allowed to appear as East-West disputes, for fear of automatic escalation;
- the capabilities to implement such a policy have to be acquired beforehand and maintained on a short-notice alert status;
- area expertise, local sympathies, transit facilities, and secure sources of accurate intelligence must be available on a permanent basis.

It is difficult for a nation, even a superpower, to design, develop, and maintain alone a worldwide capability of intervention. The United States, however, enjoys a central position within a global network of alliances, which implies fundamental responsibilities but also provides substantial allied cooperation in return. In the years to come the American aptitude to determine and utilize allied assets under every form possible will probably make all the difference between an articulate response and a rash move.

Note

*The views and conclusions expressed herein are solely those of the author and do not purport to represent those of any agency of the French or United States governments.

CHAPTER 6

Low-Intensity Conflict: The Soviet Response

Roger Hamburg

Critics and supporters of the proposed SALT II agreement in the United States and Western Europe have agreed that, whatever the final outcome of the treaty debate, the increasing Soviet presence and projection of military power will pose mounting problems for policy makers.

Shortly before and after the Cuban missile crisis, the Soviets began to construct a network of base, overflight, and mutual-support arrangements, as well as greatly increasing their ability to project payback abroad. This was clearly in evidence in the 1967 Arab-Israeli War, the Nigerian Civil War, the October 1973 Arab-Israeli War, and the Angolan War of 1975. There has also been impressive growth in the Soviet merchant marine since the early 1960s, and even an enhanced Soviet fishing fleet plays a role in communications and intelligence.[1]

The enhancement of naval strength reflected a post-Khrushchev consensus that the Soviet Union needed a wider range of capabilities to counter perceived U.S. willingness to suppress "national liberation movements" in the Third World, as revealed in Vietnam. It also sought to project a Soviet military presence in the Middle East, Africa, and the Indian Ocean as a form of "naval diplomacy" to supplement attempts to build Soviet diplomatic influence in these areas.[2]

Recently, when evidence of a Soviet combat brigade in Cuba was discovered, it was revealed that the Soviets maintained a naval and air capability for transporting, supplying, and rotating large numbers of Cuban troops to various countries, along with military transports able to deliver troops and supplies throughout the Caribbean. Some of these were used to transport military cargo to Costa Rica for the Sandinista guerrillas fighting in Nicaragua.[3]

Why has the Soviet deployment capability increased? That is, what motives, internal and external, may have impelled the Soviet moves? What is Soviet declaratory policy on the use of such forces? Can any general principles be derived from the past record of actual Soviet deployments, as distinguished from verbal statements on the potential use of such forces? Finally, what conflicting considerations are likely to govern the presence and deployment of such forces in the future?

Soviet Theory on Military Force

Soviet theory argues that strategy is always dictated by political objectives and that conflict and coercion, though not military force per se, are fundamental and pervasive in international affairs. The objective factors of power, such as size, population, social structure, and productive processes, are supplemented by subjective elements such as morale, will, timing, opportunities, and an ability to outwit and outthink a potential enemy rather than simply engaging in the ultimate test of combat.[4]

Military power, in the Soviet view, has constrained U.S. assertiveness, for example during the 1973 Middle East war. Its very existence as a force in being inhibits U.S. options. Acceptable security, to Soviet planners, entails more than equivalence. It includes a healthy margin of de facto strategic advantage. SALT, detente, and the "changing correlation of forces" in the world are all a result of the new Soviet posture of strategic and conventional equality with the United States. Foreign Minister Gromyko has remarked, for example, that "the present marked preponderance of the forces of peace and progress gives them the opportunity to lay down the direction of international policies." Furthermore, the "Soviet people have the right to have their say in the solution of any question concerning the maintenance of international peace—due to the Soviet Union's reputation as a great power." In a crisis, however far removed the area may be from the Soviet Union, "its reaction is to be expected in all capitals of the world."[5]

Internal considerations present a mixed picture. Although the buildup of military forces has been accompanied by economic growth and rising living standards, this may not be the case in the future. Even so, the Soviet practice has traditionally sought to emphasize the capacity of the economy to produce military power as a desirable end in itself, not a regrettable necessity in an insecure and threatening world. Moreover, because military and political leaders share an interest in internal discipline, suppression of dissidence, and large armed forces and deployments (usually excluding large-scale use in "no-win" wars), military forces are an instrument of national legitimation, a source of pride to Soviet citizens. Whether this visceral patriotism would survive a prolonged test of combat or substitute for the long-term capacity of the economy to produce high growth rates, enhanced capital investment, and improved quantity and quality of consumer goods is debatable. Nevertheless, the ubiquitous Soviet military presence at home, in tandem with the Soviet cult of World War II memorabilia, combines domestic fear of war with pride at the forces that presumably give the Soviet Union international respect and prevent future conflicts.[6]

Soviet Declaratory Policy

V. M. Kulish, in a widely quoted multiauthor work that is a major statement of Soviet doctrine on the use of force in international relations, avers that a state's military might must be developed in ways that do not conflict with the country's economic, political, social, and cultural life, and are congruent with the state's foreign political objectives and the prevailing international situation. War is a very dangerous means to further the ends of policy, and military threats can bring a reaction from domestic and international forces the consequences of which are impossible to anticipate when involving capitalist and socialist systems. Even a momentary advantage in one weapon or military force may be neutralized by another state, which may exploit a situation elsewhere in the world that would negate the advantage. Nor can political strategic superiority as such be expressed in simple quantitative terms, even though such terms are necessary for purposes of analysis.

The United States has a broad strategic presence and impressive strategic military forces but the presence of such mobility and the ability to use it successfully are not synonymous. The American experience in Vietnam demonstrates this.[7]

The Soviet Union, to oppose "imperialist aspirations on a world wide scale must attach great importance to a Soviet military presence in various parts of the world. Because the Soviet Union has historical, economic, and geographic peculiarities distinct from those of the USA, it will not have to maintain a military presence in remote parts of the world." But to prevent local wars and support forces fighting against "internal reaction and imperialist intervention," the Soviet Union "may require mobile and well trained and well equipped armed forces." In some situations "the very knowledge of a Soviet military presence in an area in which a conflict situation is developing may serve to restrain the imperialists and local reaction, prevent them from dealing out violence to the local populace, and eliminate a threat to overall peace and international society." Such a role is played by the Soviet navy in the Mediterranean Sea. The Soviet Union may have to restrain "the aggressive acts of imperialism. This may require an expansion of Soviet military presence and military assistance, a "very important factor in international relations." [8]

Marshall Grechko, while Minister of Defense, insisted that Soviet armed forces would not be used merely for the defense of the "Motherland and the other socialist countries," but should be prepared to resist "imperialist aggression" in "whatever distant region of our planet" in which it appears.[9] Nor is it necessary for Soviet forces to be superior in all respects to a potential opponent. This is particularly germane when deploying Soviet forces in a maritime environment, where naval units overall are inferior to the U.S. fleet. As Admiral Gorshkov has observed, a naval force has "universality, mobility, and the capability of concentrating shock power, which can be used not only in the sphere of struggle with a naval opponent, but in the sphere of operation of other kinds of armed forces. The final criterion of operations becomes, not quantity but the quality of the weapons carrier, the sum power of military capabilities concentrated in it." This can be accomplished without large numbers of ships or planes. One must "concentrate forces necessary for military success and disperse the defensive efforts of the enemy in many directions." Surprise is particularly critical, for it would "deprive the enemy of the potential of responding to the actions of the other side."[10]

The likely locus of such efforts would be in the Asian-African-Latin American areas where the usual Soviet advantages of mass and continental location would not be present. It is to this regional context that I will now turn, with subsequent references to the more escalation-prone European and Chinese theaters where appropriate.

Soviet doctrine contends that there are four kinds of wars in which socialists may participate. One would involve the defense of the homeland; second, and closely related, in the defense of other socialist countries against external aggression. Related to the latter is the preservation of the gains of socialism if they are threatened from within in other socialist countries (Czechoslovakia in 1968 and, by implication, periodic Soviet threats against China). It is the last contingency, that of repelling imperialist aggression against countries "of socialist and other friendly countries" that is the most interesting and ambiguous.[11]

The Soviets have acquired a strong but not unassailable position in supporting various Marxist regimes in Afghanistan with an increasing commitment of their own forces. They have consolidated their influence in the People's Democratic Republic of Yemen (South Yemen) with Cuban and East German assistance. Cuban proxies were instrumental in helping Ethopia repel

Somalia in the Ogaden. In this instance the Mengistu regime learned the military advantages of Soviet arms and advice. This position enabled them to exert pressure on Somalia, Egypt, and possibly Saudi Arabia. The Soviets have also assisted Libya with large quantities of arms. The Libyans have used these in policies directed against Sudan, Egypt, Israel, and other countries. The Soviets have not objected. There is an enhanced Soviet presence in the Indian Ocean. Heavy Soviet logistical support of Vietnam in its struggle against Cambodia (a Chinese client state) is well known.[12]

Boris Ponomarev, a candidate member of the Soviet Politburo and Central Committee Secretary, provides a distinct justification for such activity. Soviet force to defend such states is "no vice because it safeguards the peace and reduces the military danger." In the 1970s Vietnam was unified under socialist auspices, the peoples of Laos "stood on the path of socialism," and the "socialist orientation" of Angola, Ethiopia, Mozambique, Afghanistan, South Yemen, and other countries was proclaimed. States of a "socialist orientation" are composed of "revolutionary democrats" who have a tendency to be gradually transformed "into the vanguard organization of fighters for socialism with a program, based on scientific socialism, on Marxism-Leninism." "Imperialism" sees a threat in these countries, and threatens them with "acute pressure, blackmail, diversions and even military intervention." In such a situation the Soviet Union renders assistance to these countries, but only at the request of the legal government of liberated states. It does not use them to force a military presence or intervene in internal affairs. The very presence of the world socialist system "restricts the possibilities of imperialism resorting to the open export of counterrevolution" against such states.[13]

Soviet Experience in Deploying Military Force

Soviet use of force has been prudent and cautious, even in the case of Eastern Europe. In Hungary and Czechoslovakia, for example, there were signs of hesitation and indecision.[14] In the early postwar period, despite heated rhetoric, Soviet allies outside Eastern Europe did not receive direct support from Soviet armed forces; the Soviet role in Korea was cautious, not involving direct interference in American naval operations. No Soviet volunteers were promised to Cuba during the missile crisis. The Soviets did not run risks on Castro's behalf. Soviet assistance to the North Vietnamese armed forces, as distinguished from air defense, tended to accelerate but not to include ground forces—or, apparently encouragement of major North Vietnamese offensives in the south—until after U.S. ground forces were largely withdrawn and the risk of reescalation by U.S. forces slight. The Soviet naval deployment off North Korea in the aftermath of the *Pueblo* incident was largely symbolic, and occurred only after it was clear that the United States planned no direct retaliation against North Korea.

Soviet Third World allies received scant support beyond rhetoric until the late 1960s. Relevant situations include the Suez Canal crisis (1956), Jordan (1957), Syria (1957), Lebanon (1958), the Congo (1960 and 1964), Cuba (1961) and Laos (1961–62). The reasons included a strong U.S. stance, Soviet strategic inferiority vis-à-vis the United States, and the absence of Soviet conventional power in areas noncontiguous to the USSR. Soviet deployments were often accomplished after the crisis had peaked, as in the Syrian crisis of August 1957.

In the late 1960s the view that local wars could be influenced by the superpowers without direct Soviet-American conflict seemed to gain credence. In the June 1967 Middle East crisis, for example, the Soviets were willing to make a serious combat deployment in an area somewhat distant from the USSR to counter a major U.S. military presence. Soviet airmen began to fight in the Yemen in the late 1960s; Soviet advisers appeared in Sudan and Egypt in 1971 and in Iraq in 1974. Soviet pilots engaged Israeli aircraft in 1970–71. Soviet amphibious ships transported Moroccan troops to Israel in 1973. The Soviets established a naval presence off West Africa in November 1970 to deter a Portugese military action directed at Guinea-Bissau. The Soviet Union sought to support clients, to demonstrate it was militarily present in the region, but not to provoke a major military crisis.

Soviet naval deployments in West Africa would seem to follow Admiral Gorshkov's dicta that naval forces could "vividly demonstrate the economic and military might of a country beyond its borders," "suddenly appear close to the shores of different countries, to support friendly states"and "exert pressure on potential enemies without the direct employment of weaponry."

In the October 1973 crisis in the Middle East the Soviets did not threaten military action against the United States or Israel proper, but did appear ready to deploy ground forces to save the Egyptian army and Sadat's regime—a firm commitment to an ally involving a higher degree of risk. The Soviet Union began an arms airlift to the Arabs before the U.S. airlift to Israel and sent amphibious assault ships to the Mediterranean for the first time. A Soviet freighter that may have carried nuclear warheads for Egyptian SCUD missiles (or less apocalyptically, neutron-emitting material) entered the port of Alexandria. Even here, however, the Egyptian offensive across the Suez Canal had been indirectly countenanced by the U.S. refusal to guarantee Israel's post-1967 boundaries: the United States too did not want to see Sadat's regime overthrown. Soviet threats were not made against pre-1967 Israeli boundaries, and escalated only after it appeared that a total Egyptian defeat might be imminent.

Aside from the continuing intervention in Afghanistan, contiguous to Soviet territory and somewhat remote from American interests (although a massive Soviet deployment might threaten U.S. allies in East Asia and have a deleterious effect on overall Soviet-American relations), the major Soviet deployments with advisers and combat proxies have been in Angola and Ethiopia. In the Angolan crisis, a previous South African intervention provided a regional justification for massive Soviet logistical and Cuban combat support for the Soviet-backed MPLA—a situation offering easy pickings. In Ethiopia the Soviets risked little. They escalated slowly, and the Somalians received no practical Western support. Nor is Soviet and Cuban support against the Eritrean rebels likely to lead to spectacular results or major Western counterintervention.[15]

Soviet gains in the Third World have depended on a continued identity of interests and an ability to harmonize strategies to achieve mutual objectives. Such an identity of interests over time is rare, as the Soviets discovered in Egypt. When a government was insecure and isolated from other sources of support, when the Soviets helped a regime retain power or could, at least in regional eyes, appear to be helping a legal government that requested it (for example, the MPLA in Angola in 1975, which occupied the capital), the Soviets were successful. The Soviets used violence against China but did not seize and hold Chinese territory, did not make deep penetrations, and limited their engagement. In both the Czechoslovakian intervention in 1968 and in China, uses of force were preceded by lesser degrees of coercion along with diplomacy. Concern over possible U.S. involvement resulted in Soviet circumspection.

In the use of military power in the Third World, the Soviets have been able to minimize danger to their interests while for the most part using their capabilities cautiously and well. They were strategically cautious, used good timing, and preferred naval pressure, Cuban proxies, and covert air assistance and logistical support to the use of their own forces. Rather than issuing ultimatums, they preferred to move swiftly and decisively to create *faits accomplis*, especially where the risk of American intervention could be short-circuited by such speed and any strong *post hoc* American reaction would be limited.

The Soviets have military capabilities that can prevent an ally from being weakened. These are accompanied by deft timing and offers of assistance to counter either a U.S. friend or another nation where the West has economic, military, or political interests. The Angolan and Ethiopian interventions are examples.

Soviet leaders have probed, but the prospect of an advantage has not overridden fear that a crisis could lead to war with the United States. They may even stand by and allow an ally to be punished if the punishment is limited in severity and time frame, and no attempt is made to seize territory or overthrow the ally. Clearly, American behavior in the bombing campaign against North Vietnam, especially in the wake of the North Vietnamese offensive of 1971, revealed Soviet caution but also an American unwillingness to push its offensive actions beyond a certain point. Even when the United States was clearly strategically superior to the Soviet Union, it did not overthrow a Soviet client or deny its sovereignty. Soviet probing has been an almost irresistible temptation when the United States has shown a lack of willingness to become involved rather than prudently trying to keep the risks of confrontation with the Soviet Union minimal.

The Soviets have also been concerned about their long-term relationship with the United States, even if the immediate risks of confrontation were rather low. The wish to avoid pushing the United States or its NATO allies into augmented military buildups or diplomacy adverse to Soviet interests has been a constraint on Soviet political-military behavior. The recurring Soviet insistence that their military augmentation is no threat (as they put it, the "so-called Soviet military threat") is not only an attempt to allay Western suspicions when the Soviets take a particular action or build up forces; it also reflects real concern over an exaggerated Western response to what in Soviet eyes may be a mere tactical move or maneuver in a never-ending struggle. The same could be said concerning Soviet sensitivity to local receptivity to a Soviet and/or proxy presence; that is, the long-term effect on a particular area may, at times, counsel caution even when the Soviets are momentarily tactically successful. This seems to be the pattern in Africa after the Angolan involvement; probe, absorption, concern for adverse Western or regional response, counterprobe, and so on. The Soviet record on this is, however, a mixed one. A mere presence, however adroitly or cautiously used, can itself be of concern to regional and outside powers, particularly when the needs of the Soviet and client state diverge, as in the Egyptian case.[16]

Soviet use of naval forces in the manner suggested by Admiral Gorshkov, referred to above, offers several attractions. It is easier to deploy naval forces as a demonstration of resolve and support for a client state without the often irreversible signaling of commitment that deployment of ground forces entails. Naval forces, unlike air power, need not be used in offensive action. Although deployment of Soviet air forces can sometimes be an effective way to signal commitment, a fleet can be used in a show of diplomatic support in noncrisis times, and the line between this and crisis behavior is sometimes difficult to perceive. Opposing forces can be warned without necessarily being unduly provoked, especially if the cost of ac-quiescense to a Soviet-supported client is smaller than the hypothetical loss from unsuccessful resistance.

In such "coercive negotiations" relative force capabilities are one factor, of course, but so are the values at stake to the respective patrons. Generally, the power valuing the interest more and demonstrating this may have an edge of will in a political-military confrontation. There is also the "fact of possession"—the side in possession of the interest when a crisis begins ought to be in a stronger position than the side opposing it. There is an "inertia of the status quo." If the opposing superpower is *not* committed to the status quo, as the United States was not when Soviet naval forces protected Guinea-Bissau from attack by Portuguese forces in 1970, a superpower may use its own forces to make strategic gain for itself or a client. It may, in other instances, not be able to prevent a client's defeat but may be able to limit the client's losses. Soviet naval deployments and threats of greater intervention achieved this during the October 1973 (Arab-Israeli) war when the United States clearly signaled potential involvement. U.S. capabilities, though important, did not prevent Soviet use of coercive diplomacy even when there was overall U.S. superiority and U.S. interests were involved.

Admiral Gorshkov's words, quoted above, come to mind when the pattern of Soviet forward naval deployments reveals that rather than maintaining a force of constant size in a region, the Soviets make the most of limited forces. The Soviets use a small core in forward deployment, but augment it during crisis where it can be most effective politically. The Soviets apparently employ the notion that target audiences, both regional and outside the immediate area, are "more attentive to change than continuity." By moving forces from area to area, they "translate the physical presence of their ships into a psychological presence in the minds of the region's decision makers."

The June war of 1967, the Jordanian crisis of 1970, and the October war of 1973 were not war-related in the sense of events that might have threatened the USSR directly. Instead, Soviet moves there were attuned to local events, potential threats to Soviet communications, and U.S. Sixth Fleet maneuvers. Soviet naval force deployments in crisis reveal the use of systems that would be "irrelevant if kept in home waters" and probably inadequate for a wartime engagement with U.S. forces.[17]

If a Soviet client is struggling against a regional enemy or confronted with an internal threat, arms and/or the dispatch of Soviet or, more likely, proxy forces can be very valuable. Soviet naval and other military power in the cause of clients threatened by Israel or others helps the client deter further threats and facilitates the restoration of a balance, however tenuous. Either through manipulating an existing presence or augmenting a presence the Soviets have demonstrated their concern even where their interests might be put in jeopardy. Yet as far as is known, in no Third World crisis did the Soviets increase the readiness of strategic or conventional forces other than those such as air and naval units to be used in the immediate crisis theater.

This apparently reflected a Soviet desire to keep the crisis localized and at the conventional level. Both the Soviet Union and the United States have been equally tough and equally cautious, but neither display the same feature at the same time. The patron defending the status quo had greater credibility than that of a client seizing an interest or threatening the status quo. A dangerous pattern ensues in a crisis. The first patron defends its interest or client against the other side's client or interest. The second client reacts to defend its client against the other patron. The first patron's show of force is offset somewhat by the second patron's "limiting" show of force, which confines the threat to its client to defensive risks. The Soviets may challenge the status quo, but hesitate if they confront an armed opponent that supported the particular status quo in the past and seems to signal continued commitment. If both superpowers are committed (as was not the case in Guinea-Bissau in 1970 or Angola in 1975), forward positioning of forces seems not so much to maximize gains but to minimize losses. To overcome the status quo without taking unacceptable risks, means other than the direct deployment of Soviet forces or proxies come into play—subversion or possibly arms aid.

Although there is cause for some relief in the Soviet reluctance to use force indiscriminately to advance particular interests such a relatively cautious policy still has its dangers for U.S. interests. Not every status quo is morally acceptable, and change may be necessary. U.S. support of unjust status quos, like that of southern Africa, either by design or as a result of becoming trapped in a diplomatic cul de sac may provide the Soviet Union with openings for "opportunely timed offers of support" to impatient states and movements. Though complete victory—that is, all-out support for Soviet-assisted clients to overthrow a status quo totally—is unlikely in such a case, large-scale action may be encouraged by Soviet support if a client knows that a failed offensive would not risk the loss of everything. Soviet-assisted clients may know that for reasons of prudence the Soviet Union may not use its armed forces or proxies to help them make other than limited gains. They also know that Soviet support may insure that their losses are acceptable.[18]

Soviet intervention in the future is likely if there is a possibility of a quick victory, the United States and/or other potential adversaries are unlikely to resist forcibly, the location of the area involved is strategic to the USSR or to Western or Chinese interests the USSR seeks to undermine, and the host country can pay for its needs. Such intervention must also be acceptable to neighboring countries.[19]

But there are other possibilities because it cannot be forgotten that from the point of view of the leaders of any state, even that of a Soviet leadership committed to a progressive change of the status quo, intervention can be truly intended as defensive. A military move may be undertaken to prevent an intolerable situation from developing, or upsetting one, already developed, that carries unacceptable consequences for the potential intervening power. Soviet moves in the Third World, with few exceptions, do not involve these considerations: or they are of a mixed character, such as the successful attempt to support governments "tending toward a socialist orientation," in Ponomarev's words, quoted above. For example: in Afghanistan, prevention of a successful counterattack led by Moslem fundamentalists, with long-term implications for Soviet domestic security because of possible effects on the Soviet demographic-cultural balance in Central Asia, is mingled with attempts to exert pressure on states such as Pakistan or even India. But in many other Third World crisis situations vital Soviet security interests are not involved. The Soviets may gain a little, and support of their clients and their military power in being probably guarantees that they will not lose very much.

However, in three critical areas of Soviet concern—Western Europe, the Chinese border, and Eastern Europe—different, more pressing considerations are involved. For example, though it is unlikely, the Soviets might try to seize a portion of West Germany in a short period—and Soviet-Warsaw Pact force deployments are apparently designed, in part, with this objective in mind.[20] Such an invasion would follow some development of extreme nationalism in West Germany, or a domestic breakdown there in which Soviet-backed factions were not the beneficiary. Soviet fears of West German "revanchism," although often manipulated for political purposes in Eastern Europe and among the Soviet population, are real enough to a people living with the World War II experience. Western European audiences might also have long memories, and might be receptive to a statement of goals that followed achievement of limited military objectives with a call for cease-fire negotiations. Soviet goals might include excluding unacceptable groups from West Germany and demilitarizing and neutralizing it. Before such a dangerous move, however, the Soviets might issue increasingly serious warnings, increase deployments in East Germany, and have units mass or exercise on the West German border. Similar political-military action, if not actual force, might be used against Finland if it renounced its precariously achieved neutrality and its present arrangement with the Soviet Union.

In Eastern Europe the Hungarian and Czechoslovakian interventions demonstrate that if the Soviet leaders thought a non-Marxist-Leninist or neutralist government was about to take power or that the dissident nation's armed forces could not be persuaded to fight, Soviet intervention would be likely. Such developments could be interpreted as security threats, but even here Soviet military units would more likely be used to support Eastern European political and military leaders who were timorous about suppressing popular disorder or dissidence threatening the states. Even here, however, Soviet advice might consist of counseling firmness against possible insurrection coupled with timely concessions to limit the extent and scope of internal dissidence. Soviet policy toward Poland in 1970 concerning the rescinding of food price increases demonstrates this. The post-Tito succession in Yugoslavia provides opportunities and some danger for Soviet interests. If the Soviet leadership were not convinced that a post-Tito leadership would be weak, non-Communist, or depart from neutrality, and if they felt the Yugoslavs would resist Soviet intervention or even political-military pressure (as they did in 1948), they would be cautious and await events.

In the case of the Sino-Soviet border, current talks are apparently aimed not so much at resolving the crisis but at keeping it at a low point of potential confrontation or escalation. China might have to increase its forces and issue demands and threats to prompt Soviet action. If China issued an ultimatum over the "lost" territories the Soviets held, it would risk a preemptive nuclear strike like the one purportedly threatened in 1969. More probable, however, would be Soviet threats, augmented border forces, military demonstrations, and even limited military "lessons" like that of the spring of 1969.[21] All these of course carry the risks of even greater open-ended escalation, given the ideological and national antagonism of these powers.

Soviet-American Relations and Low-Intensity Soviet Conflict Behavior

Soviet "Americanists," in analyzing American foreign policy doctrine and behavior, know that the Vietnam war showed that American deployment of military power did not necessarily bring corresponding political influence in its train. Nevertheless, they do not doubt the ultimate strength and tenacity of the American adversary, even if American power may not be applied properly, adroitly, or judiciously in particular instances. Fear of overall American capabilities, particularly when combined with statements of American commitment and the unpredictable effect of American domestic politics on the likelihood of American military intervention, is noted in Soviet commentary.[22]

Soviet concern about uncontrolled escalation reflects this fear. An article in a Soviet "Americanist" journal indicates such concern. A. A. Kovalev, in criticizing Herman Kahn's "escalation ladder," observes that various post-World War II crises demonstrate the risk with which direct application of force is connected. Even indirect covert assistance in the form of weapons and specialists carries risks. Capitalist countries engaging in such indirect aid "find themselves moving into direct involvement as in Vietnam." Attempts to apply force "misfire," and a "positions of strength" doctrine is a "fiasco," whether the strength is directly or indirectly applied.

A rational application of force implies more than simply a proportionality of goals and means in a particular country or region. It must also take into account how relations with other countries will be affected—that is, states not taking part in the conflict and the possibility of escalation, the conflict becoming nuclear. A political demonstration of force, intervention in a conflict or direct use of force may be costly for the state. Witness the oil embargo and energy crisis after the United States supported the Israelis in the October 1973 Middle East War.

Lest all this be seen as a one-way ordinance directed against the West allowing impunity for Soviet moves of the kind described in this paper, Kovalev implies that Soviet actions can also be dangerous. The emphasis must be prevention of crisis, or "prophylaxis" for the "chain of existing contradictions" can grow and acquire a dangerous tone. The risk of confrontation and a crisis situation arising decreases and the possibility of such confrontations being resolved increases, insofar as the "mechanism for the practical implementation of detente" is created. This includes bilateral and multilateral negotiations, especially at the highest level. Kovalev calls for using available means for this, as well as adding new means that have not yet been utilized.

Deescalation of conflict must be stressed. Some criteria must be desired to determine the scope of danger of a particular crisis for the preservation of general peace. The involvement or noninvolvement of the United States, USSR or other nuclear powers that are permanent members of the Security Council is more than a "formal sign" of such criteria. It is "a very important indication of the gravity and depth of a particular conflict." Clearly, "the more powerful and dangerous the mainsprings, which have been engendered and which are impelling events dangerous for the course of peace and their spread, the greater the number of countries affected directly or indirectly, particularly vital interests, the more acute, the more difficult, the more slowly it [the conflict] is subjected to resolution and settlement."[23]

Kovalev contends that the five parameters of conflict are: (1) the level of conflict between the USSR and the United States, with the involvement of one of these two countries or some other member of the Security Council; (2) the social-political structure of the conflict; (3) the type of conflict (whether nuclear or "classical"); (4) the sphere of conflict; security, foreign policy, economics, the social area and the ideology; and (5) whether the confrontation is direct or indirect.[24]

It is possible to draw broader conclusions from what appears to be a Soviet attempt explicitly to sketch out in rudimentary form "ground rules" for competition and escalation in the Soviet-American relationship. Alexander George, in a paper delivered at the International Political Science meeting in Moscow, has observed that if the stakes are high enough a highly motivated action can challenge the status quo at an acceptable risk, even in the face of deterrence. Soviet behavior in some instances, as outlined above, demonstrates this. Capabilities and overall deterrence are but one element in a conflict situation. Each has its own time and space frame, interactions of superpowers and client states, and differing levels of risk. Deterrence used to bolster an "inept, misguided, dangerous foreign policy" is unreliable in avoiding crisis and ought to be supplemented by a "U.S.-S.U. crisis prevention regime." Like Kovalev, George contends that the two powers must move beyond crisis management to crisis prevention. Citing some of the agreements concluded at the 1972 summit, especially these designed to prevent the outbreak of nuclear war, George sketches out a set of rough criteria for crisis prevention beyond what Kovalev mentioned. Agreement on procedures to be followed to avoid the development of crisis, though useful, is insufficient. It will be necessary to develop norms and understandings in foreign policy. Limitation of behavior in Third World competition, though vital, must be supplemented by efforts to limit the stakes of the competition. Some limitations of objectives must also be accomplished. In Third World areas, objectives of second- or third-rate importance must be distinguished from vital interests. One side must not push for modest advantages in ways that would damage or threaten important national interests of the other side. Both sides should avoid the temptation to pursue marginal advantages at each other's expense. Even on less than vital issues, these can have undesirable side effects that may jeopardize the overall Soviet-American relationship. Each side must communicate its private assessment of its interests to the other side. This communication has seldom taken place, especially in the often cumbersome U.S. foreign-policy bureaucracy where with so many points of contact and conflict, consensus or agreement on such interests is painfully difficult to reach. Though more centralized, the Soviet bureaucracy also offers problems in this connection.

The two sides should agree on respective "bedrock interests," the possibility of some agreement on mutual disengagement for the area, restraints each side will observe in the interests of crisis prevention: they should provide opportunities to reassess the situation periodically and provide modification of any change in policy towards the area in question. Mutual clarification of intentions at the onset of crisis or indications that a crisis may be about to erupt may help to prevent great-power involvement.[25]

The two powers may have behaved unilaterally in crisis situations in ways that tacitly amounted to "rules of accommodation" that averted a direct clash in ground-combat or naval engagements. But the possibility of continuing to do so in the future is uncertain, and a direct clash looms as a far from remote contingency. The Third World is a dangerous, unstable area and state of mind, with regional rivalry, development crises, and domestic struggles for seizing and retaining legitimacy that can easily draw in one power or both. Nor can Third World clients be easily "disciplined" or subjected to great-power "management." Both the United States and the Soviet Union have appeared at times to be spectators at a play, where each can shout instructions but neither can be fully confident that it can control the performance. Many of the potential crises of the 1980s, especially energy matters, concern and threaten both powers: their ability to influence these crises is limited, but the chances of a clash over them is great.

It is perhaps unrealistic, and even a bit dangerous, to conceive of a Soviet-American condominium, a mutual parcelling out of influence like that of Tordesillas in 1493 between Spain and Portugal. The ideological and nationalistic forces on both sides make that difficult—particularly the Leninist legacy that the Soviet Union has a national affinity for Third World claims against the "imperialists." It is also unrealistic and unwise to expect either power to totally stay out of the other's core area of concern if that signifies total ideological, diplomatic, and economic disengagement. The United States and the USSR are more than simply states; they are rival fledgling world orders, and out of this may yet come a useful nonmilitary competition despite their permanent ideological incompatibility. In addition, neither power is likely to be willing to maintain a status quo or reestablish a previous status quo at the expense of former allies and clients—one possible require-ment of a condominium.[26]

But a mere working out of rules of disengagement may be too sterile, may assume too much about the possibilities of rational behavior in dealing with volatile situations and personalities in Third World areas. The temptation to intervene to steal a march on a rival—or the fear of leaving an area open, unchallenged to a rival if one doesn't intervene—is not easily allayed by preexisting rules. This is particularly true when internal bureaucratic momen-tum, especially in the Soviet case, may impel the use of a capability that has been developed by dint of great financial exertion and persistent lobbying.

Recently, both Western and Soviet scholars have discussed constraints that may describe a set of circumstances that *may* compel a greater degree of great-power forbearance and even cooperation than has heretofore been the case. The growing needs of economic assistance and political development in the Third World, and the increasingly close linkage between Western industralized nations, developing countries, and possibly socialist countries on the energy question have led to a stress on the notion of "interdepen-dence." Ultimately, there might be a community of fate between the United States and the Soviet Union greater than the simple desire to avoid a nuclear war that might develop by ascending steps up the escalation ladder.

"International interdependence" is the term increasingly stressed by specialists in various parts of the world to describe this linkage. It has both conflictive and cooperative elements in the life of states. Basically, it signifies "that the life of societies as organized in sovereign states becomes more or less conditioned by the life of other societies." Governmental policies increasingly affect one another, and mutual sensitivity and a sense of vulnerability increase as the barriers that used to insulate national economies from each other collapse. Societies are more sensitive to each other in areas formerly considered domestic, states find it more difficult to maintain policy coherence, and there is a possibility of linkages between issues. Force, though still available and useful in certain contingencies, carries greater costs even if used successfully. A threat to use force in a particular area may drive societies that are involved so far apart that they "cancel cooperative projects and withdraw from mutual cooperation in other fields." States that use the kind of coercive bargaining described in this essay must seek to prevent the development of total nation-to-nation or coalition-to-coalition hostility.[27]

Soviet ambivalence on this question is understandable, and is reflected in Soviet statements and actions. By admitting even the *possibility* of the integration of the socialist states into the world economy, they imply that the Soviet Union may be adjusting gradually to an international environment that is neither much to its liking nor within its control. The kinds of adjustments implied by Kovalev, and Soviet actions in implementing coercive diplomacy in recent years, do not involve basic economic-system changes nor any reconciliation with the objectionable features of such an environment. Détente in this manner makes preferred changes easier, and may offer the safest climate to effectuate them despite its limitations.

But to join in the international economic order and try to reshape it is an entirely different matter because of the basic Soviet assumption that the prevailing order exists "by and for the major capitalist powers." Usually, Soviet writers insist that the Soviet Union can insulate itself from the worst effects of the world capitalist economic system and offer trading opportunities to others on the outside, but in no way is it "responsible for nor capable of reforming the injustices of the global economic order." Arms-control agreements and tacit rules of engagement in the Third World or elsewhere mean only a partial moderation of means. Negotiating a new economic order may involve "conceding it a large degree of legitimacy." The Soviet leadership has sought to draw what it could from that order while still insulating its economy and that of Eastern Europe from it. But the logic of its growing participation in the world economy makes it difficult for it to "forever imagine a growing participation in the intercourse of the system and a continued divorce from that system's structure and rule making." How can it reconcile its stake in the international economic order with its opposition to it, and how can it accommodate particular Soviet interests by involvement in that order without serving that order's interests?[28]

The Soviets lack a comprehensive notion of international economic reform. They define their objectives narrowly but in "unimaginative and constrained terms," with major emphasis on the effect, however marginal, they may have on the socialist countries. The Soviets insist on their alliance with the demands of the south against the developed countries and seek to avoid any responsibility for the cost of a reordered world economy. The Soviets appear less concerned about delivering the less developed nations from the injustices of the old order than they are about the opportunity to capitalize on the claims of these nations to reinforce their own.

It is perhaps better from a Soviet point of view to concentrate on political, economic, and military dimensions of East-West relations than on situations in which they are at a disadvantage: better to take the reflex action of stressing conflict, however muted, in the Third World, where the military instruments and regional ideological consanguinity are present. Soviet assistance to Third World countries in 1978, for instance, was tied to large industrial projects, to the public sector (with maximum connection with a push toward "socialism"), and to arms transfers. It ignored any idea of a newer, more complex approach to development. The Soviet Union continues to ignore Third World demands for more concessional assistance, and there were few signs of any change in this attitude. Soviet reactions to a shifting international economic environment remain "instinctive and reflective, not plotted and not closely conceptualized." Soviet objectives, both intermediate and long-term, remain "rudimentary, unsystematic, even obscure, and devoid of vigor."[29]

Ultimately, for conflicts among developing nations to leave the international system unruffled, the powers must exercise restraint. But if these nations have the economic and military support of the great powers, economic interdependence, which may exert considerable influence on conflicts among Western industrial nations, "holds little prospect for similar moderation of United States-Soviet rivalries in contested regions."[30] If the involvement is muted and constrained by fear of escalation, the notion of evolving parallel, not necessarily antithetical schemes of world economic development and interaction seems fraught with unresolveable contradictions.

Examinations of Soviet attitudes toward the American energy dilemma reveal the same ambivalence. For example, castigating alleged American profligacy and "monopoly capitalism," and justifying the actions of oil-producing states which resulted in embargoes and higher prices for the American consumer, the Soviets realized that the crisis, combined with Soviet support of the Arab states, strengthened U.S. opponents of détente. They continued to deliver oil to Western markets to obtain hard currency for their own import needs from the West. The strain to meet current oil-production demands internally and the desire to continue detente may have led to the statement that "worldwide cooperation, especially between the United States and the Soviet Union, is needed to avoid any worldwide energy shortage—a new system of international economic cooperation based on "joint action and equality." There may be fear in Moscow as well as in Washington of the eventual repercussions of the energy crisis, however tempted the Soviets may have been in supporting the oil embargo, pushing for higher oil prices, and seeking to profit generally from American discomfiture. Though stressing the greater dependence of the U.S. on imported oil, the Soviets have not been able to take full advantage of this vulnerability, particularly because the energy problem is one they themselves will undoubtedly face. This is particularly the case as Soviet domestic sources of relatively inexpensive oil become fewer, less accessible, more expensive, and more demanding of the type of technology that only Western industrialized states like the United States can provide.[31]

Valkenier has noted, in examining recent Soviet assessments of economic relations with the Third World, that there are signs that the Soviets seek not so much to replace the existing economic order as to secure more advantageous Soviet participation in it.[32] The Soviets are less likely than before to argue that Third World countries must break sharply with the capitalist countries in economic relations. Soviet commentators insist less and less that Third World states deny their resources to the West or offer them at exorbitant prices and more that they should take due regard for the interests of both commodity producers and consumers.

In an equally conciliatory manner, Brezhnev at the 25th Party Congress in 1976 referred to "global problems like raw material and energy shortages and other problems that affect each state and from which the Soviet Union could not remain aloof." There is a greater stress on foreign trade as an "important artery" in the Soviet Union's "economic organism," on buying equipment from the industrialized countries on a credit basis to develop natural resources, and to create new production for domestic consumption and export. The pattern would consist of Soviet purchases of Western products with supplies of primary materials and other goods as repayment. The industrially advanced countries would help the Soviets develop raw materials and industry. The socialist countries would in turn deal with less developed countries. The latter would produce natural resources to fuel the economies of all industrialized states, benefiting from their assistance in funds and know-how for building up local processing industries. Joint Soviet-Western ventures have begun to appear. A recent economic-cooperation agreement with West Germany, for example, provides for such ventures in Third World countries. At U.N. meetings the Soviets promote long-term industrial cooperation, especially in the extractive sector, to aid in Third World problems. At home these are justified because they supply the USSR with raw materials that are either scarce or increasingly expensive to produce at home.

In summary, Valkenier contends that there is a greater Soviet tendency to view Soviet-Third World relations as part of an interdependent global economy, and that Soviet writers argue it is "impractical and counterproductive" to cut off the West from raw-material resources or engage in other unilateral and economically subversive acts. There is a cautious willingness to jettison the assumed congruity of Soviet-Third World interests against the West. The Soviet Union sees itself as a modern industrial state that, like the West, needs to promote the extraction and processing of raw materials needed to operate its own and advanced economies. If the USSR finds it profitable to involve itself increasingly in the existing order, Moscow will seek less to subvert that order but will readjust to it so that more benefits can be derived from joining it. In addition to the domestic impact on the Soviet economy that would follow from closer intermingling with the existing order, Soviet analysts accept the notion that, like the Soviet Union, Third World states can obtain development by dealing with capitalist states. This too undermines Soviet-Third World antiimperialist unity on the economic front.

But the Soviets will continue to straddle by combining "antiimperialist sloganeering" with more extensive and profitable participation in the Third World. Soviet comments reflect this straddling position, with some seeking to introduce more effective economic relations without making radical alteration in doctrine and administrative structure, others seeking practical results to aid the Soviet economy and a third group of academic specialists. The academicians have a conservative wing that combines an "uncompromising ideological stance" with a search for economic rationality and results. Its other wing acknowledges the need for extensive readjustment activity in both institutions and practices if the Soviets are to get the necessary industrial and raw materials and hard cash.[33]

Typical of the "conservative" position is the assessment of Soviet "Americanist" A.V. Nikiforov writing in *USA*, the organ of the Institute of the USA and Canada. He cites the Western literature on interdependence, especially the difficulties of states solving their problems in isolation. The United States, he contends, seeks by this to compensate for its weakened armed position by strengthening the ties of "physical interdependence" with Western industrialized countries to reduce the possibility of their developing their own interests. This is the American answer to the strengthened economic competitive position of industrial states like those of western Europe and Japan. Because it can no longer force on them methods familiar to the United States, the U.S. government seeks to find new ways of defending its foreign economic interests, "new levers of political and economic influence."

But, he avers, Western sources admit that economic interdependence can be a source of conflict as well as cooperation between states. It is an American move to accommodate to the change in the correlation of forces in the world, especially at the end of the 1960s in relation to Western Europe and Japan. It is an attempt to overcome the class struggle with capitalist states on the basis of a supposed "common interest" in industrial development. The United States seeks to "draw in" the developing countries to the Western economic system and to "subordinate the socialist states to this system and its interests." The United States in turn not only limits but even seeks to reduce its dependence in areas, such as the importation of oil and raw materials, in which it does not have superiority.[34]

American specialists, he contends, admit that generally no economic interdependence exists between the United States and the USSR. The small volume of economic, scientific, and other ties demonstrates this. Americans recognize that the balance of forces has changed in favor of socialism, but interdependence is negative but useful in drawing in the Soviet Union to global society in order to limit its ability to support a class foreign policy and gradual transformation of the social system. What is more, he insists that the Soviet Union does not need to be "drawn in" to international society because it has been and will be a member of such a society independent of United States wishes. Its foreign policy is the main factor responsible for the growing democratization of international life and United States efforts aimed at increasing political interdependence. The interests of international monopolies are incompatible with the political-economic interests of most nations. The United States, he alleges, seeks to perform the role of guarantor of the capitalist system but with unilateral advantages for itself. "As far as economic 'interdependence' is concerned, it is clear that, insofar as it exists within the capitalist system and uncontrolled development of private capitalist integration resulting in political collisions, there isn't and cannot be interdependence between socialist and capitalist countries." The socialist states must pursue their foreign economic ties to continue the development of their internal economies.[35]

Maximova's position is closer to Western themes concerning interdependence. She contends that preventing world war, insuring the availability of enough foodstuffs and other raw materials for mankind, harnessing of the world ocean, and conquering of space call for the "combined efforts of many countries." She seeks to legitimize this position by noting that Lenin did not insist that the world economy was inherent in capitalism but was a factor that could be further developed and communicated under socialism. She notes the richness of Soviet resources, the Soviet Union's industrial and scientific potential, and its need for foodstuffs and other raw materials. Furthermore, "no country, no matter how large, how developed scientifically, technologically and industrially, is able to develop fully and with optimal technical effect all the full range of its scientific research." Other countries are interested in technological and scientific links with the USSR because of its impressive scientific base and skilled personnel. Although the Soviet Union is "capable of economic self-sufficiency it does not advance it as an optimal goal." It could produce any output, but "at what price"? The USSR, large though it is, finds it unprofitable to produce an entire range of output needed to satisfy completely industrial and consumer demand. The USSR and its trading partners derive considerable economic advantages from industrial projects, productive cooperation, joint enterprises, and so on. Western economists and politicans who insist that economic cooperation between states with different social systems is to the Soviet advantage alone are wrong, as they are in their contention that such cooperation can lead to economic dependence on the USSR. Instead, such cooperation can be mutually advantageous.[36]

The Soviet Union's economic ties with the West have not made it more vulnerable to pressure, although such interaction has led to an improvement of investment and consumer goods. The Soviet Union has sought to limit its dependence on world trade and has scaled down its credit deficits accordingly in recent years. But there is a growing Soviet tendency to seek technological assistance and grain. The prospect of such assistance by the United States in the future should not be tied so much to specific actions but employed in a way that the Soviet leadership must consider in its "broader calculations."[37]

Clearly, the same doubts persist in the interdependence option as in crisis prevention. Both are vulnerable to the inherent rivalry of the Soviet-American relationship and to bureaucratic obstacles on both sides. Crisis prevention, for example, is easier for the Soviets to accept, both because it limits the need to change fundamental positions and because it recognizes the Soviet Union as a fully equal rival of the United States—a constant Soviet theme. Interdependence, on the other hand, as Nikiforov implies, puts the Soviet Union at a disadvantage. Its economic weaknesses make interdependence desirable for what it can gain, but unattractive because of the vulnerabilities it is forced to admit. It is the West that is ahead in most areas in technology, that has originated multinational corporations, and that can afford to engage in a development "race" in the Third World—not the Soviet Union. The Soviet Union is the world's "most advanced underdeveloped country."This makes Soviet commentators like Maximova vulnerable to the charge that they unwittingly promote a strategy that would make the Soviet Union a "neocolonial appendage" of the West and the United States. Furthermore, the Soviets may simply be more pressured into military action to guarantee access to energy resources, and may seek to make the Middle East, for example, a virtual protectorate.

Despite the continuing tension and rivalry in the Soviet-American relationship, low-intensity conflicts have remained low-intensity, and neither side's forces have engaged in direct combat against the other's on land or at sea. But the momentum of the rivalry is great, the Soviet tendency to derive at least marginal advantage from American difficulties and Third World radicalism greater, and the possibility that crisis prevention may fail because of miscalculation or misperception by either or both sides ever present. Whether Soviet-American interaction or low-level conflict can be put on a basis less potentially dangerous to world peace than the present one is problematic. Both sides are much affected by events and by the paradox of the Prisoner's Dilemma: cooperation is best for both sides, yet each feels the other will take advantage of its forebearance, with the result that the ensuing relationship may leave them in a poorer position than before a crisis ensued.

Nevertheless, mutual fear of escalation to nuclear war is a healthy critical reason why both sides have exercised caution in the past. Soviet strategic parity may have reduced the Soviet need for strident self-assertion, especially in the Third World, and made it more amenable to calls for "crisis prophylaxis." The volatile Third World environment, however, with its possible threats to core interests of both sides, makes intervention by either or both sides more likely.

Concern expressed in the United States at Soviet military gains and power projection abroad makes it imperative both for the United States to resist Soviet incursions abroad that threaten critical interests, and to cooperate simultaneously to lessen the dangers of escalation. Interdependence moves on a judicious *ad hoc* basis must also be applied adroitly to reduce the temptation for the Soviet Union to pursue advantages at the cost of favorable opportunities foregone in the total Soviet-American relationship. The need for such moves has never been greater. The ability to pursue such seemingly incompatible strategies simultaneously may be less than it has been, for many reasons that lie beyond the purview of this essay.

Notes

1. W. Scott Thompson, *Power Projection: A Net Assessment of US and Soviet Capabilities* (New York: National Strategy Information Center, 1978), pp. 12–13.
2. Roger Hamburg, "Soviet Perspectives on Military Intervention," in Ellen Stern, ed., *The Limits of Military Intervention* (Beverly Hills: Sage Press, Inc., 1977), p. 49.
3. Mose L. Harvey, *Soviet Combat Troops in Cuba: Implications of the Carter Solution for the USSR* (Washington, D.C.: Advanced International Studies Institute, University of Miami, 1979), pp. 29–34.
4. On these matters see Hamburg, p. 46, and Soviet sources cited there.
5. Benjamin Lambeth, "The Political Potential of Soviet Equivalence," *International Security* 4, no. 2 (Fall 1979): 33–34. The first Gromyko quote, cited by Lambeth, is from "The Peace Program in Action," *Kommunist*, no. 14, (September 1975), p. 5. For the second quote see Hamburg, pp. 50, 75.
6. For projected future difficulties in having "guns and butter" simultaneously see Joint Economic Committee, Congress of the United States, *Soviet Economy in a Time of Change* (Washington: US Government Printing Office, 10 October 1979),

I, pp. 4, 11, 12, 2, 15. For the internal political dimension see Hamburg, pp. 52, 53.

7. V. M. Kulish, *Military Force and International Relations* (Arlington, Va.: Joint Publications Research Service, 8 May 1973, JPRS58947), pp. 25, 14, 15, 23, 24, 28. The work was published under the auspices of the Institute of World Economics and International Relations of the Soviet Academy of Sciences.

8. Ibid., pp. 102, 103.

9. Andrey A. Grechko, "The Leading Role of the CPSU in Building the Army of a Developed Socialist Society," *Problems of the History of the Communist Party of the Soviet Union*, May 1974, as excerpted in *Strategic Review* III, no. 1 (Winter 1975): 88–93 and quoted in Thompson, p. 11.

10. S. Gorshkov,"Some Problems of the Naval Act"(in Russian), *Naval Collection*, no. 12 (December 1974), pp. 24, 25, 28.

11. V. F. Samoilenko, "Soviet Essence of Modern War and the Armies," paper delivered at the summer 1978 International Sociological Congress at Uppsala, Sweden, p. 15; cited in Seth Singleton, "What Are the Soviets Up To? Are They Succeeding? Regional Political Considerations and the Soviet-American Relationship," paper presented at the National Security Education Workshop, Chicago, 28 September 1979, p. 22.

12. John C. Campbell, Andrew J. Goodpaster and Brent Scowcroft, "Oil and Turmoil: Western Choices in the Middle East" (Washington: The Atlantic Council of the United States, September 1979), pp. 26, 27. See also Richard Bissell, "Soviet Use of Proxies in the Third World: The Case of Yemen," *Soviet Studies* 30, no. 1 (January 1978): 87–106.

13. B. Ponomarev, "Real Socialism and its International Significance" (in Russian), *Kommunist* 2 (January 1979): 23, 30, 32.

14. On indecisiveness in the Czech deployment see Juri Valenta, *Soviet Intervention in Czechoslovakia, 1968: Anatomy of a Decision* (Baltimore: John Hopkins University Press, 1979), esp. pp. 1–40.

15. Stephen S. Kaplan, *The Kremlin's High Card: Soviet Armed Forces as an Instrument of Defense and Foreign Policy Since the Russian Revolution*, unpublished manuscript (Washington: The Brookings Institution, 1978), 3–13, 4–6, 4–8, 4–11, 4–15, 4–22, 4–23, 5–4, 5–8, 5–15, 5–16, 5–19, 5–25, 5–28, 5–29, 5–33, 34. The Gorshkov quote is from "Navies in War and Peace," published in *Red Star Rising at Sea*, translated by Theodore A. Neely (Annapolis, Md.: United States Naval Institute Press, 1974), p. 115, cited in Kaplan, 5–28. On Soviet military policy in Vietnam, the October 1973 war in the Middle East, and the Angolan intervention, see Hamburg, pp. 60–66.

16. Stephen S. Kaplan et al., *Mailed Fist, Velvet Glove: Soviet Armed Forces as a Political Instrument*. Executive Summary sponsored by Defense Advanced Research Projects Agency (Arlington, Virginia: September 1979), pp. 10–18. The report, a summary of research conducted by a number of Western specialists on Soviet military affairs, also reveals forbearance, even in Eastern Europe where forces near Poland failed to achieve Soviet objectives by means of military pressure. In Hungary in 1956 and Czechoslovakia in 1968 discreet military pressure failed completely, and full Soviet intervention became necessary.

17. James McCornell, "The 'Rules of the Game': Superpower Coercive Diplomacy in the Third World." Paper presented to the annual convention of the International Studies Association, Toronto, March 1979, pp. 3, 7. Bradford Dismukes and James McConnell, eds., *Soviet Naval Diplomacy* (New York: Pergamon Press, 1979), paperback edition, pp. 277, 287, 292, 294.

18. Dismukes and McConnell, *Soviet Naval Diplomacy*, p. 296; idem, "Soviet Diplomacy of Force in the Third World," *Problems of Communism* 28 (January-February 1979), pp. 19, 22, 23, 24, 26, 27.
19. Singleton, p. 26.
20. Hamburg, pp. 55, 56.
21. Such measures are speculated upon by Kaplan, *The Kremlin's High Card*, 6–2, 6–4, 6–5, 6–6, 6–4.
22. See Hamburg, pp. 67–72, especially for Soviet comments on President Nixon's great severity in using force in Vietnam in some instances after a decision was made to apply it. See also the conclusions of the Soviet "moderate" camp in Morton Schwartz, *Soviet Perceptions of the United States* (Berkeley: University of California Press, 1978), 164–165.
23. A. A. Kovalev, "The Deescalation of Detente and Deescalation of Conflicts" (in Russian), *USA: Economics, Politics, Ideology* no. 4 (1979), pp. 14, 15, 18, 20, 21, 23.
24. Ibid., p. 24.
25. Alexander L. George, "Towards a US-Soviet Crisis Prevention Regime: A Proposal," Paper delivered at the Twelfth World Congress of the International Political Science Association, Moscow, 12–18, August 1979, pp 1–9.
26. For the requirements of a US- Soviet condominium and the difficulties of applying them in practice, see Alan Ned Sabrosky, "Temptation to Condominium: A Scenario for Soviet-American Relations," paper delivered at the 1979 biennial meeting of the Section on Military Studies of the International Studies Association, Pittsburgh, Pa., October 1979, pp. 3–5, esp. pp. 4–7.
27. Klaus Knorr, *The Power of Nations: The Political Economy of International Relations* (New York: Basic Books, 1975), paperback edition, p. 208. Robert O. Keohane and Joseph Nye, Jr., "Power and Interdependence," *Survival* 15, no. 4 (July/August 1973), pp. 159, 162, 163; Seyom Brown, "The Changing Essence of Power," *Foreign Affairs* 51, no. 2 (January 1973), pp. 289–90.
28. Robert Legvold, "The Soviet Role in the Restructuring of the International Economic Order," unpublished manuscript, 1977, pp. 2, 3, 4.
29. Legvold, pp. 20, 21, 28, 29, 32. Central Intelligence Agency, National Foreign Assessment Center, *Communist Aid Activities in Non-Communist Less Developed Countries* (Washington, 1978) p. 6.
30. Charles Lockhart, "Economic Issues and the Nature of Future International Conflict Activity," paper delivered at annual meeting of the Midwest Political Science Association, Chicago, 21–23 April 1977, pp. 16–17.
31. Daniel S. Papp, "International Implications of the American Energy Crisis: The Soviet View," unpublished manuscript, pp. 7, 16 (for stress on cooperation with other nations, especially the USA, see pp. 16, 17, 19, 20, 24, 25, 26, 27). See also Hedija H. Hravalis, John P. Young, Ronald G. Oechsler, and Deborah A. Lamb, "Soviet Exports to the Industrialized West: Performance and Prospects," in Soviet Economic Committee, *Soviet Economy in a Time of Change*, pp. 2, 418, 419; and Tyrus W. Cobb, "The Soviet Energy Dilemma," *Orbis* 23, no. 2. (Summer 1979), esp. pp. 355–357, 360, 361, 376, 377, 381, 384.
32. Elizabeth Kridl Valkenier, "The USSR, the Third World, and the Global Economy," *Problems of Communism* 28 (July-August 1979), pp. 20, 22, 23, 25, 26, 27. For Soviet domestic implications see pp. 30, 31, 32. The Brezhnev statement is quoted from Leonid Brezhnev, "Report of the CPSU CC. The Party's Immediate Objectives in Domestic and Foreign Policies," *Reprints from the Soviet*

Press (White Plains, N.Y.: Compass) 15, April 1976, 76–77, 20. Quoted in ibid., p. 22.

33. Brezhnev, "Report," p. 19.
34. A.V. Nikiforov, "Interdependence and Global Problems" (in Russian) *USA: Economics, Politics, Ideology*, no. 4 (1979) pp. 8–12.
35. Ibid., pp. 14–17.
36. Margarita Maximova, "The Soviet Union and Its Role in World Economy," *Social Sciences* no. 4, 1978, in *Reprints from the Soviet Press* 29, no. 4 (28 February 1979), pp. 6, 9, 13, 15, 16, 17, 21, 23, 24.
37. Thomas A. Wolf, "The Distribution of Economic Costs and Benefits in US-Soviet Trade," in *Soviet Economy in a Time of Change*, pp. 2, 337–38. Michael R. Dohan, "Export Specialization and Import Dependence in the Soviet Economy, 1979–77," ibid., pp. 367, 368; Kravalis, Young, Oeschler, and Lamb., "Soviet Exports to the Industrialized West," ibid., pp. 416–19; Cobb, p. 384.

CHAPTER 7

Low-Intensity Conflict: The U.S. Response

Frank N. Trager and William L. Scully

I

On the Risks of Terminological Inexactitude[1]

"Low-intensity conflict," a term currently in use in the Pentagon, has been variously equated, in other contexts, with "small (or minor) wars," "low-level conflict," and "low-intensity war." Is this concern over names and titles worth even limited attention here? Our answer is in the affirmative precisely because, in our estimation, there is no general consensus on the meaning of the object of this inquiry. The problem of defining "low-intensity conflict" is troubling because if we cannot find common ground the analyses and prescriptions offered in this book may prove less useful than we can otherwise hope. We have something analogous to the Aristotelian dilemma of the "mean." "Courage," Aristotle is supposed to have said by way of illustrating his "mean," is something other than (that is, the "mean" between) "foolhardiness and cowardice." But how then do we identify it? So, too, low-intensity warfare or conflict is surely not strategic (nuclear) or large-scale conventional war. Nor is it to be equated with those political-military decisions to "show the flag" or otherwise display, but not employ, military force.[2] Between these extremes of great violence and no violence at all, there are quite a few points within the spectrum of national and transnational conflict, all of which might conceivably fall within the classification of low-intensity wars. These various points reach levels of violence and hence produce casualties, and the intensity of violence escalates even as the categories change: violent coup d'état (for example, the recent Bolivian or Liberian situations or the more violent Soviet-Afghan coup of 27 December 1979), "surgical" strikes (as in the Entebbe or Mayagüez incidents), guerrilla wars (as between Morocco and Algeria or India vs. the Mizos and Nagas), insurgency/counterinsurgency wars (endemic in Southeast Asia), civil wars (Nigeria vs. Biafra or Cambodian communists vs. Vietnamese-Cambodian communists), "brush fire" and proxy wars (as in Angola, or Ethiopia vs. Somalia, or North vs. South Yemen), "punitive" wars (as between the People's Republic of China and the Democratic Republic of Vietnam). And what of organized terrorism, whether urban or rural—a contemporary, enlarged version of nineteenth-century revolutionary anarchism (Bakunin's *Propaganda of the Deed*) and Marxist-Leninist revolutionary class war? Do we stop here? What kind of "limited" conventional wars (a horrible and dangerously unclear phrase) as in Korea and Vietnam, Soviet military intervention, under the guise of "proletarian internationalism," as in Czecho-slovakia (1968), and the "border wars" between the Soviet Union and the People's Republic of China, and so on?

What—and who—determines whether a war is of "low intensity?" Is it the size of the forces and the names of the sovereign or other participants? The degree of technology employed or the lethal qualities of weapons, launchers, and platforms? The number of casualties? The location of the country or countries whose terrain becomes the battlefield? The degree of economic development enjoyed—if that be the right word—by the indigenous popula-tion? If we are to have classes, divisions, or categories of warfare they must have an inherent, consistent logic and some common, identifiable characteris-tics; otherwise, they do not form such categories. They remain a serial collection of discrete phenomena. If we cannot generalize such propositions, then we had best deal with experience as it occurs and attempt to provide, as far as possible, for the unpredictable but probable recurrence of that experience.

The difficulty of defining, analyzing, and making prescriptions for so broad a concept as "low-intensity conflict" or war is compounded by a certain rather inane U.S. defense formula offered by successive recent Democratic and Republican administrations, to wit: we must be prepared to fight simultaneously "two and one-half wars," later reduced to "one and one-half wars." What is a "one-half" war? How does one prepare for it? As if war comes in discrete sizes like wearing apparel!

In our discussion of low-intensity conflict we shall confine our analysis to two main types of security problems, regardless of how the term "security" is defined. In short, we shall define *not* by seeking the "mean" between maximum and no violence, but rather by pointing, that is, by attempting an analysis of relevant experience that then leads to particularized prescriptions (policy). We do not assume that we shall (or can) cover all points in the spectrum of war below the level of strategic and large-scale, conventional war, nor do we assume that we shall (or can) arrive at a generalized theory or model. The two classes of low-intensity conflict designed to effect change in or of the social order are here labeled: "political instability," short of sustained violence, and "war, whether declared or undeclared," short of large-scale conventional or strategic wars.

Elsewhere we have attempted to define the elusive concepts of stability and instability.[3] Generally, authors who use these terms seem to be in tacit agreement that the indicators of political stability/instability—the denotation of the concept—include:

1. the ability of the governing regime to maintain, modify in accordance with whatever constitutional charter it may have, and administer the established political institutions of the society;
2. the ability of the governing regime to persuade or otherwise influence sufficient numbers of the citizens that their economic and social expectations are or are about to be reasonably met; and
3. the ability of the governing regime so to defend the society against domestic and foreign threats and acts of violence as to gain endorsement and active support from the citizens at home and from regimes and people abroad.

The presence of these three indicators makes for stability, their absence for instability. Judgments with respect to such indicators are necessarily not "value-free." In various cases they may be persuasive to the authors and, perhaps, to others.

When instability, as here defined, leads to an alteration or change in the social order at home or abroad, such change may be brought about by peaceful means or by the display of readiness (that is, threat), but not the employment of force. Thus this, our first type of security problem, may include political agitational efforts, various forms of communication, economic pressures (such as strikes, boycotts, and lockouts), police activity, and diplomacy as well as military training exercises, weapons display, weapons transfers and "shows of force." Revolutionary violence, terror, the employment of military personnel (as in the 1958 sending of American marines to the Beirut airport or the stationing of Russian "coal miners" in Spitzbergen), interdiction or harassment at sea, and military coups—all of these move toward, and may—indeed, frequently do—fall into the second of our two types, which we have labelled "war, whether declared or undeclared" because they in fact employ or are at the threshold of using deployed force. When force is used they then belong to the arena of low-intensity conflict, our concern.

Obviously, political instability may become the domestic or international matrix out of which the use of force may occur to bring about the changes desired by the users. Therefore, political instability and potential users of force must be carefully noticed and monitored. The ascending employment of force to "war, declared or undeclared" includes not only the instruments mentioned in the preceding paragraph but also civil war, insurgency (whether indigenously or externally initiated and supported), and all levels of the interventionary use of force across international borders. The only difference—and this is no small matter—between low- and high-intensity warfare is the variation in intensity! The goal or desired outcome, whatever the intensity, is the same: to achieve one's politically desired end(s) by the military means employed. As Clausewitz observed:

> War is . . . an act of force to compel our adversary to do our will . . . the use of force is theoretically without limits. . . . [However] the greatest and the most decisive act of judgement which a statesman and commander perform is that of recognizing correctly the kind of war in which they are engaged; of not taking it for, or wishing to make of it, something which under the circumstances it cannot be. This is therefore the first and most comprehensive of all strategic questions.

And, as he added, *"we must proportion our effort to his [the enemy's] power of resistance"* (italics added).[4]

There is an obvious overlap and interrelatedness between our two types of security problems, precisely because both flow from the fact that the social order is being actually or potentially distorted and consciously disturbed by individuals, groups and movements, whether indigenous or foreign, utilizing a variety of means to effect such change. In some instances, the same "means" may appear in both types but with a variation: for example, the ships, planes and manpower on display during a "show of force" or a training exercise could be the same ships, planes and manpower employed in war. In both instances they are presumably at a "readiness" stage for combat. But only in the second type are they in use as "employed force," for then they are in combat.

We are now prepared to offer a response to the questions mentioned previously: What and who determines whether a war is of "low intensity," "half a war," small or big, conventional or strategic or both? Do size of force, casualty figures, names and numbers of sovereign participants, weaponry employed, and terrain count in the "start-up" decision making? Such questions, in our view, are not particularly meaningful; at best, they are *descriptively* answered as "history after the event." If the diagnosis seems to be one of strict political instability then prudence—or, if you will, the principle of proportionality—should apply, as it is expected that force will not be employed. If, for example, promptly withdrawing the rather substantial military and economic aid program to Bolivia (about $27.5 million) would help restore the duly elected civilian regime, recently overthrown by Colonel Alberto Natusch Busch, and if then, *mirabile dictu*, that operation and comparable ones contribute to political stability,[5] then by all means eschew the employment of force. So too, if a U.S. "show of force" in the Persian Gulf would maintain free passage through the Straits of Hormuz, thereby contributing to the peace and stability of the gulf region, as well as the continuing economic health of our 100% energy-importing ally, Japan, then such "shows of force" are infinitely superior to the actual employment of force.

History itself is replete with numerous examples of such choices. It is when (for domestic or international reasons) political stability gives way, when instability can no longer be quarantined that the issue of war, at whatever level, begins to take shape and form. "War," Clausewitz wrote, "is never an isolated act ... never breaks out suddenly and does not spread immediately."[6] Because of improved changes in communication, mobilization, and mobility in today's war systems, a more accurate comment today would tone down the "never" of Clausewitz to "almost never." What we should learn from Clausewitz and the significant military strategists and historians of the nineteenth and twentieth centuries is that answers to questions such as those raised above come not from defining "low-" or "high-" intensity warfare, nor from numerical analysis. For example, whether "half a war" requires (U.S.) divisional strength of 15,000 men rather than 30,000; or whether we should build 60,000 nonnuclear or 90,000 nuclear-driven carriers; or, whether they should be reduced to 30,000 and 45,000 tons respectively. Such rival answers in numbers are, in military terms, meaningless! Potentially usable if sometimes erroneous answers come only from one valid source: the thorough analysis on a global basis of and projection of requirements arising from, potential danger spots. Such an analysis and projection necessarily involve a systematic evaluation of one's own assets, liabilities, and interests and those of one's close allies and other friendly states, as well as a similar set of analyses of one's major and minor adversaries and their allies and friends. *When such continuing, ever-updated analyses and estimates of the situation are assembled, then and only then can a proper "force" be designed, equipped, trained, and deployed.* Such a force, with its accompanying weapons, platforms, equipment, and so on, will be as varied as the projected estimated needs call for at the time.

Let us attempt to illuminate and illustrate the central meaning of the foregoing thesis by two brief examples: (1) the case of counterinsurgency and (2) the case of the Army's "Strike Force."

The Case of Counterinsurgency

Almost two decades ago, President John F. Kennedy, in his inaugural address, sounded the tocsin for the American mission in behalf of global freedom. Kennedy, as many of us then heard, said:

> Let every nation know, whether it wishes us well or ill, that we shall pay any price, bear any burden, meet any hardship, support any friend, oppose any foe to assure the survival and the success of liberty.

It was a stirring call that was soon put to the test. Cuba was the catalyst—first, with the abysmal failure of the Bay of Pigs, undertaken not as of yore with the Marines, but with a ragtail, proxy group, inadequately trained, staffed, and equipped by the CIA, and second, when the Soviets attempted to establish a strategic missile base there. Sandwiched between these Cuban episodes the young president and his military advisor, General Maxwell Taylor, obviously concluded that the United States required, in addition to the normal use of diplomatic channels, a military option superior to the CIA proxies other than the employment of our strategic forces. In March 1962, U.S. military forces, along with the educational institutions associated with the three armed services, were ordered by the president to prepare properly for what was then called "counterinsurgency warfare." This was seen as preparation for a military capability beyond the traditional amphibious mission of the Marines. Out of this came among other things several military formations referred to generally as "Special Forces," and most notably the Green Berets—a unit appreciated by very few in or out of the Army with the notable exception of that American folk hero, the late John Wayne.

The Green Berets and all other special formations in the Army suffered from the fact that the U.S. Army did not and still does not like "special formations."[7] During the Second World War, especially in the Chinese-Burma-India theater of operations, there were similar difficulties between the regular military and such special formations—for example, Wingate's Chindits (British) and Merrill's Marauders (American) in the Burma campaign. An American Marauder even today is still apt to curse, not praise, General "Vinegar" Joe Stilwell, the alleged "hero" of the Burma campaign. By the mid-1960s—certainly during General Westmoreland's assumption of Military Assistance Command, Vietnam—MACV (1964–68)—"counterinsurgency," conceptually and organizationally, was a "goner." The Green Berets, who never had more than 3000 men posted along the 700-mile Vietnamese side of the border with Laos and Cambodia, never did recover.

"Counterinsurgency" was an early name for low-intensity warfare. It was not an integrated political-military concept. It never had the benefit of a "unified theater" or allied command—Westmoreland, for one, rejected recommendations for a combined or allied unified command and control.[8] The Army and the Marines in the South Vietnamese I Corps Area feuded over the concept of operations and organization. It was time to reexamine military strategy and tactics once again, and once again relate these to the political purpose for which the war was being fought. The literature—good, bad, and indifferent—on counterinsurgency totaled thousands of entries as early as fifteen years ago![9] It was based, perhaps too floridly, on principles and data gleaned from early American eighteenth-century wars, the experience of the British in Southeast Asia,[10] and on our academic and field experiences as "area specialists"—elements worth reviewing if we are to produce what it is we need for the 1980s.

Vietnam was thus both the testing and burial ground for counterinsurgency doctrine and organization. It should have served the same purpose for such deceptive concepts as "limited war" and "one-half wars"! Counterinsurgency doctrine and organization, however, had served the short-term purposes of U.S. policy after the failed Geneva conference on the Indochina War. Originally, the war was to be a relatively "low-cost" involvement in support of a newly acquired ally, which was to be defended against "communist aggression" by virtue of the Protocol to the September 1954 Manila Security Pact, which created SEATO. It was a feasible political-military option during the early stages[11] of the conflict between the two *de facto* and *de jure* sovereign states that occupied respectively the almost equally sized halves (some 65,000 square miles each) of the territory of Vietnam. "Insurgency" and "counterinsurgency" were the names given to the beginnings in the south of the war between North and South Vietnam. Initially, the war was fought at the lower end of the spectrum of violence: terror, kidnapping, selective assassinations, small-unit "hit-and-run" tactics, and raids, all accompanied by a steady drum fire of political propaganda and some political/welfare improvements.

As the conflict between the two Vietnams grew in intensity, there was also a marked increase in U.S. interventionary activity. By the end of 1962, more than 11,000 American military personnel were stationed in South Vietnam. Fully armed with planes and guns, the American forces, though supposedly providing only advice and assistance, were actually in part fulfilling combat roles on the ground and in the air. Counterinsurgency warfare—or warfare at the very low end of the spectrum—was gradually being escalated. However, doctrine and organization did not keep pace with the actualities of the conflict. Though attempting to assign dates to change is frequently subject to debate, perhaps the aftermath of the February 1968 Tet Offensive may be said to confirm the fact that counterinsurgency had by that time become a past doctrine. By the mid-1960s, the undeclared war had become a conflict between regular forces employing standard but not successful military strategies, and tactics more or less suitable to the terrain where it was being fought.

To this day considerable, if somewhat unenlightened, arguments arise whenever the so-called Vietcong Tet Offensive of February 1968 is discussed. At home, the event was regarded by many as at best a psychological and intelligence, if not a military, defeat for U.S. and the allied forces in Vietnam. On the other hand, the military, though accepting the charge of being open to tactical surprise, assert that because Hanoi utilized large-scale, open attacks, the American and allied ground forces were able to inflict massive damage on the DRVN's regular forces—so much so that if they had been allowed to pursue the decimated Viet Cong across the North Vietnamese border they, together with air and naval forces, could have brought the war to a military victory!

Obviously there is no resolution to that debated issue, but what can be said with certainty is that the doctrines, strategies, and tactics of "counterinsurgency" had long been superseded by more traditional military doctrines, which were sloganized under General Westmoreland's command (1964–68) as "search and destroy" (later to be followed by "clear and hold"), and a civilian doctrine of pacification.[12] Neither the military nor the civilian pacification doctrines were sufficient for the conventional, not so low-intensity, warfare that evolved in Vietnam. For the undeclared war in Vietnam had moved up the escalating ladder from very low-intensity warfare at divisional strength and defensive deployment under the advice and leadership of (MAAG) General "Hanging" Sam Williams (by 1959), and kept on escalating through the Johnson and first Nixon administrations. During the post-Tet evaluation, even the use of tactical nuclear weapons was examined but rejected. At no time during the miserable two decades of American involvement (1955–75) had there been an overall political-military war plan that could be said to exemplify the Clausewitzian (or other) approach quoted above: " ... the greatest and most decisive act which a statesman and commander perform is that of recognizing correctly the kind of war in which they are engaged; of not taking it for, or wishing to make of it, something ... it cannot be .... And we must proportion our effort to [the enemy's] power of resistance."

At no time was there developed a coherent war plan to achieve the political aims of the war. At no time under either the Johnson or Nixon administrations was there a decision to adopt the first rule of war: to use the necessary amount of power in the shortest possible time, with least possible loss of life, to make the enemy cease and desist, to destroy his will to fight, and to make him surrender.

The Case of the Army's "Strike Force"

In a press report dated 18, September 1979 it was announced that with the beginning of fiscal year 1980 the Army would "establish the headquarters and planning units for a new 110,000-man mobile strike force designed to respond to crises in the Middle East or elsewhere."[13] It was further noted that though the new mobile corps had been approved in concept, and whereas the force, when in being, is "intended for rapid deployment" and "could meet an emergency anywhere in the world," it was "clearly ... designed for action in the strategic Middle East." According to Army Chief of Staff General Edward Meyer, the force would have the "strength of several divisions" and would be drawn from "existing units" of the 770,000-man Army. Because U.S. forces assigned to NATO "make such a mobile force unnecessary in Europe," it is reasonable to infer that without additions to overall Army strength, the new strike force will draw down from forces other than those in Europe. It would, in effect, necessitate a reshuffling of existing manpower, with relevant equipment, training, and deployment capability added so as to constitute it with some kind of special function!

According to General Meyer the force "contains" (or will contain when, and if, actually in being) "a potpourri of forces all the way from very limited war types through a corps consisting of both armored and light infantry units and anti-air, Army air, and so on." Once established, he continued, it will conduct visible training exercises "to indicate to the world that we do have the capability of projecting power."

Whether these 110,000 soldiers are drawn from non-Central Front forces or are an addition to the present 770,000-man force level, or whether this new information or "potpourri" of 110,000 men will include a sufficient number of *types*—the equivalent of the earlier Green Berets, Rangers, Commandos, Light Infantry (Airborne Division), and so on—is not the basic issue. To have in being a ready force swiftly deployable to meet crises and emergencies is eminently desirable. However, there is as yet no clear indication that the missions and capabilities of these 110,000 men will be integrated with those of the three Marine divisions, despite the historic record of serious Army-Marine feuding in the crisis and emergency of Vietnam. Further the issues of command and control of related and assigned air and (other) navy units are aspects of the same problem. Without such integration of roles and missions, the U.S. ability to project power in crises and emergencies in less effective, and the defense dollar is probably spent less efficiently than it otherwise would be. Further, again, without providing for commensurate airlift capability for rapid deployment of men and materiel— *an airlift capability now largely missing*[14]—any strike force is hopelessly tied down in the crucial first days and even weeks of the crisis for which, in the first place, it was designed. And on the assumption that deployment of men and materiel can "wait" upon the use of ships, the present sealift capability of the Navy, whose overall seagoing capacity has declined from a total of 900 ships to at best 500 ships, is sorely handicapped.

The difficulty here—only dimly suggested—is not in the decision to have an Army strike force intended for "rapid deployment anywhere" or even intended especially for the "strategic Middle East." The difficult arises from a basic deficiency in the conceptualization of the problem. If the question remains: Should the Army have the capability of coping with a crisis or emergency (other than in Europe)?—*substitute*, if you wish, "Navy-Marines-Army-Air Force" for "Army"—the answer is, of course, yes! The U.S. armed forces should have a capability to meet crises and emergencies and variations of armed conflict other than at the central front in Europe. But it is not especially useful—in fact, it may indeed be wasteful—to decide on the size, shape, equipment, training, and deployment of any of our armed forces before it is decided what and why and where these forces might, in probable fact, be used. There can be no certainty in projecting estimates of the future. Yet we must arrive at a calculus of interests and commitments, and then project our estimates. Prudence, therefore—and the lead times required for various research and development production and deployment of weapons systems, platforms, and training—dictates that preparation for crisis management and other possible degrees of low-intensity warfare be neither maximalist nor minimalist, but rather proportional to the rank order of the interests and commitments that our analysis will have revealed.

The new Army strike force, the equivalent of at least three divisions, if divisions are the formations called for (we doubt this), cannot possibly cope with all the emergencies, crisis, "half wars," "limited wars," and so on that may arise outside of Europe. Nor should it be expected to do so. Such a strike force is not the only way to project power. What is required, in the first instance, is what we have called above the thorough, continuing updated analysis and ranking of potential danger spots on a regional and global basis. The analysis should be undertaken by individuals or teams of interdisciplinary experts whether in or out of uniform. Their expertise, based on continuing field experience and continuing study, should be applied as free as possible from the constraints of faction, party, promotion fears, and the like. It takes years to acquire such expertise. It should, therefore, be valued, utilized, and rewarded accordingly. The resulting analyses of assets and liabilities—ours, our friends' and allies', and our adversaries'—must be linked to a calculus of our interests and commitments.

The linkage between our interests and the analyses of global/regional threat, danger, crisis potential, emergency—call it what you will—form the bases for decision about the political-military requirements for coping with such contingencies. The organization and acquisition of projectable power—men and materiel—whether as Army strike forces, or Navy Marines, or air commandos, or mixed civilian-military CORDS personnel, or combinations of all these follows upon, does not precede such political decision making. Inasmuch as low-intensity warfare at some levels of violence is a most probable event in the real world of the 1980s, let us now turn to an examination of that probable event and suggest the terms of the U.S. response.

II

In the far less complex international environment of the early 1950s, the type of threat analysis that was linked to safeguarding interests and that concluded with both general and specific policy guidelines (which in our view then determine the force structure and the requirements for projecting power) was best exemplified in the rather well known, now declassified, *Report by the Secretaries of State and Defense on "United States Objectives and Programs for National Security," April 7, 1950*, better known by its serial number, NSC-68. It is not uninstructive to review the conclusions of that document today.[15] The basic thrust of the document leads to the conclusion "that the Cold War is in fact a real war in which the survival of the free world is at stake," and it sharply outlines and supports the policy of "containment."

Thirty years later we have modified its rhetoric, enlarged its comparative geoeconomic and geopolitical analytical framework, found or formulated other somewhat faddish vocabularies: *"detente," "deterrence," "compellence," "North-South dialogue," "Third World," "Fourth World," "Fifth World," "Nonaligned nations,"* and so on.

Despite the modifications, enlargements, and related changes in the vocabularies found in subsequent National Security Council and presidential security documents, we have *not* had (and this is a subjective judgement on the authors' part), since NSC-68, from any of the intervening presidents, a security document that provides a *total* view of the current security issue. "Total view" here, as throughout this chapter, includes analysis of global and regional threats, of assets and liabilities, of commitments—ours, as well as our friends' and foes'—linked to "interests," all in rank order, leading ultimately to political, economic, and military prescriptive policies.

President Eisenhower caused to be prepared several hundred *particularized* NSC contingency papers. Secretary of States Dulles, building on NATO and subsequent alliance policies of Truman and Acheson's last two years in office, vastly extended the U.S. collective security alliance systems. While NATO is still in place, waxing and waning with the moods of its changing political leadership, much of the remaining inter-American and

Asian-Pacific collective security systems have either "run out" or have been "run down." What remains, namely the U.S.-Japanese, U.S.-Korean, U.S.-Philippines, and ANZUS alliances, is certainly not in a healthy and vibrant state. President Kennedy's contribution, if any, was obviously limited by time. What occurred during this administration is well documented: the failure of the Bay of Pigs, the success in the Cuban missile crisis, and the failure of counterinsurgency in Vietnam. What he might have done subsequently we obviously cannot know. President Johnson had little liking for conceptualizing an overall war plan or grand strategy. He was at ease with, and retained even for theater operations, a day-to-day decision-making procedure, with fatal consequences to himself, to the nation, and to our allies. Nixon and Kissinger, on the other hand, were intellectually agreeable to the need for grand strategy but chose, in the first instance, an opportunistic "peace first" strategy that they thought would work and bring to them the blessings and laurels of the peacemakers. It worked, but only to the advantage of the adversary, North Vietnam, and did not gain any blessings for President Nixon and his successor, Gerald Ford. President Carter began his administration with PREM-10 (Presidential Review Memorandum no. 10), a global view of U.S. interests and security. The document—leaked in part to the press—was deficient in so many respects that much of it was allegedly repudiated or suppressed. The Carter administration, until the occurrence of the Iranian crisis in November and the Afghanistan crisis in December 1979, had been more preoccupied with U.S.-Soviet relations, particularly with respect to the SALT II negotiations. However, in his televised address on the U.S. response to the Soviet forces in Cuba, Carter turned his attention to the above-mentioned 100,000-man strike force. He said:

> The United States has a worldwide interest in peace and stability. Accordingly, I have directed the Secretary of Defense to further enhance the capacity of our Rapid Deployment Forces to protect our own interest and to act in response to requests for help from our allies and friends. We must be able to move our ground, sea and air units to distant areas—rapidly and with adequate supplies.[16]

Two days later, the *New York Times* returned to the President's mentioning of "Rapid Deployment Forces" and in a longer background report wrote that "Government officials report that little has been done to organize such a unit ... the Administration's plan for creating a 110,000-member rapid deployment force was made public in August 1977 ... the United States needed a special contingent for waging "brush-fire" wars in the third world." The story continued:

> The idea of creating a force to intervene in small conflicts in the third world is not new. Since the late 1960s the Pentagon has based its planning on the so-

called one-and-a-half war strategy, which suggests that the United States must have the capability of fighting a small war in Latin America, Africa or the Middle East while waging a full-scale conflict against the Soviet Union in Central Europe and northeast Asia.

Over the last decade the Army's 82nd Airborne Division, based at Fort Benning, Georgia, has been considered sufficient for small-scale third world contingencies. A third of the division, which has a strength of about 15,000, has been placed on continuous alert and, according to defense officials, could be flown anywhere in the world in 24 hours.

While this force is still judged to be adequate for coping with a crisis in Africa or Latin America, the officials contend that it would be far too small to deal with military threats to pro-Western countries in the Persian Gulf.

The Soviet Union is said to have deployed 23 divisions in its southern region. Many of the units are thought to be undermanned and poorly equipped but the officials contend that Moscow, as shown by its large military airlift to Ethiopia last year, has increased its ability to airlift troops and supplies into distant areas.[17]

Thus—to give a kind of interim summary of the current U.S. response to potential conflict situations—we are still at a level of policy analysis that calls for a capability to fight a full war (central, large-scale conventional, high-intensity, or nuclear war) against the major adversary—the Soviet "coalition"—and a "half war" (low-intensity, crisis situation, or an emergency, involving the deployment and use of force) against some hostile country or movement in the Middle East, Africa, Latin America, and, though the *New York Times* did not mention it in its analysis, Asia. However, our capability to meet the challenge of a "half war" is still limited to previously acquired resources, inasmuch as by common consent the new strike force or Rapid Deployment Forces originally announced, we are told, in August 1977 and then again in September 1979, is far from being organized, equipped, and trained.

For whatever reasons—domestic considerations or morale-building propaganda aimed at its allies—the Soviets see the matter in a much different light. A rather well known military writer, Colonel M. Ponomarev, published a short piece in *Red Star* emphasizing the U.S. development of "special strike forces" to project power and to be used to "interfere" in the internal affairs of other countries.[18] Ponomarev asserts that all U.S. forces not assigned to NATO, are committed to these two purposes. This, according to the Soviet colonel, means that the United States has more than 600,000 ground, naval, and air force personnel, commits 22% of the defense budget to power projection and what we refer to here as low-intensity warfare. He itemizes this interventionary force as including the whole U.S. Marine Corps, with their military aircraft and tanks, the 82d and 101st Airborne Army Divisions, with their tactical and airlift/transportation aviation, and a considerable section of the Navy—some thirty carriers with their 800 aircraft, plus naval landing forces, troop-transport ships, helicopters, and so on. He also writes as if the strike force (he refers to it as the U.S. Quick Reaction Corps) was already in being.

It is clear that any discussion of manpower and materiel, planned or in being, aggregated à la Colonel Ponomarev or General Meyer and designated for some "half war" in one of the gross, geographic regions of the two hemispheres, hardly advances our understanding of low-intensity warfare. It is our contention that while a further enhancement of our Rapid Deployment and related Air and Naval Forces is necessitated by recent Soviet, Cuban, and East German intrusions in the Middle East, Africa, Latin America, and Asia, the mere introduction of such forces in the U.S. military spectrum is insufficient unless it is accompanied by a much broader discussion and analysis of political and military strategy. Specifically, there should be an overall review of United States military and defense policy in light of a new and emerging strategic map that will most probably govern military and political considerations in the next decade. Geopolitical and geoeconomic analysis, constantly maintained and updated, will provide not only a coherent military context from which decisions must be made, but it will also provide a solidifying theoretical framework—heretofore missing—for the formulation of American foreign and strategic policy.

In the spring of 1977 the Joint Chiefs of Staff (JCS) undertook to prepare such a geopolitical foundation for the new president and his Secretary of Defense. A much-abbreviated, nonclassified version of this memorandum, known as "The Strategic Importance of Vital International Areas," was published in *Commander's Digest*.[19] For the JCS "vital" customarily means "to be fought for, if necessary." Seven vital areas were defined in terms of their "strategic importance" as they related to United States national interests and commitments. The vital areas are: (1) Western Europe, that is, NATO Europe; (2) the Middle East, the "strategically important corridor connecting the Eastern Hemisphere's three major continents where the interests of the major powers converge" and, in our estimation, conflict. The oil issue and the Egyptian-Israeli-Palestinian issues were obviously paramount in 1977 when the memorandum was written. The unexpected Iranian revolution has greatly exacerbated the oil issue, as well as the security problems of the Arab states and emirates on the west side of the Persian Gulf. Furthermore, the advances made by the Soviet Union in Ethiopia and South Yemen complicate the task of keeping open such "choke points" as Bab el Mandeb and the Straits of Hormuz, and its invasion of Afghanistan opens realistic vistas of Soviet dominance in Southwest Asia (that is, from the Caspian Sea south and east to India); (3) Africa warrants "attention not only for its strategic geographical position and sheer size, but as an increasingly important source of raw materials for industrialized nations." Though the JCS study recognized the importance of Africa, its analysis, already dated by the changed relationships between Somalia/Ethiopia and the Soviet Union, is too gross even for its time. It refers to the JCS' "sensitivity ... with [respect to] countries on both the Atlantic and Indian Ocean littoral" of Africa but it fails to face up to the strategic issues raised by former Ambassador Andrew Young's African policy. Young, with the support of President Carter and the Department of State, clearly espoused policies which may have been politically satisfying to the leadership of the administration but were just as clearly deleterious for U.S. military and economic interests. Tradeoffs are inevitable in a democratic society, but at least the JCS' geopolitical and strategic analysis should be clear about what is being traded off; (4) Asia and the Pacific are brought together as one of the seven strategic and vital areas. Happily, they are considered in a series of subregions, thereby receiving more attention than Asia usually receives: Northeast, Southeast, Southwest Pacific, South Asia/Indian Ocean, and Soviet/PRC relations in Asia. Of the remaining three vital areas, two—the Atlantic and North America are treated seriously but very briefly, as if their importance were so assured as to not require analytical treatment. Latin America, a typical area of neglect, as usual, receives short and woefully inadequate treatment and attention.

The importance and value of the JCS geopolitical, strategic and analytical "exercise" rests less in what it sets forth and more in that it was done at all. The JCS seemingly recognized that the analysis preceded prescriptions on force levels and materiel. The clear implication of the document is that such analysis must be a continuing annual or semiannual task not unrelated to the year-round task of budgetmaking. Less than 30 months after the unclassified report was published, it was substantially dated by geopolitical and strategic events in the Horn of Africa, Southern Africa, the Middle East, the Persian Gulf, Southwest or South Asia (depending upon where one assigns Afghanistan), the Indochinese Peninsula, and Latin America. Because change is inevitable, regular, short-term updating is most necessary. To maintain for sustained periods (five to ten years) the level of experienced (including field experience), area-trained personnel to carry on the geopolitical, geoeconomic, strategic analysis linked to consideration of vital and major interests (ours, our allies' and friends', and our adversaries') is the prime requirement for getting the job done. It may (as we believe) be better to refine the annual macrogeographical analysis into semiannual regional or subregional analyses within each macrogeographical framework. In this kind of analysis "small" should—all things being equal—be more revealing than "big."

What we see emerging today is a more complex relationship between and among pieces of geography (places, regions, lands, waters), peoples (in states, regions, regimes, movements) and various interests (political, economic, sociocultural and the like) considered as either assets or liabilities. The complex has or acquires value for those who live within its boundaries and can share it. The complex and its acknowledged value are to be defended—or subdued—when necessary, enhanced when possible. Finally, the complex is subject to challenge from within or from without. Some challenges are manageable; that is, the social order finds peaceful, accommodating solutions for the crises and emergencies inevitably arising from social change. Some challenges are violent in nature—terror, class war, revolutionary war, civil war, war across boundaries, and the like. By definition, when these violent challenges do not issue into large-scale conventional or nuclear war they are low-intensity conflicts or wars. If our method of analysis as above sketched is sound, we should be able to draw up what has been called a new "strategic map."[20] Several features of this new map are closely related and are derivative from changes that occurred in the 1950s and 1060s. Geoffrey Kemp notes four particular features of this new map:[21]

1. Breakthroughs in new weapons technology together with the widespread diffusion of arms and wealth to increasing regions of the world will impose greater constraints on the freedom of the major maritime powers, including the Soviet Union, to deploy and use military force in the southern hemisphere;
2. Steady erosion of Western base rights in important areas of the world including Southeast Asia, the Middle East, and Africa south of the Sahara; there has been a parallel, though not symmetric growth in Soviet overseas maritime facilities;
3. Partly as a result of sustained economic growth, the Western industrial countries are becoming increasingly dependent upon the transshipment of scarce raw materials, especially oil, located in, and moving through, volatile conflict areas;[22]
4. The creeping closure of the world's oceans due to unilateral extensions of sovereignty and a possible new law of the seas is eroding traditional freedom of maritime transit through areas of critical strategic and economic importance to both the West and the Soviet Union.

If, as herein proposed, the analysis is done on a continuing basis, the strategic map would begin probably to anticipate and expose various "trouble spots." For example:

• The Persian Gulf. The Shah's difficulties before his overthrow by Khomeini's Islamic Revolution were not unknown; the Gulf was or would have been on any strategic map of troubled spots. Attention was focused, however, as it should have been, on the Caspian Sea region, the Strait of Hormuz, and the Gulf of Oman. The challenge to the Shah was rightly regarded as *primarily* external and assistance to him for those challenges was being provided and improved. What was missing was the internal assessment. It was a case of misplaced confidence and inadequate independent knowledge of internal stresses and strains. It is conceivable that truly experienced analysts, full of years of field knowledge, might have placed sufficient weight on the internal factors which eventually led to the Shah's overthrow. But, excepting an Ambassador or other source, such as Eilts in the Middle East with almost two decades of experience in the area, it is doubtful that we had such personnel available for Iran. Ambassador Sullivan—steeped in a decade or more long experience in Southeast Asia—was new to Iran. The system proposed herein might have worked but we did *not* have the experienced manpower to work it.

- Oman. Since the early 1970s the Soviet- and Yemen (Aden)-supported People's Front for the Liberation of Oman (PFLO) has sought to depose the Sultan. The Shah's use of Iranian troops, naval and air operations along the Dhofar coast, and the backing of the Saudis have thus far defeated or held off the attempted advance of the PFLO. Obviously, our proposed strategic map would have already indicated that a successor to the Shah for Omani assistance must be found.[23]
- The Red Sea and the Gulf of Aden. Internal violence has marked the recent history of both Yemens, as has violence between them. South Yemen, a client state of Moscow, gives access to the Soviet Fleet at Aden and the island of Socotra. Now that the USSR has substituted Ethiopia for Somalia, it has switched ports from Berbera to Massawa. The latter and Aden can easily serve as a naval pincer to close the Red Sea's southern exit at Bab el Mandeb. The Suez Canal then no longer serves as a channel between the Mediterranean and the Indian Ocean, and pressure on Saudi Arabia can be exerted because both Jedda and the industrial complex at Yenbo are easily harassed by Soviet airplanes—as well as from the fleet at Massawa—which have access to the air facilities at Massawa and Assabin.[24]

It is possible to go around the globe in similar fashion and find other pertinent illustrations. For example:

- Southern Africa. Prior to Soviet and Cuban intervention in the Angolan civil war, the South African area received scant attention in both United States and Soviet foreign policies. During the late 1960s and early 1970s, the Soviet Navy regularly operated in the northwest Indian Ocean and around the coast of West Africa. There was little naval movement below the equator. However, after 1975 Soviet patrols were extended and intelligence ships stationed as far down the coast as South Africa permitted. The use of Angolan and Mozambican ports for resupplying Soviet vessels was essential to this extension of Soviet power. One can expect that an analysis of our proposed strategic map would indicate not only an increase in aid to various independent and insurgent forces by the Soviets and Cubans, but also an attempt to restrict Western access to African ports and thus interdict the SLOCs (sea lines of communication).[25]
- Indian Ocean Area. With the recent coup of April 1978 in Afghanistan—certainly now within the Marxist-Soviet orbit—and the increased presence of the Soviet navy in the Indian Ocean area, one may expect increasing Soviet pressures on other potential trouble spots, as for example the Baluchistan area in Pakistan.
- Southeast Asia. Of special significance for our discussion is the close, fraternal relationship existing between the Soviet Union and Vietnam. The growing influence, military and otherwise, of the Soviets in Vietnamese affairs is troubling to the PRC, and should be cause for concern within the United States (consider the signing of a Mutual Friendship and Cooperation Treaty, as well as Vietnam entry into COM-ECON). Of critical importance to the United States must be the issue of Cam Ranh Bay, the first warm-water foreign base to which the Soviet navy has been permitted access. There is little doubt but that the Soviet use of Cam Ranh Bay would have a powerful effect on the naval balance in Asia, to the advantage of the Soviet Union and the obvious disadvantage of the United States, the PRC, and Japan. For one, Moscow would gain a seapower "pincer" arm that could control vital sea lanes between China, Japan and the West, as well as a springboard for the projection of Soviet sea power northward along the rim of the Pacific. A new strategic map would make this fact eminently recognizable.

Such an analysis, carried out on a continuing basis by qualified, field-experienced personnel, linked and ranked to "interests"—ours and theirs—is certain to produce the kind of data on which military planners and strategists can requisition, acquire, prepare, and position their relevant combat arms. The diagnosis will not prove to be 100 % correct—it would be a miracle if it scored all the time. There are always imponderables, unforseeables, and accidents. But the probabilities, both in the long and short run, should be favorable to these hypothetical analysts, planners and strategists. The alternatives are to rely on intuition, hunches, and guesswork or to react, after the fact, on the assumption that belated action can still be successful action. That assumption is increasingly unreliable because contemporary warfare, much more so than in the past, can more readily achieve surprise and cut time by using technology.

Conclusion

Low-Intensity Warfare, the "Half War," and the Main Adversary

Among the recent changes we have witnessed in world power relationships is the rather remarkable growth, both in intensity and geographic spread, of Soviet "adventurism," as the Chinese communists call it. Clearly, the USSR can project its conventional military power well beyond its boundaries and those of the Warsaw Pact nations. Her ground, air and naval deployments to Cuba and the Caribbean, to most sectors of Africa (especially to those areas along both its coasts), and in Asia from the Pamirs to the Pacific and the Indian Ocean right on to the islands of Japan immediately north of Hokkaido, lands occupied and retained after World War II, are significant investments of opportunities. The Chinese communists, officially and otherwise, warn all those who will listen that the Russians are not only trying to encircle the PRC but are seeking domination or control—more than mere influence—in much of the world. They should know—until recently they were partners, albeit junior partners, in the Asian-Indian Ocean combined enterprises. The Soviet Union has found willing proxies or lieutenants in Cuba, East Germany, Vietnam, North Korea, and some others in the Warsaw Pact grouping, for example Bulgaria, for their "patronage"; in turn, these states help to gain new "clients" that then can be controlled, if not absorbed, in and through the Soviet "Marxist" Empire.

Concurrently, Soviet nuclear power has proceeded beyond the parity for which the then unlamented U.S. Secretary of Defense McNamara waited while they attained it. No one doubts this any more, not even the most rabid supporter or negotiator of the proposed SALT II treaty. The following charts state the basic facts in simple form.

Table 7.1

MANPOWER	THE UNITED STATES	THE SOVIET UNION
Army	750,800	1,825,000
Navy	524,200	433,000†
Air Force	563,000	475,000
Marine Corps	184,000	————†
Strategic Nuclear Force*	————	375,000
Air Defense Force¶	————	550,000
TOTAL	2,022,000	3,658,000§

* U.S. manpower figures included in Army, Navy and Air Force totals. The Soviet figure of 375,000 is for their offensive *Strategic Rocket Force* (SRF).
¶ There are no U.S. figures. The Soviet manpower figure of 550,000 is for their *Air Defence Force (PVO-Strany)*.
† The Soviet figure of 433,000 includes 59,000 Naval Air Force, 12,000 Naval Infantry (Marines) and 8,000 Coastal Artillery and Rocket Troops.
§ This figure excludes some 500,000 internal security forces, railroad and construction troops.

SOURCE: International Institute for Strategic Studies,
The Military Balance, 1979-80 (London: IISS, 1979), pp. 5-11.

Table 7.2

HARDWARE	THE UNITED STATES	THE SOVIET UNION
Tanks*	10,500	50,000
Artillery pieces¶	less than 6,000	more than 20,000
Major Surface Combat Ships†	180	275
Submarines§	80	248
Combat Aircraft**	3,400	4,350
SLBMs	656	1,028
ICBMs	1,054	1,398

* The U.S. figure of 10,500 medium tanks excludes 575 M-60A1 medium tanks within the Marine Corps.
¶ These figures are taken from William Schneider, Jr., "General Purpose Forces: Army and Air Force," in Francis Hoeber, William Schneider, Norman Polmar and Ray Bessette, *Arms, Men, and Military Budgets, Issues for Fiscal Year 1981* (New Brunswick and London: Transaction Books, 1980), p. 143.
† U.S. figures include 10 conventional and 3 nuclear aircraft carriers.
§ U.S. attack subs include 73 nuclear and 7 diesel. The Soviet figure of 248 attack and cruise missile subs include 86 nuclear and 162 diesel.
** U.S. figures exclude aircraft in the Strategic Air Command and NORAD, but includes those of Air National Guard and Air Force Reserve. Soviet figures exclude *PVO-Strany* and Long-Range Air Force.

SOURCE: International Institute for Strategic Studies,
The Military Balance, 1979-80 (London: IISS, 1979), pp. 5-11.

Too many words have already been said about the theory and practice of our main adversary and his successful march to the high ground behind his military might. Power has many components, and it is also true to say with Mao Tse-tung that "political power grows out of the barrel of a gun." The Soviet Union has much political power and many guns.

There is one major reason for this brief mention here of Soviet power and its many guns: What we are calling "low-intensity warfare" is, under a variety of names, a prime Soviet export, whether exported directly or indirectly through major Soviet client states. During the Khrushchev period the favorite name for this phenomenon was "wars of national liberation." These were well-nigh on being, in Khrushchev's term, "holy wars." But whether they were holy or liberating wars is truly irrelevant. What they are, in fact, is war at the lower end of the spectrum—from terrorism up to and including conventional war without nuclear weapons. They include Angola, Zaire, the various "fronts" harbored in Mozambique and Zambia, the Algerian Polisario front for the liberation of Moroccan and ex-Mauritanian "Spanish" Sahara, the Ethiopian-Eritrean-Somalian conflict in which the Soviets shifted sides, and all the other above-mentioned items. Low-intensity warfare, in whatever hemisphere it occurs, does concern us, but the concern to be activated—other than on a "knee-jerk" basis—has to be based on basic material interest, allied concern and then prompt response. (Incidentally, France has given a better account of itself and the interests it shares with former African colonies, now independent, than either the United States— with no former colonies in Africa—or England, which had, up to the Thatcher administration, badly bungled its African interests on very belated grounds of justified lack of sympathy for white supremacy in Rhodesia. England had a chance to bring off a useful multiracial settlement in 1963 if it had been willing to support the Wilenski party in Rhodesia, but that, too, is another story.)

The USSR and its proxies are the main adversary, and therefore the actions of the Soviets and their allies require monitoring in the same way as other aspects of our strategic map require monitoring. When and if a *Pax Orbis* takes place we can then relax our guard. But until it does there is no *pax*. As we have said about Asia, since the post-World War II period and the beginnings of independence, there has never been a "cold war." Literally every day since the fall of 1947, when the Cominform sent its emissaries to Bombay and then to Calcutta, the war in Asia—at least some spot in Asia— has been a "hot" war. For all these years somewhere in Asia, organized guns have been fired—not by thugs, as in preindependence India; not by dacoits, as in Burma; not sometime ethnic or religious guns, as in Mindanao where Muslim fired on Christian and vice versa, or as in Indonesia where orthodox Muslims fired on less orthodox Muslims—always there were secular political guns firing for "wars of national liberation" (or some other communist-named warfare) somehow connected to Moscow or to Peking or to both.

This brings us to what we have uncharitably characterized as a rather inane concept, the so-called half war. The concept holds that somehow the United States should be prepared to fight the "big war," possibly including nuclear weapons, against the Soviets in Europe or possibly even globally (with ICBMs, and so on), while simultaneously being prepared to fight somewhere else against an adversary. This latter would be the "half war." The big war—conventional or nuclear—is at least understandable, however tragic it would be. But what of the "half war?" Does it mean that nuclear weapons would not be used? Or that the United States would be fighting against some intermediate size or smaller power? If perchance the smaller power against which we took up arms, as for example Cuba or Vietnam, were allied with the Soviet Union, would we not expect the Soviets to stand by their comrades? And if the Soviets did come to their aid would we not be embroiled once again in a potentially "big" war?

In short, "half war" is not a meaningful concept. What is meaningful is to ask how many "fronts" we would be willing and able to engage in at any one time, with what, and with whom. A United States-NATO-Warsaw Pact-USSR front is global in nature; like World War II there really is no "front" to such a war. If that war were to spread to the Pacific, Indian, or Atlantic Oceans, there would still be one war on several fronts, and sooner or later the United States and its allies would have to cope with second, third and nth fronts. But if the war did not involve the Soviet Union and any of its satellites and client states, the United States would nevertheless be at war or would assist an ally in one form or other. The weapons to be used and the size and mobility of the forces involved should then be proportional to the opponent. The aim of such a war would be the same as that of a big war, or of any war: to use the necessary amount of force in the shortest possible time, while inflicting least damage on the civilian population so as to impose one's will on the enemy to make him surrender, so as to achieve the political goal of victory.

The only difference between high- and low-intensity warfare is the means, both quantitative and qualitative, employed to achieve the intended goal. Both types of war require analysis and forecasting, both require volumes of preparation of varied manpower and materiel, both require the political sagacity to acquire and hold allies and friends so that the obvious preponderance of one's own side acts (or so one hopes) as a deterrent to any combination in opposition. Aggregates of power, along with effective political leadership and initiative, make the difference between victory and defeat or stalemate. Nothing can substitute for the painful empirical tasks of political analysis and forecasting, of exercising intelligence, of being accordingly prepared in concert with others, where possible, to survive in battle, to defend as necessary, to advance when called for, to cause one's cherished social order and value system to thrive while contributing to the survival of equally respected, friendly societies and their value systems. The cost of this burden is what the free citizen must freely bear.

Notes

1. The term was used by Winston Churchill in a speech to the House of Commons, 22 February 1906.
2. See Ekkart Zimmermann, "Toward a Causal Model of Military Coups d'Etat," *Armed Forces and Society*, vol. 5, no. 3 (Spring 1979), pp. 387–413; and B.M. Blechman et al., *Force Without War: U.S. Armed Forces as a Political Instrument* (Washington, D.C.: The Brookings Institution, 1978).
3. Frank N. Trager and William L. Scully, "Domestic Instability in Southeast Asia," *Orbis* vol. 19, no. 3 (Fall 1975), pp. 971–89.
4. The excerpts from Clausewitz are from the *Selections on War*, Edward M. Collins, ed. and trans. (Chicago: Henry Regnery Co., 1962), pp. 63, 64, 68. The relationship between Clausewitz, Lenin and Mao may be pursued in Frank N. Trager, *Wars of National Liberation in the 1970s: Implications for U.S. Defense Planning*, monograph prepared for the Office of the Chief of Research and Development, US Army, SRI Project 8974 (Menlo Park, Calif.: Stanford Research Institute, October 1972).
5. *The New York Times*, 4 November 1979, section one, pp. 1 and 10.
6. See Clausewitz, p. 68.
7. Note similar sentiments expressed by Jacques L. Pons in his chapter.
8. See Guenter Lewy, *America in Vietnam* (New York: Oxford University Press, 1978), who writes that the "one proposal" (combined command) that might have gone a long way toward solving difficulties was rejected (pp. 121–22).
9. See D.C. Condit et al., eds., *A Counterinsurgency Bibliography* (Washington, D.C.: The American University Special Operations Office, 1963).
10. See Professor Duncanson's chapter.
11. The "early stages" may be dated 1954–60 or 1962, that is, prior to decisions of the September 1960 Third Congress of Vietnam (North) Workers Party publicized in the Jorden report known as *A Threat to the Peace: North Vietnam's Effort to Conquer South Vietnam* (Washington, D.C.: Department of State, 1961); or not later than the conversion of the U.S. Military Assistance Group (MAAG) into MACV (Military Assistance Command, Vietnam) during January-February 1962.
12. Pacification had a tortuous and unfortunate history in counterinsurgency doctrine and operations. The bewildering changes in its name, not inaccurately, conveys the bewilderment of its practice and practitioners. "Civic action," "agrovilles," "strategic hamlets," "new life hamlets," "civil operations and revolutionary development support' (CORDS) were but a few of its names. Always pacification was designed to protect and enhance local villages and town political and economic security. It was to win and hold the hearts and minds of the people by means of the military, rural militia, police and various kinds of government-supported civil action programs. Of the plethora of works on pacification, two items are particularly useful: U.S. Department of the Army, Office of the Deputy

Chief of Staff, Operations, *A Program for the Pacification and Long Term Development of South Vietnam (PROVN)* (March 1966), and Robert W. Komer, *Bureaucracy Does Its Thing*, R. 967 (Santa Monica, Calif.: Rand-ARPA Study, 1973). Komer, a civilian, was then chief of CORDS under the commander of MACV.

13. *Los Angeles Times*, 18 September 1979, p. 2. All quotes in the following two paragraphs are from the same press report.
14. Major General Paul X. Kelley, Deputy Chief of Staff for Requirements and Programs of the Marine Corps, is reported to have said that by 1983, it is hoped, the Corps would be able to move 16,500 fully armed Marines, supported by tanks, artillery and aircraft, into any troubled area within six days and to sustain them for 30 days before their resupply (see Richard Halloran, "Marine Corps to Provide Seagoing Units in Rapid Deployment Force," *New York Times*, 6 December 1979, p. B15.) General Kelly has been assigned as Commander of the Rapid Deployment Task Force, MacDill Air Force Base, Florida.
15. For a full text, see *Naval War College Review* 27 (May-June 1975): 51–108.
16. *New York Times*, 2 October 1979.
17. *New York Times*, 4 October 1979, p. A3. Nixon and Kissinger were the proponents of the "one-and-a-half" war approach, reducing this from Johnson's "two-and-a-half" wars.
18. M. Ponomarev, "Strategy of the World Policeman" *Red Star (Strategiia Mirovoyo Zhandarma, Krasnaja, Zvezda)*, *Red Star*, 12 August 1979.
19. *Commander's Digest*, vol. 20, no. 6 (17 March 1977).
20. Cf. Geoffrey Kemp, "The New Strategic Map," *Survival* (March-April 1977).
21. Ibid.
22. The source of the following chart is OECD, Royal Institute of International Affairs and Economic Intelligence Unit, as published in *Barron's* (5 February 1979).

Strategic Metals
Their Availability Has Begun to Worry the Western World

Key Minerals	Percentage of World Reserves		Percentage of World Production	
Cobalt	Zaire	30%	Zaire	53%
	New Caledonia	19%	Zambia	9%
	USSR	14%		
Manganese	South Africa	45%	South Africa	22%
	USSR	38%	USSR	35%
Chrome	South Africa	74%	South Africa	26%
	Rhodesia	22%	Rhodesia	8%
	USSR	1%	USSR	36%
Gold	South Africa	49%	South Africa	60%
	USSR	22%	USSR	21%
Platinum-group metals	USSR	16%	USSR	31%

Of 26 essential minerals required by U.S. industry and commerce, we import 100% of chromite, cobalt, columbium, tantalum, manganese, rubber, thorium, and tin; 80–90% of antimony, asbestos, bauxite, mercury, nickel, zircon; 40–60% iron ore, oil, potash, titanium, tungsten and zinc. Source: *U.S. Lifelines* (Washington, D.C.: Office of Chief of Naval Operations, Department of the Navy, January 1979), p. 85.

23. Alvin J. Cottrell, "Iranian and Saudi Arabian Security Interests," *Washington Review of Strategic and International Studies* (May 1978), pp. 51–52.

24. For a more complete discussion of the Horn of Africa, see "The White Paper: Horn of Africa," Special Supplement, *Washington Review of Strategic and International Studies* (May 1978).

25. Cf. Richard Bissell, "Soviet Policies in Africa," *Current History* (October 1979).

Bibliography

Adelman, Kenneth L. "African Security: Facts and Fantasies." *Comparative Strategy* 2, no. 1 (1980): 97–108.

Albright, David E. "The USSR and Africa: Soviet Policy." *Problems of Communism* (January-Febraury 1978): 20–39.

Asprey, Robert B. *War in the Shadows*. New York: Doubleday, 1975.

Barber, Willard F. and Ronning, C. Neale. *Internal Security and Military Power: Counterinsurgency and Civic Action in Latin America*. Columbus: Ohio State University Press, 1966.

Barclay, C.N. "Countermeasures against the Urban Guerrilla." *Military Review* 52 (January 1972): 83–90.

Bigeard, Gen. Marcel Maurice. *Pour une parcelle de gloire*. Paris: Presses de la Cité, 1975.

Binkin, Martin and Record, Jeffrey. *Where Does the Marine Corps Go from Here?* Washington, D.C.: The Brookings Institution, 1976.

Bissell, Richard. "Soviet Policies in Africa." *Current History* (October 1979): 124–28.

Bissell, Richard. "Soviet Use of Proxies in the Third World: The Case of Yemen." *Soviet Studies* 30, no. 1 (January 1978): 87–106.

Black, Robert J. "A Change in Tactics? The Urban Insurgent." *Air University Review* 23 (January-February 1972): 50–58.

Blaufarb, Douglas S. "Another Look at Counterinsurgency." *Freedom at Issue*, no. 51 (May-June 1979).

Blaufarb, Douglas S. *The Counterinsurgency Era: U.S. Doctrine and Performance, 1950 to the Present*. New York: Free Press, 1977.

Blechman, Barry M. et al. *Force without War: U.S. Armed Forces as a Political Instrument*. Washington, D.C.: The Brookings Institution, 1978.

Bloomfield, Lincoln P. and Leiss, Amelia C. *Controlling Small Wars*. New York: Knopf, 1969.

Bradford, Zeb B. "U.S. Tactics in Vietnam." *Military Review* 52 (February 1972): 63–76.

Cable, James. *Gunboat Diplomacy: Political Applications of Limited Naval Force*. New York: Praeger, 1971.

Callwell, Sir Charles E. *Small Wars: Their Principles and Practice*. Rev. ed. London: Harrison and Sons, 1896.

Calvert, Michael. "Some Aspects of Guerrilla Warfare: Socio-Economic Polwar and Psywar." *RUSI: Journal for Defence Studies* 117 (September 1972):20–24.

Catroux, Gen. Georges. *Deux actes du drame de l'Indochine, Hanoi 1940–Dien-Bien-Phu 1954*. Paris: Plon, 1959.

Clayton, Anthony. *Counter-insurgency in Kenya: A Study of Military Operations against Mau Mau*. Nairobi: Transafrica, 1976.

Clutterbuck, Richard. *Guerrillas and Terrorists*. London: Faber and Faber, 1977.

Clutterbuck, Richard. *Kidnap and Ransom: The Response*. London: Faber and Faber, 1978.

Clutterbuck, Richard. *Living with Terrorism*. London: Faber and Faber, 1975.

Clutterbuck, Richard. *Protest and the Urban Guerrilla*. New York: Abelard-Schuman, 1974.

Clutterbuck, Richard. *Riot and Revolution in Singapore and Malaya, 1945–1963*. London: Faber and Faber, 1973.

Cogley, William L. "A New Look at People's War." *Air University Review* 28 (July-August 1977): 44–55.

Condit, D.C., et al., eds. *A Counterinsurgency Bibliography*. Washington D.C.: The American University Special Operations Office, 1963.

Cottrell, Alvin J. "Iranian and Saudi Arabian Security Interests." *The Washington Review of Strategic and International Studies* (May 1978): 50–56.

Crozier, Brian. *Strategy of Survival*. London: Maurice Temple Smith, 1978.

Darcourt, P. *De Lattre au Viet-Nam: une année de victoires*. Paris: La Table Ronde, 1965.

David, Steven. "Realignment in the Horn: The Soviet Advantage." *International Security* (Fall 1979): 69–90.

Darling, Roger. "A New Conceptual Scheme for Analyzing Counterinsurgency." *Military Review* 54 (June 1974): 54–56.

Deitchman, Seymour J. "Limited War." *Military Review* 51 (July 1971): 3–16.

Deitchman, Seymour J. *Limited War and American Defense Policy*. Cambridge, Mass.: MIT Press, 1969.

de la Gorce, Paul-Marie. *The French Army: A Military Political History*. New York: George Braziller, 1963.

DeWeerd, Harvey A. "Is US Again Preparing for the Wrong War?" *Army* 28 (February 1978): 26–30.

Dodd, Norman L. "Counter Insurgency and Internal Security Operations." *Defence* 10 (May 1979).

Fall, Bernard B. *Last Reflections on a War.* Garden City, N.Y.: Doubleday, 1967.

Galula, David. *Counterinsurgency Warfare: Theory and Practice.* New York: Praeger, 1964.

Gershman, Carl. "Africa, Soviet Imperialism, and the Retreat of American Power." *Commentary* (October 1977): 33–45.

Glassman, Jon D. *Arms and the Arabs: The Soviet Union and War in the Middle East.* Baltimore: Johns Hopkins University Press, 1975.

Golan, Galia. *The Soviet Union in the Middle East.* New York: Columbia University Press, 1977.

Gras, Gen. Yves. *Histoire de la guerre d'Indochine.* Paris: Plon, 1979.

Gray, Colin. *The Geopolitics of the Nuclear Era: Heartland, Rimlands, and the Technological Revolution.* New York: Crane, Russak and Company, 1979.

Grinalds, LTC John, USMC. "Structuring the Marine Corps for the 1980s and 1990s." *National Security Affairs Monograph.* Washington, D.C.: National Defense University, Research Directorate, May 1978.

Grivas, George. *Guerrilla Warfare and EOKA's Struggle, A Politico-Military Study.* London: Longmans, 1964.

Guerard, Albert. *France: A Short History.* New York: W.W. Norton and Co., 1946.

Halperin, Morton H. "War Termination as a Problem in Civil-Military Relations." *The Annals,* 392 (November 1970): 86–95.

Heilbrunn, Otto. *Warfare in the Enemy's Rear.* New York: Praeger, 1964.

Hyde, Douglas. *The Peaceful Assault: The Pattern of Subversion.* London: Bodley Head, 1963.

Hyde, Douglas. *The Rehabilitation of Detainees.* London: Faber, 1972.

Hyde, Douglas. *The Roots of Guerrilla Warfare.* Chester Springs, Pa.: Dufour editions, 1968.

"Irregular Warfare: Legal Implications of the Facts, Policies, and Law from World War II to Vietnam." *Proceedings of the American Society of International Law* (April 1976).

Jacobs, Walter D. "Urban Guerrilla Warfare: Scenarios for the 1970s." *NATO's Fifteen Nations* 16 (August-September 1971): 62–68.

Johnson, James R. "People's War and Conventional Armies." *Military Review* 54 (January 1974): 24–33.

Jones, Christopher D. "Just Wars and Limited Wars: Restraints on the Use of the Soviet Armed Forces." *World Politics* 28 (October 1975): 44–68.

Juin, Marechal. *Trois siècles d'obeissance militaire (1650–1963)*. Paris: Plon, 1964.

Kelly, Francis J. *U.S. Army Special Forces, 1961–1971*. Washington, D.C.: Department of the Army, 1973.

Kemp, Geoffrey. "The New Strategic Map. " *Survival* (March-April 1977): 50–59.

Kitson, Frank. *Low Intensity Operations: Subversion, Insurgency, Peacekeeping*. London: Faber, 1971.

Klonis, N.L. *Guerrilla Warfare: Analysis and Projection*. New York: R. Speller, 1972.

Knorr, Klaus. "On the International Use of Military Force in the Contemporary World." *Orbis* 21 (Spring 1977): 5–28.

Knorr, Klaus. *On the Uses of Military Power in the Nuclear Age*. Princeton: Princeton University Press, 1966.

Krulak, Victor D. "The Strategic Limits of Proxy War." *Strategic Review* 2 (Winter 1974): 52–57.

Laqueur, Walter. *Guerrilla: A Historical and Critical Study*. Boston: Little, Brown, & Co., 1976.

Laqueur, Walter, *The Guerrilla Reader: A Historical Anthology* . Philadelphia: Temple University Press, 1977.

Legvold, Robert. *Soviet Policy in West Africa*. Cambridge, Mass.: Harvard University Press, 1970.

Legvold, Robert. "The Super Rivals: Conflict in the Third World." *Foreign Affairs* (Spring 1979): 755–78.

Lewy, Guenter. *America in Vietnam*. New York: Oxford University Press, 1978.

Long, William F. "Counterinsurgency: Corrupting Concept." *U.S. Naval Institute Proceedings* 105 (April 1979): 57–64.

Mangold, Peter. *Superpower Intervention in the Middle East*. London: Croom Helm, 1978.

Massu, Gen. Jacques. *Le torrent et la digue*. Paris: Plon, 1972.

McConnell, James and Dismukes, Bradford. "Soviet Diplomacy of Force in the Third World." *Problems of Communism* (January-February 1979).

McCuen, John. *The Art of Counter-Revolutionary War*. Harrisburg, Pa.: Stackpole, 1966.

McIntyre, Capt. John J., ed. *The Future of Conflict*. Washington, D.C.: National Defense University Press, 1979.

Novik, Nimrod. *On the Shores of Bab Al-Mandab: Soviet Diplomacy and Regional Dynamics (FPRI Monograph No. 26)*. Philadelphia: Foreign Policy Research Institute: 1979.

Osgood, Robert E. *Limited War: The Challenge to American Strategy*. Chicago: University of Chicago Press, 1957.

Paget, Julian. *Counter-insurgency Operations: Techniques of Guerrilla Warfare*. New York: Walter, 1967.

Palmer, George E. "The Strategy of Unconventional Warfare." *Military Review* 56 (August 1976): 58–62.

Paret, Pierre. *French Revolutionary Warfare from Indochina to Algeria*. New York: Praeger, 1964.

Pauker, Guy J. *Military Implications of a Possible World Order Crisis in the 1980s*. Santa Monica Calif.: Rand Corporation (November 1977).

Quester, George H. "The Guerrilla Problem in Retrospect." *Military Affairs* 39 (December 1975): 192–96.

Race, Jeffrey. "Vietnam Intervention: Systematic Distortion in Policymaking." *Armed Forces and Society* 2 (Spring 1976): 377–96.

Robinson, D.F. "Irregular Warfare: An Outline of Historical Development, Causes, and Counter-Measures." *Army Quarterly and Defense Journal* 104 (July 1974): 427–36.

Ro'i, Yaacov. *The Limits to Power: Soviet Policy in the Middle East*. London: Croom Helm, 1979.

Rustin, Bayard and Gershman, Carl. "Africa, Soviet Imperialism and the Retreat of American Power." *Commentary* (October 1977).

Schlaak, Thomas M. "The Essence of Future Guerrilla Warfare: Urban Combat." *Marine Corps Gazette* 60 (December 1976): 18–26.

Schlacter, David C. and Stubbs, Fred J. "Special Operations Forces: Not Applicable?" *Military Review* 58 (February 1978): 15–26.

Scott, Andrew M. *Insurgency*. Chapel Hill: University of North Carolina Press, 1970.

Scott, Harriet Fast and Scott, William F. *The Armed Forces of the USSR*. Boulder, Colo.: Westview Press, 1979.

Sella, Amon. "Patterns of Soviet Involvement in a Local War." *RUSI: Journal for Defence Studies* 124 (June 1979): 53–55.

Simpson, Benjamin M. "Current Strategic Theories." *Naval War College Review* 24 (May 1972): 76–85.

Spjut, R.J. "A Review of Counterinsurgency Theorists." *Political Quarterly* 49 (January-March 1978): 54–64.

Stern, Ellen P., ed. *The Limits of Military Intervention*. Beverly Hills: Sage, 1977.

Strategic Studies Institute. *Organization, Missions, and Command and Control for Special Forces and Ranger Units in the 1980's*. Carlisle Barracks, Pa.: US Army War College, 1979.

"The United States Role in Counterinsurgency." *Naval War College Review* 25 (January-February 1973): 88–99.

"The White Paper: Horn of Africa." Special Supplement. *Washington Review of Strategic and International Studies* (May 1978).

Thompson, Robert. "The War in Vietnam: Reflections on Counterinsurgency Operations." *RUSI: Journal for Defence Studies* 118 (March 1973): 20–27.

Thompson, W. Scott. *Power Projection: A Net Assessment of US and Soviet Capabilities*. New York: National Strategy Information Center, 1978.

Thompson, W. Scott and Frizzell, D. Donaldson. *The Lessons of Vietnam*. New York: Crane, Russak, 1977.

Trager, Frank N. *Wars of National Liberation in the 1970s: Implications for U.S. Defense Planning*. Monograph. Prepared for the Office of the Chief of Research and Development, US Army. SRI Project 8974. Menlo Park, Calif.: Stanford Research Institute, October, 1972.

Tucker, Robert. "Further Reflections on Oil and Force." *Commentary* (March 1975).

Tucker, Robert. "Oil: The Issue of American Intervention." *Commentary* (January 1975): 21–31.

United States Air Force Academy. Department of Political Science and Philosophy. *American Defense Policy*. 4th ed. Baltimore; Johns Hopkins University Press, 1977.

United States Congress. Special Subcommittee on Investigations of the Committee on International Relations. *Oil Fields as Military Objectives: A Feasibility Study*. Washington, D.C.: Government Printing Office, 1975.

United States Naval Amphibious School. *Counterinsurgency Studies*. San Diego, Calif.: 1978.

Valenta, J. *Soviet Intervention in Czechoslovakia 1968: Anatomy of a Decision*. Baltimore: Johns Hopkins University Press, 1979.

Valkenier, Elizabeth K. "The USSR, the Third World, and the Global Economy." *Problems of Communism* (January-February 1979).

Vought, Donald B. "Preparing for the Wrong War?" *Military Review* 57 (May 1977): 16–34.

Weinrod, W. Bruce. "Counterinsurgency: Its Role in Defense Policy." *Strategic Review* 2 (Fall 1974): 36–40.

Weller, J. "Arms for Guerrilla War." *Ordnance* 57 (November-December 1972): 208–13.

Whelan, Joseph and Inglee, William B. *The Soviet Union and the Third World: A Watershed in Great Power Policy?* Washington, D.C.: Government Printing Office, 1977.

Whetten, Lawrence. *The Political Implications of Soviet Military Power*. New York: Crane, Russak, 1977.

Whetten, Lawrence. "The Soviet-Cuban Presence in the Horn of Africa." *RUSI: Journal for Defence Studies* 123 (September 1978): 39–45.

Wolynski, Alexander. "Soviet Aid to the Third World." *Conflict Studies* no. 90 (December 1977).

Zagoria, Donald S. "Into the Breach: New Soviet Alliances in the Third World." *Foreign Affairs* (Spring 1979): 733–54.

About the Authors

DENNIS J. DUNCANSON, OBE, M.A., Ph.D, is a reader in Southeast Asian Studies at the University of Kent, England. He has served as a military administrator in Eritrea, colonial administrator in Malaya and Hong Kong and a diplomatic adviser in the Republic of Vietnam. Dr. Duncanson has published widely, his most recent book being *Government and Revolution in Vietnam*.

HOWARD D. GRAVES is a colonel, U.S.A., currently commanding officer, 20th Engineer Brigade, XVIII Airborne Corps, Fort Bragg. He has also recently served as special assistant to the deputy commandant, U.S. Army War College. Colonel Graves is a 1961 graduate of the United States Military Academy and holds M.A. and B. Litt. degrees in political science from Oxford University. He has commanded a combat engineer company in the 82nd Airborne Division and a combat engineer battalion in Germany. His staff assignments include engineer battalion operations officer and military assistant to the secretary of defense.

ROGER HAMBURG is a professor of political science at Indiana University at South Bend. His publications include articles on Soviet foreign and military policy; among these are "Soviet Views on Intervention" in Ellen Stern, ed., *The Limits of Military Intervention*, and "American and Soviet Views on Human Rights," forthcoming in the journal *Conflict*.

GEORGE K. OSBORN III is professor of international and comparative politics at the U.S. Military Academy. He has been visiting fellow at the Institute of Southeast Asian Studies (Singapore), and served in the U.S. Embassy in Bangkok. He is the author of *Balances of Power in Southeast Asia*, and numerous articles on Asian affairs and military subjects.

207

JACQUES L. PONS is a colonel in the French Army serving as liaison officer with the United States Army Training and Doctrine Command (TRADOC), Fort Monroe, Virginia. In 1978 he was an international fellow at the U.S. Army War College. Colonel Pons has served in Tunisia, Vietnam, Algeria, and Germany. He is a qualified paratrooper and aircraft observer. His other specialties include national security policy, regional studies (Mideast, Africa, and Eastern Europe), and nuclear warfare.

SAM C. SARKESIAN is professor and chairman, Department of Political Science, Loyola University of Chicago. Dr. Sarkesian includes among his publicatons *The Military-Industrial Complex: A Reassessment; The Professional Army Officer in a Changing Society; Revolutionary Guerrilla Warfare;* and *Politics and Power: An Introduction to American Government,* as well as a variety of articles on the military profession, national security, and civil-military relations. He has served as Executive Secretary of the Inter-University Seminar on Armed Forces and Society, and is currently the associate chairman of that organization. He began his service in the U.S. Army as an enlisted man, retiring as a lieutenant colonel, having had duty in Germany, Korea, Vietnam, and the U.S. Military Academy.

WILLIAM L. SCULLY recently held the position of research associate professor at New York University, serving both as an analyst for the Burma Research Project and the National Security Education Program. He has previously taught at Siena College and has been a frequent panel member at scholarly symposia. Professor Scully has contributed many articles on both national security and Asian topics, including "Burma in 1979: The Slow Road to Development" (*Asian Survey*) and "Domestic Instability in Southeast Asia' (*Orbis*). He is currently a foreign policy analyst specializing in Asian and Pacific affairs for The Heritage Foundation, Washington, D.C. He is preparing a monograph about the Rapid Deployment Force.

DAVID TARR is a professor of political science at the University of Wisconsin-Madison. He has also served as a national defense analyst in the Legislative Reference Service of the Library of Congress and as a research associate at the Washington Center of Foreign Policy Research (Johns Hopkins University), as well as at Harvard University. At Wisconsin he has served as director of the National Security Studies Group and as chairman of the Department of Political Science, and is a recipient of a Rockefeller Foundation Fellowship. He has published many scholarly articles, and is the author of *American Strategy in the Nuclear Age* and coeditor of *Modules in Security Studies.* In preparation is *Strategic Weapons: A Disarming Proposal.*

WILLIAM J. TAYLOR, Jr., colonel, U.S.A., is professor of social sciences at the U.S. Military Academy. He teaches courses in national security and

American Foreign policy, and is director of the West Point Debate Council and Forum. A frequent contributor to various books and journals, his most recent articles appear in *American Defense Policy, Public Administration Review*, and *Air University Review*. He is coauthor of an undergraduate text, *U.S. National Security: Policy and Process*, forthcoming. His institutional memberships include the Council on Foreign Relations and the International Institute for Strategic Studies.

FRANK N. TRAGER serves as professor of international affairs and director, National Security Program, New York University, and as director of studies, National Strategy Information Center. He has served on the faculties of Johns Hopkins and Yale Universities and the National War College, and is a board member of the Foreign Policy Research Institute and chairman of the American-Asian Educational Exchange, as well as of the Chinese Cultural Center (Republic of China). Dr. Trager was director of the U.S. Economic AID Mission to Burma and has been a consultant to many research institutes and government agencies. He is the author or editor of numerous books, articles, and monographs, including *Economic Issues and National Security*.

Index

Aboukir, 129
Aden, 96, 98, 100, 102, 104, 108, 109, 113, 117, 118, 119, 122, 124n, 191
Affaires Indigènes, 133, 140
Afghanistan, vii, 4, 9, 13, 19, 28, 31, 44n, 49, 50, 97, 106, 147, 152, 153, 155, 159, 176, 186, 188, 189, 191
Africa: and Great Britain, 100, 194; and France, 131, 144, 194; and Soviet Union, 149, 152, 188; and United States, 187, 188-89
Africa, Central: and France, 132; and Great Britain, 132
Africa, East: and United States, 84
Africa, Horn of, 4, 98, 106, 198n; and Soviet Union, 33; and proxy conflicts, 106
Africa, South. *See* South Africa
Africa, sub-Saharan, 31, 34-36, 97; and United States, 28, 31, 34-36; and the West, 35; and Soviet Union, 35-36; and Cuba, 36
Africa, West: and Soviet Navy, 191
Afrique du Nord Française, 131
Afrique Occidentale Française, 131
Agrovilles, 196n
Alexander II (Tsar), 96
Algeria: and France, 98, 119, 128, 129-30, 132, 134, 139-43, 176

Algiers, 129-30
American Declaration of Independence, 19
American Revolutionary War, 129
Andren, N., 45n
Angola, 36, 44n, 106, 145, 149, 153, 155, 156, 158, 171n, 176, 191, 194
Annual Defense Planning Questionnaire, 77
ANZUS, 186
Arab-Israeli conflicts: 1967 war, 33, 149, 157; 1973 war, 33-34, 149, 150, 157, 161, 171
Aristotle, 175
Aron, R., 55
Arctic Warfare School, 87
Asia: U.S. regional interests in, 28, 30, 50; United States Air Force in, 81; and Great Britain, 96; and France, 131; and *The New York Times,* 187; and Soviet Union, 188, 191; and JCS memo, 189; and cold war/hot war, 194
Asia, Central: and Soviet Union, 159
Asia, East: and United States, 26, 29-30; and PRC, 30
Asia, Northeast: and superpower conflict, 69; and non-NATO contingency, 78; and U.S. military capabilities, 78; and JCS memo, 189

Asia-Pacific region: and JCS memo,
189
Asia, South: and U.S. interests, 31;
and Soviet Union, 31, 33; and JCS
memo, 189
Assabin, 191
Atlantic Ocean: United States and, 50;
and Soviet advances, 189; and
possible war, 195
Atlantic Partnership. See NATO
Atlantic region: and JCS memo, 189
Australia, 124n
Austria-Hungary, 24
Bab el Mandeb, 188, 191
Bakunin, M., 176
Baluchistan, 191
Bao Dai government, 102
Bay of Pigs, 180, 186
Beila, 98
Belgium, 20, 71, 98, 145-46
Berbera, 98, 108, 191
Berlin Wall, 61
Bernhardi, 24
Biafra, 176
Binh-Xuen sect, 137
Bissell, R., 171n, 198n
Black Africa. See Africa, sub-Saharan
Blaufarb, D., 47n
Blechman, B., 15n, 44n, 93n, 196n
Bokassa, 147
Bolivia, 114, 176, 179
Bonaparte, Napoleon, 119, 129
Borneo, 95
Borodin, A., 103
Branley, B., 94n
Brazil, 38
Brezhnev, L., 166, 172n, 173n
Brown, H., 76, 77, 93n, 94n
Brown, S., 172n
Bugeaud, Gen., 119
Bulgaria, 192
Burma, 19, 106, 180
Busch, Col. A., 179
Callwell, C., 98, 116, 119, 124n
Cambodia, 61, 124n, 131, 153, 176,
180

Cameron, J., 94n
Campbell, J., 171n
Cam Ranh Bay, 191
Canada, 38
Canadian Armed Forces, 88
Can Bo, 136
Cao Dai, 137
Caribbean: Soviet support of Cuban
troops in, 150; Soviet forces to, 191
Carney, L., 94n
Carter, J.: administration of, 13, 33,
56, 186, 189
Cartier, R., 143
Castro, F., 153. See also Cuba
Central African Republic, 40. See also
Bokassa
Central Intelligence Agency (CIA):
and Bay of Pigs, 180
CENTO, 100
Chad: and France, 40, 131, 145
Chamberlain, N., 27
Chiang Kai-shek, 137
Chicago Council on Foreign
Relations, 58-59, 64
Chile: Guevarists in, 114
China card, 30
Chindits, 180
Chinese Nationalist troops, 135, 137,
138
Chinese Turkestan, 107
Church, F., 61
Churchill, W., 196n
Civil Reserve Air Fleet (CRAF). See
United States Air Force
Clausewitz, C., 24, 45n, 95, 112,
178, 179, 182, 196n
Clayton, A., 125n, 126n
Clyde, Baron, 108
Cobb, T., 45n, 172n
Cochin China, 131
Coffey, K., 46n
Cohen, B., 67n
Cold war, 50, 58, 59, 60, 106, 147,
185, 194
Collins, E., 196n
Collins, J., 45n

COMECON, 18, 191
Cominform, 107, 194
Comintern, 100, 101, 107, 115
Commander's Digest, 188
Committee for Public Salvation, 140
Comte, A., 102-03, 105
Concept 67, 144-45
Concept 77, 145
Condit, D., 196n
Conflict Spectrum, 3, 5-6
Congo, 98, 106, 114, 131, 154
Constantinople, 97
Containment: Truman doctrine of, 56
CORDS, 185, 196n
Costa Rica, 150
Cottrell, A., 198n
Counterinsurgency, 179, 180-82
Cripps, Sir S., 115, 116
Crusades, 97
Cuba, 17, 19, 37, 54, 61, 62, 106,
    149-50, 152-53, 154, 155, 180, 186,
    191, 192
Cyprus, 95, 97, 98, 101, 102, 104,
    113, 117, 118, 120, 122, 124n, 143
Czechoslovakia, 152, 153, 156, 159,
    171n, 176
De Gaulle, C., 40, 134, 143
De Lattre, Gen., 124n, 138
De Montalembert, C., 114
Dervishes, 97, 122
De Tocqueville, A., 44n, 55
Dhofar, 113, 119
Dien Bien Phu, 138
Dismukes, B., 171n, 172n
Dixon, J., 44n
Djibouti, 144-45
Dohan, M., 173n
Dragon Team X. *See* United States
    Army.
Dulles, J.F., 25, 185
Duncanson, D., 125n
East Germany, 19, 106, 153, 159, 192
Eden, A., 110, 125n
Egypt, 31, 33, 34, 97, 99, 129, 154,
    155, 156, 188
Eisenhower, D., 185

Elits, Amb., 190
Entebbe, 176
EOKA, 101, 113, 117
Eritrea, 96, 155, 194
Ethiopia, 36, 44n, 115, 153, 155, 176,
    187, 188, 191, 194
Eudin, K., 125n
Eurocommunism, 58
Europe, Central: and United States,
    187
Europe, Eastern: and Soviet Union,
    159, 164
Europe, Western: and United States,
    28, 29, 30, 38-41; and Soviet
    Union, 39-40; and JCS memo, 188
European monetary system, 39
Fashoda, 132
Fenians, 103, 105. *See also* Sinn Fein
Finland, 45n
Finlandization, 29, 40, 45n
First Republic: and Napoleon, 129
Force: employment of. *See* Low-
    intensity conflict
Force de frappe, 40
Ford, Gerald, 186
Ford Doctrine, 24
Fourth International, 121
France: and Zaire, 20, 40, 71, 145-47;
    and Chad, 40; and Mauritania, 40,
    145; and Central African Republic,
    40, 132-33; and Egypt, 99; and
    experience in low-intensity conflict,
    127ff; and colonial expansion,
    128-33; and New World and India,
    128-29; and decolonization, 128,
    133-43; and Indochina war, 128,
    131-32; and Algeria, 98, 128, 132,
    134, 139-43; and policy of
    cooperation, 128, 143-47; and
    Foreign Legion, 128, 132, 140, 144,
    164; and pacification, 130-31; and
    native forces, 132-33; and Concept
    67, 144-45; and Concept 77, 145
French Declaration of the Rights of
    Man, 19
French Revolution, 44n

French Union: and Indochina, 134, 135, 139
Front de Libération Nationale (FLN): and Algeria, 140, 141, 142
Gabon, 144
Geneva Conference (Indochina), 99, 110, 125n, 138-39, 181
George, A., 161, 162, 172n
German Democratic Republic. *See* East Germany
German Federal Republic. *See* West Germany
Ghana, 106, 114
Goldsborough, J., 46n
Goldstein, W., 15n
Goodpaster, A., 171n
Gorchakov, A., 96, 106, 107, 109, 121
Gorman, T., 45n
Gorshkov, S., 152, 154, 156, 157, 171n
Great Britain: and Europe, 25; and Northern Ireland, 89, 95, 101-02, 103, 112, 113-14, 117, 118, 119, 120, 123; experience in low-intensity conflict, 95-124; and Northwest Frontier, 95, 98, 103, 121, 122; and Palestine, 95, 108, 188; and Cyprus, 95, 97, 98, 101, 102, 104, 113, 117, 118, 120, 122, 143; and Malaya, 95, 98, 100, 101, 104, 105, 107, 108, 113, 115, 117, 118, 119, 120, 121, 122; and Borneo, 95; and Indonesia, 95; and Indochina, 96, 110; and Rhodesia, 96; and Oman, 96, 113, 118, 119; and Eritrea, 96; and Java, 96; and South Vietnam, 96ff; and Aden, 96, 98, 100, 102-04, 108, 109, 113, 117, 118, 119, 122; and Kenya, 96, 97, 100-01, 104, 105, 112, 116, 117, 118, 119, 121, 122, 123; and Mau Mau, 96, 97, 98, 100-01, 104, 112, 116, 117, 123; and Sudan, 97; and Afghanistan, 97; and Somaliland, 97, 98, 103, 121; and Egypt, 97, 99; and Suez Crisis (1956), 99; and

Great Britain *(continued)* India, 100; and Singapore, 100; and terrorist fronts, 105-06; and Middle East, 108-09
Grechko, A., 152, 171n
Greece, 101
Green Berets. *See* United States Army
Grivas, G., 112, 125n
Gromyko, A., 150, 171n
Guadeloupe, 144
Guinea, 131
Guinea-Bissau, 154, 157, 158
Hackett, J., 44n
Hadhramaut, 97, 113
Hague Conventions, 99
Haig, A., 78
Halloran, R., 197n
Halperin, M., 44n, 47n
Hamburg, R., 170n, 171n, 172n
Harding, Gen., 117
Harvey, M., 170n
Hinsley, F., 66n
Hitler, A., 109, 122, 125n
Hoa Binh Guerrilla School, 100
Hoa Hao sect, 137
Ho Chi-Minh, 115, 134, 135, 138
Ho Chi-Minh Trail, 110
Hoffmann, S., 55, 58
Hokkaido, 192
Home, D., 110
Hong Kong, 115
Hormuz, Straits of, 21, 26, 27, 179, 188, 190
Howard, M., 45n
Hravalis, H., 172n, 173n
Hungary, 153, 159, 171n
India, 19, 31, 100, 106, 115, 128-29, 159, 176
Indian Army (British), 122
Indian Ocean: importance of, 31; and Soviet Union, 28, 149, 153, 191; and JCS memo, 189; and strategic map, 191
Indochina, 96, 97, 101, 110, 114, 121, 131, 132, 134-39
Indochinese Communist party, 134

Indonesia, 19, 24, 95, 194
Infanterie Coloniale, 132
Infanterie de Marine, 144
Infantry School. *See* United States
    Army
International Press Correspondence,
    115
International Red Aid, 101, 115, 120
International Red Cross, 120
Iran, vii, 4, 9, 31, 32, 49, 50, 54,
    62, 96, 108 109, 147, 188
Iraq, 34, 108, 154
Irish Republican Army (IRA), 105,
    106, 113, 117, 122, 125n
Israel, 31, 33, 34, 83, 143, 153, 154,
    159, 188. *See also* Arab-Israeli
    Wars
Ivory Coast, 144
Janowitz, M., 46n
Jansen, M., 94n
Japan, 26, 28, 29, 30, 32, 37, 40,
    179, 186, 191
Java, 96
Jedda, 191
Jefferson, T., 110
Jihad, 98, 106
Johnson, L., 56, 63, 182, 186, 197n
Joint Chiefs of Staff memo (JCS),
    188-89
Jordan, 34, 154, 157
Jordan, A., 45n, 46n
Jorden Report, 196n
Jungle Warfare School (Panama), 87
Kahn, H., 160
Kaplan, S., 15n, 171n
Katanga, 145
Kelley, P.X., 197n
Kellogg-Briand Pact, 51
Kemp, G., 46n, 190ff, 197n
Kennedy, J.F.: administration of, 8,
    61, 180, 186
Kenya: and Great Britain, 96, 97,
    100-01, 104, 105, 112, 116, 117, 118,
    119, 121, 122, 123, 124n
Kenya African Union, 105
Kenyatta, J., 100, 105, 116

Keohane, R., 172
Khablyian rebellion, 140
Khomeini, A., 54, 190
Khrushchev, N., 149, 194
Kikuyu, 104, 112
Kissinger, H., 25, 28, 39, 40, 45n,
    46n, 56, 110, 186, 197n
Kitson, F., 124n
Knorr, K., 51, 52-53, 57, 58, 66n,
    172n
Kolwezi (Zaire), 145-47
Komer, R., 197n
Konfrontasi, 95
Korea. *See* North Korea and South
    Korea
Korean War, 5, 8, 10, 12, 20, 21, 50,
    58, 61, 63, 123, 137, 176
Kovalev, A., 160, 161, 162, 164, 172n
Kulish, V., 151, 171n
La Compagnie des Indes, 129
Lamb, D., 172n
Lambeth, B., 170n
Laos, 110, 114, 131, 153, 154, 180
Laotian Patriotic Front, 124n
Latin America: and United States,
    36-38; and JCS memo, 189
Lawrence, G., 44n
League of Nations, 51
Lebanon, 154, 177
Leclerc, Gen., 135
Lee Tuan-huat, 124n
Legvold, R., 172n
Leighton, M., 45n
Lenin, V.I., 102, 103, 104, 106-16,
    117, 121, 122, 125n, 168
Lewy, G., 15n, 124n, 196n
Liberia, 75, 176
Libya, 106, 153
Lockhart, C., 172n
Low-intensity conflict: definition and
    concept, 2-5, 20-24, 175-80,
    180-82, 192-98; conflict spectrum,
    5-6; political constraints and
    limitations, 7-11, 49-66; military
    requirements and capabilities, 11-14,
    69-93, 183-85; policy guidelines,

Low-intensity conflict *(continued)*
14-15, 185-92; U.S. interests and,
27-41; and employment of force,
41-43, 49-66; international
restraints, 51-55; national
constraints, 55-61; other constraints,
61-64; and Great Britain, 95-124;
and France, 127-48; and Soviet
behavior, 160-70
Lowenthal, A., 46n
Loyola Workshop, vii-viii, 1-2
McConnell, J., 171n, 172n
McNamara, R., 192
MAAG, 182, 196n
MacDonald, M., 110
Machiavelli, N., 102, 118
MACV, 180, 196n
Mahdiya, 97, 103
Makarios, 105
Malacca, Straits of, 21
Malaya: and Great Britain, 95, 98,
100, 101, 104, 105, 107, 108, 113,
115, 117, 118, 119, 120, 121, 122,
124n
Malaysia, 95
Malta, 129
Malthus, T., 4
Manila Security Pact, 181
Mao Tse-tung, 107, 112, 125n, 128,
136, 139, 140, 194
Martinique, 144
Marx, K., 103
Massawa, 191
Massu, Gen., 141
Mau Mau, 96, 97, 98, 100-01, 104,
112, 116, 117, 123
Mauritania, 40, 145
Maximova, M., 168-69, 173n
Mayagüez, 46n, 62, 86, 176
Mayer, J., 44n
Mazzini, G., 112, 125n
Mengistu regime, 153
Meo, 114
Merrill's Marauders, 180
Meyer, E.C., 78, 91, 94n, 183, 188

Middle East: and U.S. interests, 28,
31-34; and Soviet Union–United
States rivalry, 32-33; and Great
Britain, 96, 123; Soviet expansion
in, 108-09, 149; and U.S. Strike
Force, 183-84; and JCS memo, 188;
and strategic map, 190
Military Advisory Assistance
Command, Vietnam. *See* MACV
Military Advisory Assistance Group.
See MAAG
Military Airlift Command. *See* United
States Air Force
Military Sealift Command. *See* United
States Navy
Mindanao, 194
Mizos, 176
Mobile Training Teams. *See* United
States Army
Mobutu, Gen., 145
Mogadishu, 40
Mongolia-Tannu Tuva, 107, 109
Monnerot, J., 108
Morgenthau, H., 66n
Morocco, 20, 71, 131, 132, 133, 139,
142, 154, 176, 194
Mountbatten, Earl, 125n
Mozambique, 104, 153, 191, 194
MPLA, 155
Mueller, J., 63
Mughal monarchy, 96
Munzenberg, W., 115, 121
Mutual Assured Destruction (MAD),
25, 26
Myers, D., 46n
Nagas, 176
Namibia, 36
Napoleon III, 130
Nasser, 33, 113
NATO, 5, 9, 12, 20, 24, 26, 28, 29,
32, 33, 39-40, 50, 69, 70, 77-79,
100, 156, 186, 188, 195
Navarre, Gen., 138
Neely, T., 171n
Nelson, H., 129

Netherlands, 98
New Caledonia, 144, 197n
New life hamlets, 196n
New Zealand, 124n
Nguyen Ai-Quoc. *See* Ho Chi-Minh
Nicaragua, 150
Nietzche, F., 24
Niger, 131
Nigeria, 35, 149, 176
Nikiforov, A., 167-68, 169, 173n
Nixon, R.: administration of, 33, 56, 172n, 182, 186, 197n
Nixon Doctrine, 24
North, R., 125n
Northern Ireland, 89, 95, 101-02, 103, 112, 113-14, 117, 118, 119, 120, 123
Northern Theatre, 28-29, 39
North Korea, 100, 106, 125n, 153, 192
North Sea, 39
North-South conflict, 30
North-South dialogue, 35
Northwest Frontier, 95, 98, 103, 121, 122
Norway, 27, 28, 29, 42
Nye, J., 172n
OECD, 18, 19, 26
Oechsler, R., 172n, 173n
Office of Strategic Services, 96
Olson, R., 45n
Oman, 42, 96, 113, 118, 119, 191
Oman: Gulf of, 190
Osgood, R., 8, 15n
Ottoman Empire, 97, 107
Pakistan, 31, 159, 191
Palestine, 95, 108, 188
Palestine Liberation Organization (PLO), 54
Panama Canal, 12-13, 37
Papp, D., 172n
Paret, P., 45n
Pathans, 97, 115
Pax Americana, 60-61
Payne, J., 66n
People's Front for the Liberation of Oman (PFLO), 191

People's Republic of China (PRC), 26, 29, 30, 58, 59, 104, 106, 107, 147, 152, 155, 160, 176
People's War, 4
Peres, S., 46n
Persia, 97, 106
Persian Gulf, 32, 188, 190
Philippines, 7, 106, 186
Pickett, J., 94n
Pipes, R., 45n
Poland, 160
Polisario, 145, 194
Polynesia, 144
Ponomarev, B., 153, 159, 171n
Ponomarev, M., 187-88, 197n
Portugal, 157, 163
Potsdam, 134
Presidential Review Memorandum (PREM), 186
Pritt, D., 115, 116, 125n, 126n
Pueblo incident, 47n, 153-54
Purcell, H., 125n
Pye, L., 104, 125n
Qaddafi, Col., 100
Quigley, C., 45n
Race, J., 47n
Ranger battalions. *See* United States Army
Rapid Deployment Force. *See* United States Army
Ravenal, E., 8-9, 15n, 46n
Ready Reserve Force of the National Defense Reserve Fleet. *See* United States Navy
Red Star, 187
Rhodesia, 96, 104, 114, 147, 194, 197n
Rielly, J., 66n, 67n
Rogers, B., 78, 94n
Roosevelt, F.D., 63, 134
Roy, M., 108
Royal Lao force, 110
Russett, B., 63-64
Russia, 96, 97, 98, 108-09. *See also* Soviet Union

Russian Civil War, 44n
Sabrosky, A., 172n
Sadat, A., 154
Salihiya, 98
SALT negotiations, 28, 33, 149, 150, 186, 192
Samoilenko, V., 171n
Sandinista guerrillas, 150
Satow's Guide, 99
Saudi Arabia, 32, 34, 191
Saunders, H., 45n
Schelling, T., 44n
Schwartz, M., 172n
Scowcroft, B., 13, 15n, 171n
Scully, W., 196n
Sea Lines of Communication (SLOC), 191
Seal Teams. *See* United States Navy
Sealift Readiness Program. *See* United States Navy
SEATO, 31, 100, 124n, 181
Secret Armed Organization (OAS), 142
Sections Administratives Specialisées (SAS), 141
Security Assistance Force. *See* United States Army Special Forces
Security Assistance Teams. *See* United States Army
Selassie, H., 115
Seminole Indians, 7
Senegal, 71, 131, 144
Shaba. *See* Zaire
Shah (Iran), 24, 190, 191
Sidey, H., 15n
Simonstown, 21, 26
Singapore, 100, 108
Singleton, S., 171n, 172n
Sinn Fein, 105. *See also* Fenians
Sino-Soviet conflict, 26, 29, 160, 176
Slater, J., 46n
SLOC. *See* Sea Lines of Communication
Socotra, 191
Somalia, 36, 145, 153, 176, 191, 194

Somaliland, 97, 98, 103, 121
South Africa, 36, 155, 191, 197n
South America, 37
South Asia. *See* Asia, South
South Korea, 24, 119, 186
Soviet Union: and political-military policy, vii, 9, 41, 43-44; relations with United States, 9, 13, 28, 31, 44, 59, 70, 160-70; military capabilities, 9, 28, 41, 149, 150-51, 155; and Africa, 9, 35, 54, 149, 154, 191; and Middle East, 9, 31, 32-33, 108-09, 149, 150, 169; and Afghanistan, 9, 13, 19, 49, 147, 153, 155, 176, 188, 191; and central war, 17; goals of, 18-19; economy, 19; and economic assistance, 19; advisors, 19; and military intervention (general), 19; and split with PRC, 26, 29, 160, 176; and NATO, 28; and Northern Theatre, 28-29, 39; and Western Europe, 29, 39, 159; and Finlandization, 29, 40; and Turkey, 29; and international system, 29; and East Asia, 29-30; and China card, 30; and Southeast Asia, 30; and South Asia, 31, 33; Navy in Indian Ocean, 33, 149, 153; and Horn of Africa, 33; and Egypt, 33, 154; and Angola, 36, 149, 155, 171n, 191, 194; and Ethiopia, 36, 155; and Somalia, 36; and Cuba, 37, 61, 62, 149, 152, 153, 154, 186; and SS-20, 40; and Tillemma, 57; and Pathans, 97; and Comintern, 100, 115; and Lenin, 102, 103, 106-16 passim; and Ho Chi-Minh, 137; and low-intensity conflict, 149-73; and Arab-Israeli Wars, 149, 154, 157; and Nigeria, 149; and merchant marines, 149; theory on military force, 150-51; declaratory policy of, 151-53; Navy in Mediterranean, 152; and South Yemen, 152, 154, 171n; and East

Soviet Union *(continued)*
Germans, 152; and Libya, 153; and Vietnam, 153, 171n, 191; experience in deploying military force, 153-60; and Eastern Europe, 153, 159, 164; and Hungary, 153, 159; and Czechoslovakia, 153, 155, 159, 171n, 176; and Korea, 153-54; and Third World, 154, 157, 159, 162-63, 164, 165; and Jordan, 154, 157; and Syria, 154; and Lebanon, 154; and Congo, 154; and Laos, 154; and Sudan, 154; and PRC, 155, 159; and Guinea-Bissau, 157; and Central Asia, 159; and Poland, 160; and Yugoslavia, 160; and U.S. strike force, 187-88; and wars of national liberation, 194; and Zaire, 194; and Cominform, 194; and strategic metals, 197n

Spain, 163
Spanier, Jr., 55
Spanish Sahara, 194
Special Forces. *See* United States Army
Spitzbergen, 177
SS-20, 40
Stalin, J., 115, 125n
Stern, E., 46n, 170n
Stilwell, J., 180
Strategic Air Command (SAC). *See* United States Air Force
Strategic hamlets, 196n
Strategic map. *See* Kemp, G.
Strike force. *See* United States Army, Rapid Deployment Force
Sudan, 97, 131, 153, 154
Suez Canal, 191
Suez Crisis, 99, 143, 154
Sukarno, 95
Sullivan, W., 191
Sun Yat-sen University, 100
Sweden, 40
Switzerland, 40
Syria, 34, 132, 133, 154

Ta Khek, 96
Taylor, M., 180
Technical Assistance Teams. *See* United States Army
Teheran, 21
Templer, Gen., 117
Tet Offensive, 63, 181, 182
Thailand, 113, 124n
Thatcher, M., 194
Third World, vii, 3-4, 9, 12, 18, 19, 20, 24, 53, 59, 154, 157, 159, 162, 163, 164, 165, 166, 167, 169, 170
Thompson, W., 170n, 171n
Tillemma, H., 56-58, 62, 64, 65, 66n
Tirailleurs Marocains, 132
Tirailleurs Sénégalais, 132
Tito, J., 147, 160
Toilers-of-the-East Universities, 100, 106, 116
Tonkin, 131
Tonkin Gulf Resolution, 63
Tordesillas, 163
Trager, F., 196n
Treverton, G., 46n
Truman, H.: administration of, 50, 56, 63, 134
Truman Doctrine, 96
Tudeh, 21
Tunisia, 131, 139, 142
Turkey, 29, 101, 106, 108, 109
Uganda, 106
UNCTAD, 18
United Nations, 3, 35, 51, 65, 109, 123
United States: and low-intensity conflict (general), vii, 2-15 passim, 20-24, 175-98 passim; and Third World, 3-4, 10, 12, 24; and Vietnam War, 4, 7-9, 10, 12, 20, 21, 23, 24, 26, 50, 58-60, 62, 63, 75, 78, 89, 97, 110, 122, 149, 151, 153, 180-82; and insurgency/counterinsurgency, 4, 20, 180-82; and Korean War, 5, 8, 10, 12, 20, 21, 50, 61, 63; and NATO, 5, 9,

United States *(continued)*
12, 25, 26, 27, 32, 33, 39, 50, 70,
77, 78, 79, 80, 185; and Soviet
Union (relations), 5, 9-10, 13, 17,
22, 28-29, 30, 32-33, 43-44, 150,
154-60 passim, 160-70, 186, 191,
192-98 passim; and J. Kennedy, 8,
61, 180, 186; policy constraints and
low-intensity conflict (general),
10-11; and military requirements and
capabilities for low-intensity
conflict (general), 11-14; and
Panama Canal, 12, 37; and J.
Carter, 13, 33, 186; policy
guidelines for low-intensity conflict,
14-15; and central wars, 17, 20; and
linkage, 22, 24-28; and R. Nixon,
24, 110; and G. Ford, 24; and D.
Eisenhower, 25, 185; and Persian
Gulf, 26, 27; and Japan, 26, 29,
30, 32; and OECD, 26; and
Norway, 27, 29; and international
system, 29; and East Asia, 29-30;
and China card, 30; and PRC, 30;
and South Asia, 31; and SEATO,
31, 181; and Middle East, 31-34;
and SALT negotiations, 33, 149,
186; and Israel, 33-34; and sub-
Saharan Africa, 34-36; and South
Africa, 36; and Latin America,
36-38; and Western Europe, 38-41;
and employment of force for low-
intensity conflict, 41-43, 49, 69;
and H. Truman, 50, 56, 63, 96,
185; and international restraints to
employment of force, 51-55; and
national values and intervention,
55-61; and Tillemma's theory of
restraints, 56-58, 62, 64; and other
constraints, 61-64; and Berlin Wall,
61; and Iran, 61-62; and F.D.
Roosevelt, 63; and L. Johnson, 63,
186; and War Powers Act, 63;
military requirements and
capabilities for low-intensity
conflict (specific), 69-93; and

United States *(continued)*
Pueblo incident, 153-54; and Green
Berets, 180; and JCS memo,
188-89; and strategic map, 189-92
United States Air Force, 69-93
passim; Special Operations
squadrons, 72; and Rapid
Deployment Force, 80; and Saudi
Arabia, 81; and low-intensity
conflict, 81-83, 91; Military Airlift
Command, 81; airlift operations and
capabilities, 81-82; Civil Reserve
Air Fleet (CRAF), 82, 83; Strategic
Air Command (SAC), 83; and
multilateral training exercises,
87-90 passim; equipment shortfalls,
90; manpower, 91-92
United States Army, 69-93 passim;
Special Forces, 7, 11, 12, 72, 73,
74-75, 76; and Rapid Deployment
Force, 10, 77, 78, 79-80, 81-87
passim, 183-85, 186-87, 187-88;
Ranger battalions, 11, 72, 73-74,
80, 91, 92, 183; Security Assistance
Teams, 71, 72, 75-76, 92; Technical
Assistance Teams, 71, 75; Military
Training Teams, 71, 75; and Shaba
(Zaire), 71; Security Assistance
Force, 74; and S. Yemen, 75; and
Liberia, 76; conventional
capabilities of, 76-81 passim;
posture statements of, 78; 101st Air
Assault Division, 78; 82nd
Airborne Division, 79-80, 81, 88;
4th Mechanized Division, 80, 84;
XVIII Airborne Corps, 80, 87-88;
and low-intensity conflict, 84,
89-90, 91; and multilateral training
exercises, 87-90 passim; DRAGON
TEAM X, 88; equipment shortfalls,
90; and Green Berets, 180
United States Congress: House Armed
Services Committee, 78
United States Marine Corps, 69-93
passim; Marine Amphibious Forces
(MAF), 73, 78, 80, 84; and NATO,

U.S. Marine Corps *(continued)*
78; and Rapid Deployment Force,
80; manpower, 84-85, 91; and
multilateral training exercises,
87-90 passim; equipment shortfalls,
90
United States Navy, 69-93 passim;
Seal Teams, 73, 92; and low-
intensity conflict, 83-84, 91;
Military Sealift Command, 83;
Ready Reserve Force of the
National Defense Reserve Fleet, 83;
Sealift Readiness Program, 83; and
multilateral training exercises,
87-90 passim; manpower, 91
USA, 167
USSR. *See* Soviet Union
Valenta, J., 171n
Valkenier, E., 166-67, 172n
Vance, C., 45n
Venezuela, 2
Versailles, Treaty of, 51, 107
Vienna, Congress of, 99
Viet Cong, 7, 182
Viet Minh, 134, 135, 136-37, 138, 140
Vietnam, Democratic Republic of
(DRV), 30, 124n, 149, 153, 156,
171, 176, 182, 191, 192
Vietnam War, 4, 7-9, 10, 12, 20, 21,
23, 24, 26, 40, 50, 56, 58-60, 62,
63, 64, 74, 75, 78, 79, 89, 97,
102, 110, 122, 124n, 149, 151, 153,

Vietnam War *(continued)*
160, 176, 180-82, 183
Vishinsky, A., 115
Vought, D., 94n
Waltz, K., 45n
War Powers Act, 42, 63
Warsaw Pact, 12, 20, 60, 69, 89, 159,
192, 195
Wayne, J., 180
Weinland, R., 46n
West Germany, 24, 34, 40, 159
Westmoreland, W., 180, 181, 182
Wilenski party, 194
Williams, S., 182
Wilson, Gen., 78
Wingate's Chindits, 180
Witherspoon, R., 45n
Wolf, T., 173n
World Peace Council, 121, 123
Wyatt, D., 46n
Yankelovich, D., 45n
Yemen: North, 42, 75, 171, 176
Yemen: South, 44n 113, 152, 153,
154, 171n, 176, 188, 191
Yenbo, 191
Young, A., 189
Young, J., 172n, 173n
Yugoslavia, 104, 160
Zaire, 20, 40, 71, 145-47, 194, 197n
Zambia, 194, 197n
Zimbabwe, 36
Zimmermann, E., 196n